Timeless Tools
for Every Generation

J.N. Whiddon

BROWN BOOKS
PUBLISHING GROUP

The Old School Advantage
Timeless Tools for Every Generation

Brown Books Publishing Group
16250 Knoll Trail Drive, Suite 205
Dallas, Texas 75248
www.BrownBooks.com
(972) 381-0009

A New Era in Publishing®

ISBN 978-1-61254-881-4 (HC)
ISBN 978-1-61254-910-1 (PB)
LCCN 2015958699

Printed in the United States
10 9 8 7 6 5 4 3 2 1

For more information or to contact the author, please go to
www.TheOldSchoolAdvantage.cool

To Johnathan, Analiese, Daniel, Alexandra, and
the next generation . . . and the next.

CONTENTS

INTRODUCTION

While speaking to an audience of college upperclassmen in March of 2014, I opened with this question: "What is the symbol of this generation?" With startling swiftness and *in unison*, they answered, "The smartphone!" (Many raised their own gadgets in the air as they said it.) This small, electronic device is a tool the likes of which the world has never seen. And it has become "mobiquitous" (a term for the ubiquity of mobile devices).[1] Imagine—there is more computing power in our smartphones than in the Apollo lunar module that landed a man on the moon![2]

Like most people, I stand in awe of what has been accomplished through technology. I don't know how any of it works, but I am thankful for it. To be able to carry my entire personal library with me wherever I go on a tablet weighing less than one pound; to instantly communicate—with few exceptions—with anyone, anytime, anywhere on the planet; to know that my loved ones are safe on the open highway; and to have, literally at my fingertips, the entirety of human history and knowledge in a machine the size of a deck of cards—the convenience is great and the advantages are extraordinary. And so it is not the use of technology that creates a challenge, but rather the *misuse* and *overuse* of it.

With the average person checking his or her phone over two hundred times per day, many are living in a state of technological dependency. Some have labeled this as "IDD," or Internet Distraction Disorder. Sadly, this preoccupation has made many in this generation less equipped—and less motivated—to function at a high level of interpersonal communication. Our close contact with people face-to-face fades in importance as we increasingly withdraw into the virtual world. When this occurs, trust in others tends to erode. Many of the relational skills that were learned naturally by previous generations have been hindered as our attention spans shorten amid the overwhelming sea of data, which is already doubling every eighteen months, with this rate growing shorter.[3]

Americans now rarely take the time to read a good book, go on a walk in the woods, or sit down to have dinner with family. These are the commonplaces through which, for generations, the values of our culture were handed down through interpersonal interactions. We have lost some of those fulfilling experiences that come from relating to one another on a frequent and personal basis. We are settling for virtual encounters with hundreds or even thousands of people, and we are not truly present with any of them. In many ways, the electronic rectangles that surround us are robbing us of a life of purpose and thereby limiting our access to the greatest resource of all—*wisdom*.

Adding to this dilemma is the fact that, as a nation, we have drifted away from a classical form of education. We have wandered gradually from the classics in literature and from learning meaningful history and government (or "civics," as it was once called).

In our curricula, these subjects have been replaced in recent decades by "more important" areas of study, in which the goal seems to be to teach *what* is to be learned instead of teaching students *how* to learn.

> Tomorrow's illiterate will not be the man who can't read; he will be the man who has not learned how to learn.
>
> —Alvin Toffler, *Future Shock*

This shift in emphasis is having an effect. One survey indicated that only 44 percent of employers believe that college graduates have what it takes for any real advancement in their organizations. According to other studies, only a quarter of college graduates have the writing and thinking skills necessary to do their jobs. Another survey of 318 companies found that 93 percent cite "critical thinking, communication, and problem-solving skills as more important than a candidate's undergraduate major." Graduates are said to have trouble working in teams and often struggle to see complex problems from a variety of angles. Even engineering programs have started to recognize the importance of giving their students a base in the liberal arts, precisely because technical information has a limited shelf life while skills of thinking and communication last a lifetime.[4]

Any successful business leader recognizes that the person who has technical expertise *plus* the ability to express ideas usually demonstrates leadership that inspires others. Given this common understanding, you would think that every college in the country would offer a concentrated course to develop this most valued of abilities. But I have not yet seen such an offering.

So I asked myself this question: "Where are the opportunities for enterprising individuals to take advantage of the 'gap' in communication and leadership skills that exists today?" After reading over four hundred books in six years, I wrote this book to address that question. My desire is to provide the training you need to support you in reaching your full potential academically, vocationally, and personally.

But first, you must understand three major concepts:

A. Opportunities are most often disguised as challenges.
B. Learning is a lifelong process.
C. It is not only *what* you do but also *who* you are that truly makes the difference.

The first concept can be summarized through a loose adaptation of a classic scientific theorem:

With every challenge comes an equal or greater opportunity.

Challenge and opportunity are two sides of the same coin. But in order to seize the opportunities born out of challenges, training is needed. The majority of your contemporaries are limited by the general retreat from classical academic training, and this provides you with a phenomenal chance to differentiate yourself and flourish—even in the midst of economic or political turmoil. You must understand the value of recognizing temporary defeat and pressing through it when most would stall or give in. This is a mode of thought that is rare and is irreplaceable on a determined journey of success. You will soon see how the Old School Advantage is the key to making this happen.

In regard to *lifelong learning*, author Stephen Mansfield stated it well:

> Most great men [and women] in history have become great because they aggressively pursued knowledge. They overcame gaps in their early education. They studied to understand the world at a level well beyond their years. They took responsibility for their education and did not wait for the knowledge they needed to come to them.
>
> Winston Churchill read so ravenously when he was a young officer in India that a biographer later wrote that "he became his own university." Lincoln was also enflamed by a hunger to learn. He read every book he could buy or borrow.
>
> Devotion to self-education is unquestionably one of the marks of an exceptional man. Passive men wait for knowledge to come to them. Weak men assume what they need to know will seek them out. Men of great character and drive search out the knowledge they need. They take responsibility for knowing what they must know to live effectively in their generation and to prosper. It is a lesson for today. In fact, it may prove to be one of the most important lessons.[5]

The third concept is one to embrace because it will change the course of your life: it is not only *what you do* but also *who you are* that truly makes the difference.

Schools today do an adequate job, in most cases, of preparing you to apply the knowledge from a college degree to a chosen field. This is "what you do." "Who you are," on the other hand, is a different proposition altogether. "Who you are" includes mastering the "soft skills," which include written and oral communications, social skills (other than social media), an ability to engage and motivate, and business etiquette and professionalism. All are vital to your success and to a thriving and exceptional society.

Your uniqueness can never be replicated because no one but you has your talents and expertise, and no one has had your experiences. The primary "makers" of *who you are* might very well be summed up in the following quote:

> You will be the same person in five years as you are today except for the people you meet and the books you read.
>
> —Charlie "Tremendous" Jones

The Old School Advantage is designed to move you from the "curriculum to the conversation," from the "scholarship to the relationship."[6] The idea is to synthesize what you know with what you learn and then have the tools to pour it into your interpersonal connections, which will enable you to thrive in any endeavor—while also benefitting all those around you. This involves showing aptitude for every kind of learning, along with being well informed, quick to understand, and qualified to serve in any circumstance where life takes you. It also means being tactful and winsome in all your interactions. These characteristics, when combined with courage and conviction, will lead you not only to promotion and prosperity but also to a life of significance. You can be a citizen who stands above the rest, one who has wisdom and understanding that far exceeds the standards set by our culture.

You will begin by learning a handful of interpersonal skills that are familiar to us all but are almost universally misapplied or under-applied in our population.

These five skills are:
1. Recall
2. Words
3. Influence
4. Reason
5. Storytelling

First, you will learn how to develop and utilize your short-term memory through techniques of *ready recall*. (If you can't recall important information *at the moment* it is needed, then it is as if *you don't know it*.) Chapter 1 will provide you with the capability to forgo the reliance on electronic devices when the situation calls for it. This will be a tremendous advantage if you are preparing for an exam or whenever you need to recall an important list or concept. These techniques will also allow you to set aside memory crutches, such as charts or notes, when making any presentation, which will not only impress your audience but will enhance your ability to "stay connected" with them personally as you maintain eye contact throughout the discussion.

Conducting successful dialogue requires that you not only understand which words fit well in every conversation but also deliver the right words at the right time when you want to make a real impact. Chapter 2 focuses on ways to use words that get attention. You will learn many words and phrases that "*wow!*" and others that I call "fit" words—ones that pleasantly and subtly add flavor to your dialogue. This could make the difference between a successful negotiation and a failed one; a thriving relationship and a strained one; a winning campaign and a losing one. You will come to understand that "it is not what we say, but what people hear"[7] that is important. If "what people hear" is not expressed or framed in an optimal manner, then unnecessary challenges could develop, or opportunities could be lost.

Once the building blocks of *recall* and *words* are set in place, we build on these skills by entering the arena of *influence* in chapter 3. The discussion will include the psychology associated with the six major influence techniques and fifteen persuasive phrases—plus other valuable concepts.

Chapter 4 builds on the art of influence and persuasion and takes you into the domain of *reason*. I will present some classic argumentation techniques using rules of logic, reason, figures of speech, and probing questions. This discussion will make an immediate impact on your speaking *and* listening skills.

In chapter 5, you will learn the final interpersonal communication skill and the secrets and techniques of the ultimate communication tool—*storytelling*. If a picture is worth a thousand words, then a story is worth a thousand pictures. You will learn the three conversations that constantly occur in any storytelling scenario. It will become clear that being able to tell stories effectively is the most valuable skill you can develop in order to persuade others.

In chapter 6, we will make some practical applications of what you have learned by delving into the intricacies of a formal interview and analyzing how to make a great first (and lasting) *impression.* You are *always* interviewing for something every minute, whether to get into the college of your choice, acquire the perfect first job, or rise to the next level in your career.

Chapter 7 centers on *leadership.* Here, you will find practical questions concerning your personal purpose, the disciplines and habits of life-changing leaders, and finding your *place* to *lead,* as well as a quantitative method for making good decisions.

Concluding the book, chapter 8 (on *lifelong learning*) will provide you with perhaps the most important topic of the book—the Wisdom Factor. You will learn the keys to taking your newly acquired wisdom and skill set to a place where a "360-degree view" of the world will be a constant companion. There are four major subject-area quadrants of learning that will equip you to not only lead well but also to *live* well. All of this will combine to provide you with an enhanced perspective, attitude, and depth of knowledge that will make you a world changer.

I have endeavored to write a book of which I can say, "I wish someone had given me this book when I was a young man. It would have made such a difference." If no longer for me, then for my children and grandchildren— and for you and yours.

Herbert Spencer said, "The great aim of education is not knowledge, but action." The Old School is a movement

NOTE: While there is a large amount of instructional material in this book, please know that you are not expected to master everything at once. The idea is to read through the first time while gaining the concepts that are *most* useful to you *right now.* It will then become a reference book for decades to come.

to promote the tenets and skill sets that will help students of *every* age not just to be successful but also to live a life of significance and purpose. I invite you to join this quest.

School might at times get old, but you must get old school in these times.

Now, let's get to work!

CHAPTER 1
Recall

The secret of a good memory is attention, and attention to a subject depends upon our interest in it. We rarely forget that which has made a deep impression on our minds.

—T. Edwards

Failure was only a few moments away.

Ms. Wright, a distinguished professional, was set to lecture a group of three hundred engineers at a large technology convention. She and her team had prepared a dynamic presentation complete with the latest special effects. Each frame had been carefully edited at least a dozen times. She was prepared to "knock 'em dead" with her expertise and presentation skills.

Ms. Wright settled in at the podium, taking one last sip of water. Suddenly, she lost her grip on the glass—soaking her laptop. The screen went dark. She stared into the crowded hotel ballroom as frantic AV personnel rushed to assist. What would she do?

Undeterred, she waved off the rescuers, thanked them for their help, and politely requested two flip charts with markers. She then calmly set the glass upright, mopped up the water as best she could, and stepped off the podium and toward the audience. As she began to speak, she seemed to make eye contact with every person in the room.

She was flawless. She used the easel to deliver each concept just as it had been prepared so tirelessly in the six weeks preceding the event. Her performance captured the audience's undivided attention and earned their utmost respect.

Imagine the confidence they now placed in her. Imagine the influence she could now exercise. Imagine the stories that would be repeated about this "great presentation."

How did she do it? How did she find the wherewithal to pull off such a feat?

By implementing a simple technique she had learned many years prior— known as *ready recall*—Ms. Wright was able to communicate her ideas with precision and poise, even in the midst of difficult circumstances.

Ready recall is one of Ms. Wright's secret weapons, and part of the Old School Advantage.

On surveys that ask what people fear most, public speaking consistently ranks even higher than death. This situation with Ms. Wright is a nightmare scenario for any of us. You might never be called on to give a presentation while facing this kind of difficulty. But will there come a critical moment when technology fails you? Almost certainly.

What if you were not only prepared to *react* to such a challenge but also knew how to use classical recall skills *proactively?* Could you gain an advantage by *intentionally* setting aside technology, if only temporarily and in certain situations? It could well allow you to make an indelible impression on your audience—whether you're speaking to three thousand or a single person.

As the opening quote by Tryon Edwards implies, I want this short story about Ms. Wright to make a "deep impression." The skills and concepts we are about to study can launch your academic and professional careers, placing you well ahead of your contemporaries.

This study of *recall*, a simplified term for *functional short-term memory*, will build a foundation for the other four Old School Advantage competencies.

But first, a brief tutorial in three areas that affect recall:

1. Working memory
2. How we forget
3. How we remember

Let's get to work.

Working Memory

Our brain's most essential function is memory. Without it, we have no ability to draw on past experiences, which makes learning impossible.

Research has provided limited understanding of the mysterious process that permits us to store bits of passing time. This includes studies that have shown that "an average thought lasts no more than a minute before we lose it. What's more, most of us find it impossible to learn more than one new concept every ten minutes."[1]

Have you ever wondered how information was passed to each generation before the common use of the written word? Perhaps this seems a strange question. Haven't people always written things down? No, they haven't.

Many centuries ago, learning depended almost exclusively on having an incredible memory. (Cyrus, king of Persia, could reportedly give the names of all the soldiers in his army.)[2] Without exceptional recall abilities, one had little chance of excelling in education or employment.

Memory was so revered that there was great resistance to a "new technology" known as *writing*. In fact, Socrates, who lived in the fifth century BC, was in no way a fan of the written word. He feared that memories would deteriorate because of it. Fortunately, Plato—the prime pupil of Socrates—wrote down his teacher's aversion to the written word and its "memory-stealing" properties.[3]

The art of memory was also a crucial part of a classical education in the United States up until the 1800s. Since then, the study and practice of memorization has been largely absent. In the last decade, memory work has been even more rare due to the ease with which external memory is available via electronic devices. (One third of people under the age of thirty can't remember their own phone number without pulling it up on their cell phone.)[4]

NOTE: Lest you worry that you have to compete with the "chosen few" who have the fabled "photographic memory," I have news for you: *there is no such thing.* (Unless you count the single case that has been described in scientific literature.)[5]

In his best-selling book on memory, *Moonwalking with Einstein*, Joshua Foer explains how we remember:

> In 1956, a Harvard psychologist named George Miller published what would become a classic paper in the history of memory research. His paper was titled "The Magical Number Seven, Plus or Minus Two: Some Limits on Our Capacity for Processing Information." Miller had discovered that our ability to process information and make decisions in the world is limited by a fundamental constraint: We can only think about roughly *seven* things at a time. When a new thought or perception enters our head, it doesn't immediately get stashed away in long-term memory. Rather, it exists in a temporary limbo, in what's known as short-term, or, *working memory*, a collection of brain systems that hold on to whatever is rattling around in our consciousness at the present moment.[6]

Foer establishes that short-term memory is quite short. That is why you can't recall even the sentence from two sentences back. He points out:

> Dividing memory between short-term and long-term stories is such a savvy way of managing information that most computers are built around the same model. They have long-term memories in the form of hard drives as well as a working memory cache in the CPU that stores whatever the processor is computing at the moment.[7]

Isn't that ironic? We are continuously looking for ways to improve our computers' electronic storehouses, yet the very concept is based on the inner workings of our own brains. Foer continues:

> Miller's work basically says that most people can, on average, hold seven pieces of information in their head at any given time. Some five, others can do nine. But the "magical number seven" seems to be the universal carrying capacity of our short-term working memory. To make matters

worse, those seven things only stick around for a few seconds, and often not at all if we're distracted.[8]

Miller's research now gives you license to stop worrying about your recall inadequacies. You don't have to clog up your brain's synapses with useless information. You can focus on "optimal situational recall utility"—otherwise known as *ready recall*.

How We Forget

"The Curve of Forgetting," originally based on research by German psychologist Hermann Ebbinghaus, describes how we retain and forget information. His research used a one-hour lecture as the basis for testing how this process works.

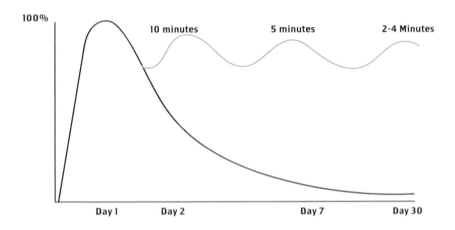

On day 1, at the beginning of the lecture, you go in knowing nothing, or 0 percent (where the curve starts at the baseline). At the end of the lecture you know 100 percent of what you know, however well you know it (where the curve rises to its highest point). By day 2, if you have done nothing with the information you learned in that lecture, didn't think about it again, read it again, etc., you will have lost 50–80 percent of what you learned. Our brains are constantly recording information on a temporary basis: scraps of conversation heard on the sidewalk, what the person in front of you is wearing. Because the information isn't necessary, and it doesn't come up again, our brains dump it all off, along with what was learned in the lecture that you actually do want to hold on to! By day 7, we remember even less, and by day 30, we retain about 2–3 percent of the original hour!

This can be depressing if you are staring final exams in the face. But knowing the mechanics of this human attribute allows you to create solutions. The article continues with some good news on how to combat this memory shortfall.

When you are exposed to the same information repeatedly, it takes less and less time to "activate" the information in your long term memory and it becomes easier for you to retrieve the information when you need it.

Here's the formula and the case for making time to review material: within 24 hours of getting the information—spend 10 minutes reviewing and you will raise the curve almost to 100 percent again. A week later (day 7), it only takes 5 minutes to "reactivate" the same material, and again raise the curve. By day 30, your brain will only need 2–4 minutes to give you the feedback, "yes, I know that . . ."

Often students feel they can't possibly make time for a review session every day in their schedules—they have trouble keeping up as it is. However, this review is an excellent investment of time. If you don't review, you will need to spend 40–50 minutes re-learning each hour of material later—do you have that kind of time? Cramming rarely stores information in your long term memory successfully, which makes it harder to access the material for assignments during the term and exam preparation.

Depending on the course load, the general recommendation is to spend half an hour or so every weekday, and 1.5 to 2 hours every weekend in review activity. Perhaps you only have time to review 4 or 5 days of the week, and the curve stays at about the mid-range. That's OK, it's a lot better than the 2–3 percent you would have retained if you hadn't reviewed at all.

Many students are amazed at the difference reviewing regularly makes in how much they understand and how well they understand and retain material. It's worth experimenting for a couple weeks, just to see what difference it makes to you![9]

No All-Nighters!

FOR COLLEGE STUDENTS: Rest and memory are highly correlated. For both scientific and practical reasons, "pulling an all-nighter" is not a good idea. Kevin DeYoung explains:

> Because you stayed up all night on Thursday, you'll invariably crash on Friday. If not on Friday, you'll sleep an extra five hours on Saturday. If you don't catch up on sleep over the weekend, you'll likely get sick the next week. And if you don't get sick and you keep pushing yourself on empty, your productivity will slide. Or you'll get into a car accident when you are beyond exhaustion. Or you'll snap at your friend and cause a relational meltdown that takes weeks to mend. The time you thought you stole cannot be so easily filched. You cannot cheat sleep indefinitely. And the longer you try to borrow against sleep, the more your body will force you to pay for those hours—plus interest.[10]

The reason we forget so easily lies in what scientists have labeled *neuroplasticity*. This is sometimes referred to as *brain plasticity* and theorizes that the neural pathways in the brain change continuously. With every word you read, your brain literally changes.[11] Unfortunately, like the rest of your body, aging results in less malleability in the brain, and thus less functionality. You face other challenges as well.

"If we stop exercising our mental skills, we do not just forget them: the brain map space for those skills is turned over to the skills we practice instead."[12] This statement has alarming implications when you consider that our current dependence on technology is the greatest influence changing our brains and altering the *way* we think. Our deep contemplation skills—which come from extended and concentrated periods of reading and studying—are being replaced with multitasking and hyper-connectedness. This brings up another enemy of memory: *distraction*.

We have plenty of options in America to fill our free time, but nothing has diluted our attention more than the World Wide Web. Americans are spending as much as a third of their leisure time online. (In China, it is approaching half.)[13] If we are to improve our memories, we must obtain new skills that enhance our ability to focus through deep, contemplative engagement with content, as opposed to the sporadic and surface-level skimming that is fostered in online environments.

Now, let's explore how we remember, which will enable you to deal with the tsunami of information that is constantly vying for your time and attention.

How We Remember

First, some *seemingly* bad news. "The nonlinear associative nature of our brains makes it impossible for us to consciously search our memories in an orderly way. A memory only pops directly into consciousness if it is cued by some other thought or perception—some other node in the nearly limitless interconnected web [of the brain]."[14] The good news is that the disorderly search of our memories is natural. There are certain associative properties of remembering. What does "associative properties" mean?

Let's look first at an area familiar to all of us—music. If I asked you to sing the words to the 1965 Beatles hit "Yesterday," you could probably do it even without hearing the first note. How about "Sweet Home Alabama" by Lynyrd Skynyrd? Just hearing the notes to these songs in your head triggers the associative property of memory. Classics like these, which have been played by cover bands for decades, are recognizable across multiple generations. And when songs from your own generation are included, it is amazing to think that you could probably recognize *hundreds, if not thousands,* of songs just from the first several notes in the opening stanzas. Even as children, we learned the alphabet to the tune of a famous song we otherwise know as "Twinkle, Twinkle Little Star," which was itself a poem put to the tune of a French melody once arranged by Mozart more than two centuries ago.

Music has a powerful way of triggering poems (lyrics) in our brains that we could not otherwise remember without the notes. The Greeks recited or sang poetry long before they learned to write prose, and music was a form of moral training many centuries before their thinkers turned to ethics.[15]

Marketing experts on Madison Avenue have used jingles in radio and TV commercials for years because of the exceptional properties of memory stickiness they possess. And it is all because of the power music has to help us remember.

In a similar way, pictures show the associative properties inherent in re-membering events and their details with ease.

Imagine that you go to a famous art museum, such as the Louvre in Paris. If you take a tour on your own and then take the same tour with a docent or a self-guided audio tour, the paintings will "come alive" with meaning on the second encounter. Knowing the history behind the scene—or details about the artist's life—creates an enriched learning experience as you view the masterpiece.

Consider the painting in the Metropolitan Museum of Art in New York City entitled *Washington Crossing the Delaware.* You can likely explain the general circumstances surrounding this famous scene: It was freezing cold, Christmas night, and Washington was on his way to a surprise attack against the British forces in New Jersey at the Battle of Trenton. You remember this from eighth grade history class.

Additional facts concerning the backstory of this work:

- It was painted in 1848 by a German American, Emanuel Leutze, who completed it in Germany because he wanted to use it to encourage Europe's liberal reformers through the example of the American Revolution.

- In 1942, during World War II, it was destroyed in a bombing raid by the British Royal Air Force (which has led to a persistent joke that the raid was Britain's final retaliation for the American Revolution). Leutze fortunately made multiple copies.

- The people in the boat represent a cross section of the American colonies. Not all are actual people. (Although the man standing next to Washington and holding the flag is Lieutenant James Monroe, fifth president of the United States.)

- The flag depicted is the original flag of the United States (the "Stars and Stripes"), a design that did not exist at the time of Washington's crossing.

- The boat is the wrong type and is too small to carry all occupants and stay afloat. But this emphasizes the struggle of the rowing soldiers.

- The rising sun can be seen on the face of the front rower, and there are shadows on the water, but the crossing took place in the dark of night.

- At what is now called Washington Crossing, the Delaware River is far narrower than the river depicted in the painting. It was also raining.
- The men did not bring horses or field guns across the river in the boats but instead had them transported by ferries.
- Washington's stance, obviously intended to depict him in a heroic fashion, would have been hard to maintain in the stormy conditions. Standing in a rowboat would have risked capsizing it.

Do you *need* to know these particular facts about this painting? Perhaps, if you are studying art history. But the point is that when you see this painting, your experience is now laced with new details, some of which stay with you and animate the scene each time you revisit it.

Music, rhymes, and paintings all provide structure and patterns for associations and, thus, for remembering. We can all remember some things better than others if we are interested in the topic (I knew the final scores of the first thirty-five Super Bowls), but remembering a series of words or numbers usually doesn't trigger easily in our brains. However, visual imagery allows us "to take the kinds of memories our brains aren't good at holding on to and transform them into the kinds of memories our brains were built for." This is known as "elaborative encoding."[16]

Foer quotes one of his mental-athlete friends:

> The general idea with most memory techniques is to change whatever boring thing is being inputted into your memory into something that is so colorful, so exciting, and so different from anything you've seen before that you can't possibly forget it. The natural memory is that memory which is embedded in our minds, born simultaneously with thought. The artificial memory is that memory which is strengthened by a kind of training and system of discipline. In other words, natural memory is the hardware you're born with. Artificial memory is the software you run on your hardware.
>
> Artificial memory has two basic components: *images* and *places*. Images represent the contents of *what* one wishes to remember.

Places—or *loci*, as they're called in the original Latin—are *where* those images are stored.

The idea is to create a space in the mind's eye, a place that you know well and can easily visualize, and then populate that imagined place with images representing whatever you want to remember. Known as the "method of loci" by the Romans, such a building would later come to be called a "memory palace."[17]

The *memory palace* technique Foer mentions will be the foundational technique you will employ to enable ready recall. When you create images for a memory palace, the more humorous or bizarre they are, the more memorable. This is a key concept because ordinary things are not easily remembered. "The more vivid the image, the more likely it is to cleave to its locus. What distinguishes a great mnemonist is the ability to create these sorts of lavish images on the fly, to paint in the mind a scene so unlike any that has been seen before that it cannot be forgotten."[18]

Again, this methodology is designed to give you the ability to recall important information *without* the aid of electronic devices, charts, or notes (think of Ms. Wright). If you can't extract critical information *at the moment* it is needed, then you might as well have never learned it. (And your audience—or your professor—will assume you didn't.)

Another advantage to the memory palace technique is that it gives you complete confidence in what you know (remember) so that you can maintain continual eye contact with a person or audience during any significant discussion or presentation. Making this eyeball-to-eyeball connection is of critical importance in the human relational experience. ("The eyes are the window of the soul.")

Exhibiting ready recall relays to your audience that you have internalized your story and you "know it by heart." This capability is invaluable when seeking to be persuasive.

Ready to learn the memory palace technique? It's time.

Entering the Palace

First of all, relax, take a deep breath, and clear your thoughts—and get ready to see how incredibly well your brain works.

In your mind's eye, walk into a classroom. There are fifteen items—or *loci*—within the room. Pretend that I am reading them to you slowly . . . pausing five to eight seconds between each. Better yet, read the list aloud to yourself. Do *not* write the list down.

Visualize and concentrate on the items.

Number *one* is . . . the whiteboard.

Number *two* is . . . the light switch.

Number *three* is . . . the carpet.

Number *four* is . . . a chair.

Number *five* is . . . a book (on a desk in the center of the classroom).

Number *six* is . . . a telephone (the old-fashioned kind with the piggy-tail cord and a rotary dial).

Again, take this slowly . . . every five to eight seconds or so. (If you have been reading this list at a normal silent reading pace, please start over and read slowly with the pauses.)

Number *seven* is . . . the door.

Number *eight* is . . . the window.

Number *nine* is . . . a table.

Number *ten* is . . . a bottle of water.

Number *eleven* is . . . a dry-erase marker.

Slowly . . . five to eight seconds . . . concentrate . . .

Number *twelve* is . . . a filing cabinet.

Number *thirteen* is . . . the light fixture.

Number *fourteen* is . . . the drapes.

Finally, number *fifteen* is . . . a video projector.

Now, pause and close your book or e-reader. Write numbers one to fifteen on a blank sheet of paper. Take five to eight minutes to list as many of the items as you can—in order. I will be here waiting.

How did you do? Here are the items again:

1. Whiteboard	6. Telephone	11. Dry-erase marker
2. Light switch	7. Door	12. Filing cabinet
3. Carpet	8. Window	13. Light fixture
4. Chair	9. Table	14. Drapes
5. Book	10. Water bottle	15. Projector

Most students correctly name between four and eight items in this first exercise. But whether you only got two correct or twelve, there is a foolproof way for you to get them *all* correct.

Now, let's go slowly through the items again—but *this* time, we'll give you a clue (association) for each.

Please put down your pen and concentrate on the associations you see in your mind.

Ready?

Number *one* is . . . the whiteboard. Picture in your mind a large, black number one drawn on the board. Make it a "1" like you see on a dollar bill.

Number *two* is . . . the light switch. Most conventional light switches have *two* positions—up for on and down for off. Additionally, they typically have *two* switches on each plate with *two* screws holding the switch plate on the wall.

Number *three* is . . . the carpet. Imagine a heroic, *three*-legged German shepherd tracking in mud on a white carpet—and his paw prints look just like the number *three*!

Number *four* is . . . a chair. The chair has *four* legs, and when you turn it upside down, it looks like the number *four*.

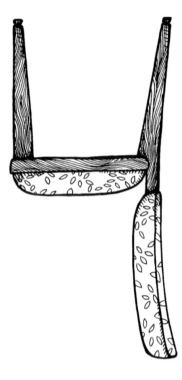

Number *five* is . . . a book. Imagine that the book cost *five* dollars. It has *five* chapters with a total of *five* hundred pages. You hold it with *five* fingers to read.

Number *six* is . . . a telephone. When you pick up the old-fashioned hand piece, it looks like a number *six*. Can you see it? How long is the call you are on? *Six* minutes. What was the cost of a call in the day of rotary phones? *Six* dollars per minute. (No kidding.)

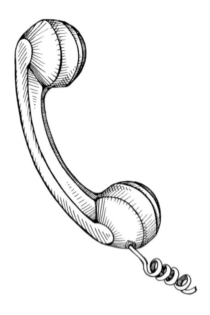

Again, take this slowly . . . every eight seconds or so . . .

Number *seven* is . . . the door. Picture half of the doorframe. It looks like the number *seven*, doesn't it? How high is the doorframe? *Seven* feet.

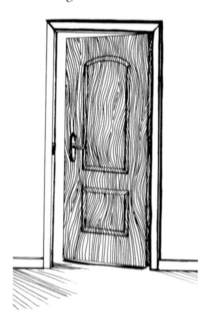

Number *eight* is . . . the window. Visualize the window as a square *eight*: two panes, one on top of the other. How far can you see out the window? *Eight* miles. How much do you pay the window cleaner? *Eight* dollars per hour.

To reiterate, this process is all about creating simple clues to remind you of the item that is associated with each number.

Number *nine* is . . . a table. It is *nine* feet long. Imagine a large, oval *nine* drawn on the tabletop. There is room for *nine* chairs around the table.

Number *ten* is . . . a bottle of water. A *ten*-ounce bottle, of course. Return the bottle to the grocery store, and get *ten* cents back.

Number *eleven* is . . . a dry-erase marker. If you had two markers and held them upside down side by side, they would look like the two ones in the number *eleven*. There are *eleven* different colors of markers available.

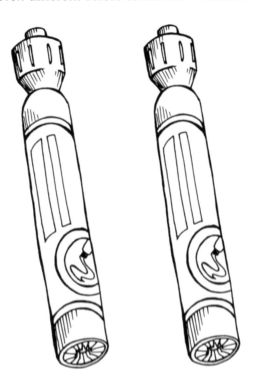

Slowly . . .

Number *twelve* is . . . a filing cabinet. Guess how many drawers are in the cabinet? *Twelve*—one for *each month* of the year. How many file folders does each drawer hold? *Twelve*.

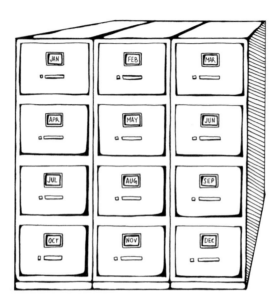

Number *thirteen* is . . . the light fixture. Imagine *thirteen* bulbs. Each bulb is *thirteen* watts and is expected to last *thirteen* years. They were expensive— *thirteen* dollars each.

Number *fourteen* is . . . the drapes. They happen to be *fourteen* feet tall with sunlight coming in *fourteen* hours per day.

Finally, number *fifteen* is . . . a video projector. It takes *fifteen* minutes to warm up, but it projects a very clear image as long as you don't get more than *fifteen* feet away from the screen. It also cost *fifteen* hundred dollars—including installation.

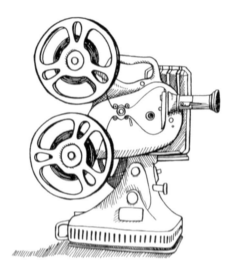

Now, you get a second chance. Close your book or e-reader. Number one to fifteen, and take five minutes to list the items in order.

Check your answers. Let me guess: you answered between eleven and fifteen correctly. This is typical. How did you learn this so quickly?

By making associations between the objects (loci) and their assigned numbers, you easily remembered them. This is a simple technique that allows ready recall. And now you own it. Momentarily, we will make a practical application to show the real value.

But first, you need a break.

Get up, get a soda or a bottle of water (number *ten*), and take a walk. As you do, slowly go over the fifteen locations of the classroom memory palace *three* times.

Oops . . .

If only presidential candidate Rick Perry had used a memory palace in 2012.

Governor Perry said "oops" during a nationally televised debate after failing to remember the third of three government departments he would close down if he became president. The lack of ready recall on such a short list as important as this—the platform cornerstone of his campaign—was not just embarrassing, but unthinkable. His campaign never recovered.

A man who would be the holder of the most powerful position on the planet was sunk by a simple lapse in short-term memory.

I will be prepared, and then perhaps my chance will come.
—Coach John Wooden

Welcome back!

You might be wondering what you have gained by learning fifteen items in an imaginary classroom. Let's find out.

Suppose you need to learn the presidents of the United States from George Washington through the Civil War for an exam in three days. How can you use the memory palace technique for this assignment? (Don't forget to read slowly and pause after each association in order to embed it in the proper locus.)

Here we go . . .

Number *one* is the whiteboard. What is on it? A big number *one*, like on the back of a dollar bill—the same dollar bill that has a picture of George *Washington*. Obviously, you won't miss the *first* president—the "Father of our Country." But notice that the association is still there.

Number *two* is the light switch, which goes up and down like an Adam's apple does when someone with a prominent one talks or swallows. Imagine that our *second* president, John *Adams*, had this conspicuous feature.

NOTE: Number two is a good example of how the association with an object or person does not have to necessarily be true. It only has to be *memorable*. Whether John Adams had a protruding Adam's apple is not the point. Let your imagination go unfettered.

Number *three* is the carpet. Who is on the white carpet with muddy paws? The president's heroic, *three*-legged dog—aptly named *Liberty*.

Number *four* is a chair, and when the fourth president of the United States walks in and sees what has happened to the white carpet, he gets really *mad* at Jefferson's dog, grabs a chair, and smashes the chair into *four* pieces. President James *Mad-i-son* is number *four*.

Number *five* is the book, and it happens to be a hardbound copy of a very famous document: the *Monroe* Doctrine. James *Monroe* is the *fifth* president.

Number *six* is the telephone. Guess who is calling? It's *John Quincy Adams* calling his father John Adams for advice. He has become the *sixth* president and needs *six* minutes to visit. Can you see them talking on the telephone on a split screen in your mind? The anachronistic nature of this scene makes it memorable.

Number *seven* is the door. On the door is a famous performer's name, placed over a star. "Jackson," it says. But this "Jackson" is Andrew *Jackson*—the *seventh* president. He was known for the *seven*-hundred-mile Trail of Tears, which starts after you walk through the *seven*-foot door.

Number *eight* is the window, through which you see a van burning! It is an Aston Martin van. (I did not know they made those; did you?) It reminds us of our *eighth* president, Martin Van Burning . . . I mean, *Martin Van Buren*.

Again, take this slowly . . . every eight seconds or so . . .

Number *nine* is a table. It has a hairy, cowhide tablecloth that has brown and white spots. Can you see the president's hairy, *nine-year-old* son sprawled across it? *William Henry Harri-son*—our *ninth* president.

Number *ten* is the water bottle, which comes in handy when you have a headache and need to take *Tyler*nol. John *Tyler* is chief executive number *ten*.

Number *eleven* is a dry-erase marker, which makes a great instrument with which to *poke* someone. James K. *Polk* is the eleventh president.

Number *twelve* is the filing cabinet. Its *twelve* drawers can be used for keeping clients' measurements if you are a *tailor*. Zachary *Taylor* measures in at number *twelve* on the list.

Number *thirteen* is the light fixture. Each bulb has a *fil*ament inside. If you had more bulbs, you could *fill more* of the room with light. Millard *Fillmore*—president number *thirteen*—also had a *bulb*ous nose.

Number *fourteen* is the drapes. When they are open slightly, you can see sunlight *pierce* through them. Franklin *Pierce* is our man at number *fourteen*.

Number *fifteen* is the projector, which happens to be a *Canon* brand. It costs a few *bucks* for sure (*fifteen* hundred). The life story of James *Buchanan* was the first movie we watched on it. (Not really. But now you won't forget his motion picture debut as "Buck Cannon." It's a western.)

Again, number from one to fifteen, and calmly think through the clues. Each president is just waiting for you at his location (loci) in the classroom. You don't have to be in a hurry. Relax, and recall each one. They are there in the classroom. They are not going anywhere.

If you forgot a few, that's OK. The key is to revisit the fifteen presidents in your memory palace *seven* times over *three* days (seven times three) to guarantee success on your exam. (And for good measure, number *sixteen* is Abe Lincoln. His successor, number *seventeen*, is Andrew Johnson—who was impeached— and number *eighteen* was General Ulysses S. Grant. You now are almost halfway to knowing them all.)

The Magic of Writing Things Down

Have you ever noticed that when you write things down, they are easier to remember? This is no fluke. By some estimates, you are *five times* more likely to recall something if you apply pen to paper.

According to the *New York Times*, children who learn to write by hand rather than by typing read more quickly and are better able to generate ideas and retain information. Even as adults, memory and learning ability are enhanced when we write information rather than type it. The more fully we engage the information, the more it informs and shapes us.[19]

It makes sense when you consider that while the movement of typing uses dozens of movements, the natural motion of the fingers when writing with a pen requires *thousands* of movements, so it causes deeper and more nuanced thinking—as well as better recall. Notice how often the top leaders in organizations write things out while many of their employees prefer typing.[20] (Students and test-takers, take note!)

Another example of why "there's no school like the old school."

LEVERAGING YOUR READY RECALL

You can double your ready recall capacity with a second memory palace. Here is one I created called the *car palace* (with associations):

1. Windshield (See a big red number *one* on it?)
2. Front bucket seats (There are *two* of them.)
3. Speedometer (Go *three* miles over the limit, and you will get a ticket.)
4. Tires (There are *four* of them.)
5. Radio buttons (*Five* of them are programmed.)
6. Engine (It has *six* cylinders.)
7. Middle armrest ("On the *seventh* day, God rested.")
8. Back window (You can see *eight* miles back.)
9. Side mirrors (They're shaped like the top of a number *nine*.)
10. Steering wheel (It makes the zero in the number *ten* and is *ten* inches in diameter.)
11. Horn (It goes "beep, beep" or "one, one [11—*eleven*].")
12. Trunk (It holds twelve items and is twelve cubic feet.)
13. Seatbelt (If you get in a wreck, you are *unlucky*—like the number *thirteen*.)
14. Moon roof (When it's open, you see *fourteen* billion stars.)
15. Tailpipe (This car gets only *fifteen* miles to the gallon and pollutes a lot.)

Can you learn the presidents using the car memory palace? How about John Adams with his Adam's apple protruding as he sits in one of the *two* front seats? Or *six*-year-old John Quincy Adams sitting on the hood where the *six*-cylinder engine is? This is easy.

You can also create your own palace using your house or apartment (loci can be the TV, arm chairs, couch, refrigerator, etc.). You can create a palace using your favorite sports stadium or the route you travel daily, using buildings, streets, or other landmarks as the loci. Use your favorite vacation spot. You can have multiple palaces for an exam, a presentation, an interview, a casual conversation, or something as ordinary as a grocery list. You have the ability to recall *what* you need *when* you need it.

More on the Origin of the Memory Palace

Another historical validation of the memory palace concept comes from a story concerning the Greek poet Simonides in the sixth century BC. Legend has it that he was celebrating a great military victory with a leader named Scopas and his relatives at a great banquet. Simonides received word that two men were waiting to speak with him outside. When he went to meet them, the visitors had disappeared, and the palace dining hall collapsed behind him. Scopas and all in attendance died in the tragedy.

From the event, Simonides reportedly derived a system of mnemonics—thus giving birth to the "memory palace." (He supposedly used a memory palace to lead family members to the location of their deceased loved ones in the rubble, having recalled where they were sitting.)

The story was later dismissed as fictional by Quintilian because "the poet [Simonides] nowhere mentions the affair, although he was not in the least likely to keep silent on a matter which brought him such glory."[21] The legend endures.

MORE TECHNIQUES

Acronyms have been used by all students at one time or another. You can take a cue from Harvard psychologist George Miller—mentioned earlier—and use acronyms in instances where you have between five and nine items to remember.

Once you become proficient with memory palaces, you can also incorporate acronyms within them. If you were using the classroom memory palace to study for a science exam, you could make number *one*, the whiteboard, the place to write an acronym for biological classifications, such as KPCOFGS ("King Phillip Came Over For Good Soup"): Kingdom, Phylum, Class, Order, Family, Genus,

Species. Or, for the string order for beginner guitar students, EADGBE: "Eddie Ate Dynamite, Good Bye Eddie." This enhances the capacity of a memory palace. (Tip: See www.AcronymFinder.com for more aids.)

Another leveraging tool is the *shadow palace*. For example, after you have learned the presidents, you will come to know them so well that each one can actually become like a number for his corresponding place in presidential history. When I see a three, I think "Thomas Jefferson." A seven is always "Andrew Jackson" to me. As nine follows eight, Harrison follows Van Buren. It will become second nature. When you know a list thoroughly, you can make it a memory palace and then remember another list by assigning characteristics—whether true or not—to that specific person. Remember, the more creative you make the associations, the more complex and numerous are the items you can then access through this ready recall technique.

Let's say you work for—or are interviewing with—a company that has a list of "The Six Characteristics of an Exceptional Associate." Here they are (along with the "presidential" association that goes with it):

1. Highest Personal Integrity (Washington is known for his honesty.)
2. Fully Embraces the Company Culture (Adams is hugging me with his big Adam's apple.)
3. Innovative Spirit (Jefferson wrote the Declaration of Independence, which led to free-market opportunities.)
4. Discerning Thinker (See Madison sitting in a chair, pensively considering the Constitution.)
5. Lifelong Learner (Monroe Doctrine—book. Easy.)
6. People-Centered (I see John Quincy on the phone helping a customer.)

I could have easily used the standard classroom palace for this short list, or simply used an acronym. But from any core list you need to learn—whether the US presidents or perhaps the periodic table of elements—all the items can be used as a shadow memory palace themselves.

One more fun method: If you are an art buff or have a favorite personal photograph full of memories, you can walk into any scene, like we did with

Washington Crossing the Delaware, and fill it with associations. This transforms something familiar to you into a memory palace. The possibilities are endless.

Group Activity!

You can enjoy using the *memory palace* technique in group settings. If you have a group project at school or work, develop unique palaces out of any location. The more bizarre or humorous, the better! This can make learning and working fun by creating camaraderie and building rapport amongst your peers. In fact, it might become more like play than work. And you won't ever forget it.

THERE ARE TOO MANY THINGS IN MY PALACE!

You might be asking a common question: "If I am using the same palace(s) repeatedly, will I get everything 'jumbled up' in my mind?" This *can* happen. But when it does, you will just need to go back and strengthen your memory link. The funnier and more bizarre you make your memory palaces, the more memorable they will be. Remember this billboard:

CREATIVITY = OPTIMAL RECALL

Picture a bridge with two tall towers on either side. The left tower is the location, or *loci*, in your palace (numbered one to fifteen—whiteboard, light switch, etc.). The tower on the right represents a person, thing, or concept to be recalled. The bridge in between is the *association* between the number (loci) and the person, thing, or concept. We also refer to this bridge as the *creative zone* where the linkage or connection you need for remembering occurs.

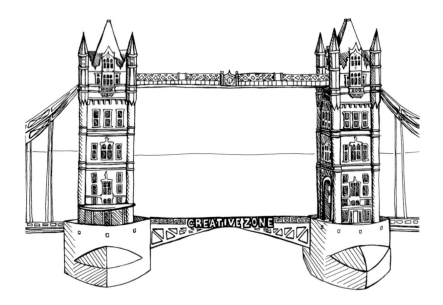

Consider the example you learned for the third president of the United States. The locus is the carpet, or number *three* (left tower). The person we want to remember is Thomas Jefferson (right tower). The humorous and bizarre connection used to create a memorable association/linkage was his heroic, three-legged German shepherd tracking muddy 3s on a white carpet.

In the example of Characteristics of an Exceptional Associate, I used the president shadow palace. For number *three*—"Innovative Spirit"—I associated Thomas Jefferson as the one who wrote the *Declaration of Independence*, which ultimately provided free-market opportunities for entrepreneurs.

If I had wanted to instead use number *three* in the classroom palace, then I could think of a carpet made of one hundred-dollar bills, which would provide the solid financial foundation—or a "ground-floor opportunity"—that any good entrepreneur seeks.

You can easily change the thing to be remembered yet stay in the same palace for different lists. The creative zone provides *unlimited* associations between the loci (in the memory palace you are using) and the person, thing, or concept to be recalled.

Again, humorous, crazy, bizarre, and vivid imagery equates to easier recall. You can place anything you wish in the palace, walk away, and return when you are ready to recall it.

But remember, if the link is not strong enough, it can crumble, and ready recall will be weakened. If this happens, simply go back and reform a more creative, memorable "bridge" between the two "towers."

When you have three or four palaces at your disposal, you have plenty of capacity to alleviate the "getting things jumbled up" problem. (Competitive mental athletes have *hundreds* of memory palaces.) And remember: adding acronyms leverages your ready recall abilities even further.

One more tip adopted from memory athletes is that, before they go into a competition, they imagine the memory palace they are walking into "has the shades wide open so that images will be as clear as possible."[22] You can do the same before a test or a presentation.

Extra Credit:

If you have an interest in learning more memory techniques, I strongly recommend that you go to www.MemoryPower.com. I consider Scott Bornstein to be the foremost memory expert in the United States. The "classroom" memory palace was adapted from his work in this area. But to get the full menu of his expertise, including many more memory techniques, you can learn all you need and more by visiting his website.

CONCLUSION

Technology provides us many advantages that our ancestors did not have. But if you can cultivate memory skills like the ones they needed just to survive, you will seize a great and untapped opportunity to thrive in the twenty-first century.

The great news in this regard is that ready recall can be easily and quickly acquired and is a skill that you can continually improve. It is the foundation on which we will build the interpersonal relationship prowess you need to communicate, persuade, and teach your way to a significant life. Congratulations. You are off to a great start to developing the Old School Advantage.

And Ms. Wright is smiling.

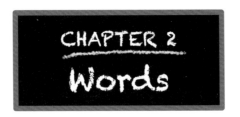

CHAPTER 2
Words

The limits of my language mean the limits of my world.

—Ludwig Wittgenstein

Words matter.

Words are at the center of the human experience. The words we use are the very *currency* of communication—and, as such, have an untold impact on the world around us. Words can even have the power of life and death.[1]

Our second building block on the way to the Old School Advantage in interpersonal communication concerns choosing words that set you apart. You only get one chance to make a first impression, and the cornerstone of every relationship is laid at "hello." Your appearance first, and then the words you use, make up the essence of the initial response you draw from your audience—whether an audience of one or of many. How we speak (and write) is how we define ourselves.

At minimum, when you use ineffective words and poor grammar, you are assessed—fairly or not—as less intelligent, less capable, and less desirable in all facets of life. This puts you in a disadvantageous position. This chapter is dedicated to preventing a poor showing caused by your words. You will be instructed in the use of words and phrases that call *overt positive attention* to your abilities to communicate in an impressive or even profound way. They can make an immediate impact on a conversation or presentation. I call these, "Words that WOW!"

Other words and phrases you learn will be those that support a subtle undercurrent of politeness, sophistication, and discernment. These are called *fit words.*

Both Words that WOW! and fit words will become second nature to you. And believe me, there has never been a better time to speak well. Why?

Strong, effective communication skills in our society are generally lacking and are arguably on the decline. There are many reasons this is the case, but the effects of technology and a dwindling curriculum in the "classics" are two key drivers. You can witness communication deficiencies every day at school or at your workplace.

Ironically, this situation has created a rich environment for people who are willing to work hard to improve and differentiate themselves. With a little extra training and dedication, *you* can be an exceptional conversationalist, public speaker, and writer. You can achieve practically anything with effective communication skills.

Let's get to work.

The Essence of Words

This ancient proverb is very instructive:

```
A word fitly spoken is like apples of gold
in a setting of silver.²
```

This quote speaks to the extraordinarily high value of words chosen well. Implicit in this concept is that using words well is not strictly about using the *correct* words at the *correct* time—it also involves improving skills that allow relationships to be built.

As you learned in chapter 1, our technology-laden culture is also adversely affecting our brains and memory. The Millennial Generation (born 1980–2000) has never known a world *without* the Internet. (They were born into an age where typewriters and fax machines are practically museum relics.) But our world of technological efficiency, along with the accompanying increased production of the American worker, has made it increasingly difficult for this age group to "get a leg up" on the competition in the marketplace. I have a particular affinity for Millennials because I have four of them. I'm passionate about giving them the tools they need to succeed.

But these concepts concerning proper word selection are not just for Millennials. Regardless of your age, imagine what might happen if you were one of the small minority of the population who is dedicated to using words fit for every occasion. What value might be derived from using *exactly* the right word or phrase at *exactly* the right time and place? Could it make a difference in your success trajectory? Could you be more influential? Could you "WOW!" those around you?

We all know the value of being bilingual. What if you could become *bi-gen-lingual?* Or even *tri-gen-lingual?* That is, speak with a "timeless voice" that reaches across generations—older to younger and younger to older.

Business owners and CEOs: What advantage would there be in having a team whose members understood the importance of every word they spoke? Could your organization become more people-centered, making a greater impact in the lives of current customers and a more effective appeal to prospects? What would this do to the bottom line?

Regardless of your position, what could fit words do for your career? For your relationships? For your life?

In short, using proper words provides *power.* As Mark Twain said, "The difference between the right word and the almost right word is the difference between lightning and a lightning bug."[3]

Applying the Old School Advantage words as a communication filter will present you as "wise beyond your years." This is a huge compliment when offered by any member of the generation ahead of yours. Furthermore, using fit words at *any* age deems you to be not only wiser but also more intelligent, well read, and highly qualified in your chosen field.

This chapter is divided into four areas:

1. Fifteen words and phrases that show the Old School wisdom
2. Fifteen power words for success
3. Additional words and phrases that are *fit*
4. Bonus tips

Dr. Frank Luntz is one of the premier wordsmiths of our day, and I refer often to his exceptional work concerning the following lists of words and phrases. I like his powerful quote, "It is not what you say, it's what people hear," which he used for the subtitle of his best-selling book, *Words That Work*. It relates perfectly to the "perception is reality" world in which we must operate. It is a mantra I want to keep in the back of your mind throughout this chapter.

FIFTEEN WORDS AND PHRASES THAT SHOW THE OLD SCHOOL WISDOM

> Words can light fires in the minds of men.
> —Patrick Rothfuss

Words and phrases can connote either a positive or negative tone. For example, the word "catastrophe" is difficult to use in a positive sense; conversely, the word "pleasant" is very positive.

This section contains words and phrases that not only are positive in meaning and usage but also indicate the life and character of the user. In other words, *they are terms that present you as a person of a certain depth and substance universally viewed as favorable.* These words will often contain a nostalgic or "old-school" tone. But that is the point of this first list.

The favorable impression you receive from using these words and phrases in conversation or written communication is what I call the *magic of attribution.* When using these terms, the positive aspect of their meaning is imputed or attributed to you, the speaker. And whether consciously or unconsciously, the listener might instinctively give you credit for ability far above that which you actually possess.

Simply by using the term "people-centered," for example, you are considered to be a friendly person who cares genuinely for others. Or, if you are concerned about the "consequences" of doing something, you must be a responsible person who thinks things through. This "magic" can be a double-edged sword, however. How?

The words we use are an initial indication of our character, and our character speaks to our trustworthiness. If you are earnest in your character, right actions will generally follow. Actions are important because *what we do* comes out of *who we are*. But, if our words lack authenticity because they are contradicted by our behavior, then the influence we are hoping to have will be justifiably diminished. Because there is such power in the words we use, there is an accompanying *responsibility*. We must speak not only with sincerity but also with integrity.

As you increase your usage of these words and phrases, they will have an effect on *you*. They can make you a better person. We are all familiar with the expression "Garbage in, garbage out." "Good in, good out" is true as well. The words and phrases that follow will become habit-forming. You should well see some constructive changes occur in your life as a result.

With each term, I will offer the Old School Advantage meaning and application.

NOTE: In order to make the ready recall applicable from chapter 1, the memory palace *association* is included [in brackets] at the end of each entry using the *classroom* memory palace. This will provide you with some good practice to reinforce how the memory palace operates. And this is an excellent first list of items to have at your ready recall disposal.

1. **"First things first" ("First principles")**

The phrase itself harkens back to a time when things were simpler. It exemplifies the following characteristics: follows the rules, does not rush through work, is a logical sequential thinker, knows how to set priorities.

[The word "first" makes this one easy. See the big "ONE" on the *whiteboard* (number *one*).]

2. **"Consistent"**

This word exemplifies people who will do what they say they are going to do. These people work well with others, and their views and actions are dependable. They are "someone you can count on."

   [The *light* always comes on when you flip the *switch* (number *two*). It is *consistent*.]

3. **"People-centered" ("Customer-centered")**

If you are people-centered, you ask thoughtful questions and listen. You are saying, "I hear you. I get it. I respect you. I care about you."[4] Using this term shows that you care about these aspects of a relationship and focus on the needs and desires of others.

   [Picture *three people* in the *center* of the room sitting on the *carpet* (number *three*).]

4. **"Peace of mind"**

Defined as "the absence of stress or anxiety," this term represents a universal human wish. Contentment, joy, and security are related terms. If you have peace of mind, you are also better equipped to keep your composure under pressure.

   [As you relax in your favorite *chair* (number *four*) at the end of a good day, you have no worries—you have *peace of mind*.]

5. **"-ability" words**

   A. Responsibility
   B. Predictability
   C. Accountability
   D. Reliability
   E. Stability

These *five* "ability" words describe characteristics we all admire. These are also known as *quality attributes*. Having these attributes means you "do what you say you will do" and "exceed expectations." If you have these "abilities," you can write your own ticket.

[You are reading a *book* (number *five*) about golf, and you want to make sure your scores all "R PARS"—an acronym for the *five* "-*ability*" words.]

6. **"Simple truth" ("Truth-based")**

Simple truth implies that you break things down to get at the core issue or problem. You are not interested in the "spin." You are a problem solver. *Truth-based* is a more modern term that is akin to "evidence-based" or "fact-based."[5] All of these terms signal your interest in openness and integrity.

[Picture someone on the *telephone* (number *six*) telling the *simple truth*.]

7. **"Let's get to work"**

This phrase indicates a positive attitude and an eagerness to engage the task. It describes a "go-getter." Any member with this attitude is an asset to the team. This is also a phrase you can use to spur action.

[When you say, "*Let's get to work*," you must "hit the *door* (number *seven*) running!"]

8. **"Consequences"**

This word deals with outcomes and is the only word in this list that could be construed as negative.[6] However, it is positive in that everyone appreciates those who recognize that *choices have consequences*. If you are concerned about the adverse consequences of doing something, you must be a responsible person who carefully considers alternatives.

[The *consequences* of jumping out of the *window* (number *eight*) are not good. Avoid them.]

9. **"Determined"**

This word brings to mind other words like "resolved" and "resolute." If you are determined, then success is the only ultimate outcome. You are committed to it. You will persevere.

[You pound your fist on the *table* (number *nine*), expressing that you are *determined* to successfully complete your mission.]

10. "A hands-on approach" ("Can-do")

Using this phrase indicates that you are not afraid of "getting your hands dirty" or getting involved in the *real* work.[7] You will "get in there and fix things" *when* and *how* they need to be fixed.

[You have both *hands on* the *water bottle* (number *ten*).]

11. "In my opinion"

These three words signal strength—"for what I'm about to say, I take full responsibility." That shows confidence. The more certain you are about something, the more likely you are to preface or conclude your remarks with "in my opinion."[8]

[You stand before the class, *dry-erase marker* (number *eleven*) in hand, ready to give your *opinion*.]

12. "Common sense"

"Why is common sense so uncommon?" Precisely. That is why you are valuable if you have it. You are a clear thinker. You have sound practical judgment—a sort of native intelligence. This could be considered a component of the fabled "it factor."

[Thomas Paine kept his pamphlets, *Common Sense*, in a *file cabinet* (number *twelve*). It sold *twelve* million copies.]

13. "No excuses"

You *will* succeed, period. Also characteristic of someone who does not complain or whine.

[There is *no excuse* for not replacing the *thirteen* bulbs in the *light fixture* (number *thirteen*). You need good light to study or work!]

14. "Extraordinary" and "exceptional"

These words are used sparingly today and indicate "above and beyond." [9] They carry far more weight than pedestrian words such as "cool," "nice," or the overused "awesome." If you have exceptional or extraordinary character, you will be invaluable to your family, team, or employer.

[The *fourteen*-foot-high *drapes* (number *fourteen*) in the ballroom were *extraordinary* and *exceptional*. (Say with a British accent for effect.)]

15. "Nothing is more important than _____."

If you use this phrase in a speech—especially at the beginning or the end—you will have undivided attention. It also conveys passion. [10]

[*Nothing is more important than* the last thing you show using your *projector* (number *fifteen*).]

FIFTEEN POWER WORDS FOR SUCCESS

> Language is the apparel in which your thoughts parade before the public.
>
> —George Crane

This section contains words and phrases that have a more modern-day feel, but they are packed with power.

To reiterate, there is *nothing* more powerful than words. More than any other single thing we experience, they have the greatest influence on our lives. I take this simple truth seriously and realize the personal responsibility I have as an author when I share it with you.

As before, I will offer Old School Advantage meanings and applications. The memory palace *association* is again included in brackets at the end of each entry to allow ready recall. [This time using the *car* memory palace.]

1. **"Imagine"**

This word could be the *single most powerful word* in the English language because it has more than 320 million different meanings (in the United States).[11] When you hear "imagine," *your* vision is seen in *your* mind, and it blends with *your* heart and life experiences. Only humans can see things as they *ought* to be—and that is what this word is all about.

   [As the most powerful word, it has to be number *one* in this palace. You can go anywhere you can *imagine* as you look out of your front *windshield* (number *one*).]

2. **"Mission"**

This word deals with an important goal or purpose that is accompanied by strong conviction. It means a vitally important endeavor. It is a calling.

   [You are sitting in the *front seat* (number *two*) and turn the ignition to start the *mission*.]

3. **"My commitment"**

When you give your commitment, you are offering a level of assurance that is dependable and forthright. You are saying, "I will be involved and sincere in my actions." It is essentially a vow. It is stronger than a promise.

   [I have made a *commitment* to watch my *speedometer* (number *three*) and never exceed the limit.]

4. **"Fully aligned"**

This phrase connotes cooperation amongst team members, which often occurs after rigorous debate and argumentation—thus yielding the correct way to proceed on any issue, problem, or challenge.

   [The *tires* (number *four*) need to be *fully aligned,* or your car can eventually swerve off the road.]

5. **"Life-changing"**

This term connotes comprehensive change—usually positive. It goes beyond *transformational*, which is a more difficult concept to understand.[12]

> [You can hear a *life-changing* message by choosing one of the *five* buttons on the *radio* (number *five*—radio buttons).]

6. **"Optimize"**

This word is more effective than "maximize" in a business setting because it means "best in class," with opportunity for even more improvement as discoveries allow. (For customers, "more efficient and effective" is more appropriate.[13]) In plain words, it is "to make the most of."

> [You want to *optimize* the performance of your car's *six*-cylinder *engine* (number *six*).]

7. **"Certified"**

This indicates a level of reliability and might even imply a guarantee. When you certify something, you are saying it has been confirmed, verified, and validated as "good to go." It often connotes professional competence (e.g., MD, JD, CPA, CFP, etc.).

> [You can *rest* (arm rest—number *seven*) assured that your car is *certified*.]

8. **"Authenticity"**

If you are authentic, you are friendly, easy to get to know, and trustworthy. It is a trait that is honored in American culture. It combines genuineness and substance.

> [As you look to the past—out the *back window* (number *eight*)—there were many wise and *authentic* people.]

9. **"Insight"**

If you are insightful, you have an intuitive discernment for underlying truth. Wisdom, understanding, acumen, and right judgment would all be components. In business, "it is the ability to identify what is missing and bring it to life."[14]

[*Insight* requires surveying your surroundings through *side mirrors* (number *nine*) before making a move.]

10. "Impact"

This word implies a *measurable* difference.[15] You make an impact when you effect a desirable outcome. The proper impact can "move the dial," allowing you to dominate.

[Keep both hands on the *steering wheel* (number *ten*) because the air bag deploys on *impact*.]

11. "Because"

Research has shown that saying "because" triggers an automatic compliance response.[16] Even when no good reason follows "because," people still often allow you to do what you requested.

[Get out of my way *because* I am honking my *horn* (number *eleven*).]

12. "Bold approach"

This phrase says you are thinking beyond the conventional or usual limits. A bold approach speaks of courage, initiative, and spirit. Many of the great military battles in history were won because of a "bold stroke."

[It would be a *bold approach* to sneak a spy into Berlin during WWII in the *trunk* of a car (number *twelve*).]

13. "No surprises / no worries"

You are not going to shock anyone at the last minute—something most people dislike. You are saying, "I will handle this for you. Trust me." You stand behind your promises, and things are going to go "as advertised."

[You will drive safely, with hopefully *no surprises / no worries*, so the *seat belt* (number *thirteen*) won't be needed—but still used.]

14. "Breakthrough"

This word connotes surpassing expectations—even something game-changing—something never seen before.[17] It is more than just innovation. It is "gaining by leaps and bounds," not just mere progress. This speaks more to a completely new discovery—not just an improvement. Another modern-day synonym could be "disruptive technology."

> [You envision a *breakthrough* as you look through the *moon roof* (number *fourteen*).]

15. "Hassle-free"

This means eliminating the difficulties that result from missed deadlines, deliveries, or other costly (in time or money) inconveniences. (It is the opposite of the dreaded Department of Motor Vehicles experience.)

> [A bumper to bumper (*tailpipe*—number *fifteen*) warranty means my car maintenance is *hassle free*.]

Now you have these words and phrases at your ready recall "fingertips" to enhance your capabilities in every mode of communication. I encourage you to use the memory palaces until they are firmly and naturally entrenched into your vocabulary. Conveniently, there are thirty of them, which allows you to review one per day throughout a month. Practice them in this manner for three months, and they will be yours for life. (I call this little exercise "Ninety Days to WOW!") Once you have them, you will be amazed with the results!

Now, it's your turn.

ADDITIONAL WORDS & PHRASES

In this section, there are ninety additional words and phrases that will multiply your capacity right away. Your job is to use them in a way that will reflect your personality and character. They are listed in alphabetical order.

- A balanced approach
- A fresh approach
- Aspirational
- At last
- Change
- Choice
- Classic
- Coachable
- Comfortable
- Compare
- Continuous improvement
- Convenience
- Culture of _____
- Customize
- Deserve
- Dialogue
- Distinguished
- Easy
- Effective
- Efficient
- Exclusive
- Experienced
- Expert
- Faithful
- Fresh
- Help
- Humility
- Improve[ment]
- Independent [thinker]

- Indispensable
- Initiative
- Integrity
- Intentional
- Investing in your future
- Last chance
- Lasting solutions
- Let me fight for you
- Life is an adventure
- Maturity
- Money-saving
- My pleasure
- Naturally
- New
- Now
- Originality
- Overcome
- Passion
- Performance driven
- Please
- Popular
- Powerful
- Practical
- Prevention
- Priority
- Profitable
- Promise
- Prosperity
- Proven
- Pursuit of perfection

- Real-time
- Recommended
- Re-engineer
- Relentless
- Remarkable
- Renew
- Research
- Results
- Risk-free
- Safety
- Satisfaction
- Save
- Secret
- Security
- Simplify
- Single-minded focus
- Soothe
- Specialist
- Striking
- Surefire
- Thank you
- Timely
- Traditional
- Trusted
- Ultimate
- United
- Unlimited
- Valuable
- We deliver
- Wow
- You're right

There are scores of additional words we could have included in this discussion. We are continually adding to the list. Have ones you want to share? Send them. I want to hear about it!

Ninety Days to WOW!

Here is an easy daily exercise to allow you to take ownership of the 120 WOW!/fit words and phrases introduced in this chapter:

Starting on the first day of any month, write on your daily task list/calendar the word or phrase that corresponds to the number on the list. For example, on the Old School list of fifteen, write "First things first" in a prominent place—perhaps writing it in a noticeable color like red. Also write "#1" beside it for the memory palace clue. On the second of the month, you would write "consistent" and "#2, light switch"—and so on each day. On the sixteenth through the thirtieth, you would use the Power Word List of fifteen with the car memory palace clues.

The idea is to speak or write each word or phrase at least *three* times on its "day" to embed both the word/phrase and the memory palace clue deep into your brain. Repeat this for ninety days, and you will have these words forever in your vocabulary—*and* they will come naturally.

As your memory palace skills continue to grow, you can do the same exercise with the additional ninety words and phrases, expanding your WOW!/fit words capacity and usage to even greater extent over the course of just one year.

Try it, and see what a difference it makes in your influence with others and the change it makes in you!

Bonus Tips

1. **The two biggest word outlaws of our time.**
   - "Like." This verbal tick might be the worst of our time.
   - "So." Stop using this word at the beginning of every answer. It is a nervous transition word.

   Eliminate these, and you will raise your IQ in the eyes of others by twenty points.

2. **Put thesaurus and dictionary apps on your electronic devices.**
   Refer often to these word apps and watch your WOW! and fit words multiply exponentially.

3. **Avoid jokes and anger in e-mails.**
   Your voice tone and inflection can't be determined. Humor and sarcasm can be misinterpreted and thus offend. Similarly, you should avoid sending an e-mail when you are emotional—especially when angry. (Whenever Abraham Lincoln felt the urge to tell someone off, he would compose what he called a "hot letter." After composing it, he would then put it aside until he cooled down. He would write on it, "Never signed, never sent.")

4. **Join Toastmasters International.**
   This organization holds meetings on a weekly basis at over fourteen thousand locations around the world. A Toastmasters meeting is a learn-by-doing workshop in which participants hone their speaking and leadership skills in a low-pressure atmosphere. Members evaluate one another's presentations and provide key feedback for improvement. It is exceptional "graduate level" training to supplement the Old School Advantage—especially for recent college graduates or young professionals. Learn more at www.Toastmasters.org.

CONCLUSION

Years ago, a construction supervisor was ready to retire. He told his employer of his plans to leave the house-building business and live a leisurely life with his wife. He was getting older, and he wanted to see his grandchildren more. He would miss the paycheck but felt like it was time to slow down.

The builder was saddened to see him go and asked if he would build one more house for the company as a personal favor.

The supervisor agreed; however, he never put his heart into this last project. He resorted to shoddy workmanship and inferior materials. It was an unfortunate way to end his career. When he finished his work and it was time to inspect the house, his employer never set foot inside. He smiled and handed the key to his longtime employee. "This is yours," he said. "It's my gift to you!" The retiree now had to live in the home he had built.

Eventually, we will all live in what we build. Every day, we're constructing a life, and the materials we use are our *words*. With our words, we hammer a nail, place a board, or erect a wall. All of us must recognize the power of the words we use—for better and for worse—because we're going to live in what we build with them.

A limited vocabulary limits your life. Whether on an essay exam, a first date, a job interview, a sales presentation, or as a keynote address at a national convention—words make the difference. In fact, they can—and always do—*change the world*.

Words are the only things that last forever.

—Sir Winston Churchill

CHAPTER 3
Influence

By simply changing three words in a standard infomercial line from "Operators are waiting, please call now" to "If operators are busy, please call again," product sales skyrocketed.[1]

Food servers who simply parroted their customers' orders back to them *exactly* as they said them—word for word—increased their tip size by almost 70 percent.[2]

In an office break room where employees were asked to pay for their drinks on the "honor system," a picture of eyes was placed on the wall above the coffee pot. This increased the payments by more than two and a half times.[3]

What is happening in each of these scenarios shows the power of influence and persuasion techniques. You have acquired a recall system, which is available to you at a moment's notice, and learned words and phrases that allow you to speak powerfully in any situation. By combining those skills with the powers of influence and persuasion, you are garnering a formidable arsenal of rhetorical weaponry.

But the realm of influence is one where your natural inclinations and sensibilities as a decent person can be exploited. Therefore, you must also learn how to "play defense." This means you have to be paying attention. In *The Invisible Gorilla*, by Christopher Chabrois and Daniel Simons, there is a fascinating and now well-known experiment described that teaches us about what we see.[4] In other words—how we pay attention and to what.

The experiment was conducted at Harvard and involved students moving around and passing two basketballs. One team wore black shorts and the other white. The scene was filmed so that the student participants could go out on the campus grounds to run the experiment.

They asked fellow students to watch the approximately one-minute film and count the number of passes made by the players wearing white shorts and to ignore those wearing black. *Stop here* and go to www.TheInvisibleGorilla.com to watch the video yourself before the results of the experiment are revealed.

After watching the video, the subjects were asked how many passes they counted. The correct answer is fifteen. But the task of counting was just meant to be a distraction from the gorilla-suited girl who casually walked right through the middle of the players in the game. Incredibly, *half* of the students did not notice the gorilla in the film as they counted the passes. The experiment has been conducted in multiple countries with diverse audiences, and the results are always consistent.

Chabrois and Simons explain that the gorilla was so often missed because of our lack of attention when we see an unexpected object. The scientific name for this is "inattentional blindness."

They go on to say, "When people devote their attention to a particular area or aspect of their visual world, they tend *not* to notice unexpected objects, even when those unexpected objects are salient, potentially important, and appear right where they are looking."[5]

If we are this blind to such an obvious distraction half of the time, imagine how vulnerable we are when experts in the art of influence and persuasion use their techniques on us. And, unlike in 1999, when the experiment was first conducted, this attention deficit is made worse by the electronic rectangles that take up more and more of our time and attention.

Because our brains simply don't allow us to be aware of all that surrounds us, we should learn the influence techniques so well that they become second nature to us.

We will look at three areas regarding influence and persuasion:

1. Influence techniques
2. Influence phrases
3. Bonus tips

Let's get to work!

Six Influence Techniques

Why do some things "come naturally," and others don't? Why can you do many things "without thinking about it," yet other tasks are elusive? These are key questions to consider if you are to learn how to use influence and persuasion techniques effectively and also defend against them when necessary.

In his book *Thinking Fast and Slow*, Daniel Kahneman explains the two systems of thinking:

> *System I*, or fast thinking, operates automatically and with little effort (such as you have when you are an experienced driver. Or soon, with your *memory palace!*)

> *System II*, or slow thinking, requires effort, such as with complex computations[6] or tasks.

NOTE: For me, learning to play the guitar is a perfect example of how complex System II tasks are "converted" into System I tasks. At first, it was a torturous process, as my fingers would not reach the frets and I had to concentrate on every position and every chord intensely. Remarkably, within a few days, I found myself changing chords quickly and strumming to the beat without thinking about the individual actions. The chords had "moved" from System II to System I. This gives a clearer insight into what you already know: "practice makes perfect."

The art of influence and persuasion depends on System I for its advantage because System I cannot be turned off. The instinctive nature of System I leaves room for errors of intuitive thinking. System II, on the other hand, is in charge of self-control and therefore takes on the role of overtaking any impulses of System I that might be disadvantageous.[7]

Kahneman explains:

> Several psychological studies have shown that people who are simultaneously challenged by a demanding cognitive task and by a temptation

are more likely to yield to the temptation. Imagine that you are asked to retain a list of seven digits for a minute or two. You are told that remembering the digits is your top priority. While your attention is focused on the digits, you are offered a choice between two desserts: a sinful chocolate cake and a virtuous fruit salad. The evidence suggests that you would be more likely to select the tempting chocolate cake when your mind is loaded with digits. System 1 has more influence on behavior when System 2 is busy, and it has a sweet tooth.[8]

In other words, when you are working on a task that requires more concentration (System II) and an influence technique (or temptation) is introduced, you are more likely to indulge in compliant behavior than you otherwise would be. In addition to preoccupation, fatigue can be a factor that might cause you to comply more readily.

The propensity to "blindly follow along" as marketers, salespeople, and politicians of all stripes take advantage of your brain's operating system is also referred to as *fixed-action patterns*.[9] These patterns occur in the same mode and order almost every time—almost like a recording being played. Compliance expert Robert Cialdini, author of the seminal book *Influence: The Psychology of Persuasion*, calls this the *click . . . whirr* response. When you are on a date, the date tape kicks in: *click . . . whirr*. When you are taking care of children, the parent tape kicks in. When a clothing salesperson asks, "May I help you?" *Click . . . whirr*: "No thanks, I'm just looking." We have behavior responses that occur without thought. This is why empty, persuasive messages like television commercials work so well.[10] This is also why it is important to understand how and when influence tools are being employed against you.

You can also learn how to use these techniques to your advantage. And because these techniques ramp up your influence skills to an even greater level, it is important to maintain high personal integrity when applying these skills.

INFLUENCE TECHNIQUE ONE: RAPPORT & LIKABILITY

We all enjoy working and being with people whom we like on a personal level. This is why we comply with friends' requests and often have a difficult time saying "no," even when we should. This is also an issue when we interact with someone who comes across as likable, even when we first meet them.

Building rapport and likability is typically the first persuasion technique we use—or have used on us. There are several ways this is done.

- **Physical attractiveness.** It is commonly understood that good-looking people have a distinct advantage in social and business settings. But the scope of that influence appears to have become even greater as social scientists have studied the "halo effect." This occurs when "one positive characteristic of a person dominates the way that person is viewed by others."[11] Physical appearance fits this definition.

  What's more, we automatically ascribe nice-looking people qualities such as talent, compassion, trustworthiness, and intelligence. And the scariest part is that we do this without even being aware of the role attractiveness plays in our judgment.[12]

- **Compliments.** In *The Theory of Moral Sentiments*, Adam Smith wrote this concerning flattery:

  > "It is only the weakest and most superficial of mankind who can be much delighted with that praise which they themselves know to be altogether unmerited. A weak man may sometimes be pleased with it, but a wise man rejects it upon all occasions."

  Yet, flattery seems to always work because many lack wisdom. Even when it is obviously being used in the form of insincere praise with an ulterior motive—called "strategic flattery"[13]— it still often gets the desired result for the perpetrator. Recognize when flattery is being used as a weapon of persuasion against you. And always use compliments authentically yourself.

Perfect vision is to see the faults in yourself and the good in others.

—Anonymous

- **Similarity.** Simply dressing like the person you are trying to persuade can provide an immediate likability connection (highly prevalent among teen-agers, for example). Also, relating to people based on vocation, hobbies, children/grandchildren (particularly effective), or other interests is very powerful.

  The great Greek father of philosophy, Socrates, went about Athens talking to as many people as he could, asking them questions all his life. He was always interested in trades and occupations and how they were conducted—and his questions gradually broached more complex matters of beliefs, morals, and opinions.[14]

  Understanding the geography and landmarks of a hometown and otherwise being well read in a variety of areas also contributes to your ability to relate through similarity. Even though some of these areas appear to be insignificant, they aren't. Small connections add up to big influence.

- **Postural echo.** This is another way to say "mirroring." By adopting a physical posture that is similar to—but not exactly like—that of the person you wish to persuade, you can build instant rapport. It could be as simple as holding your arms in a comparable manner, or crossing your legs, or leaning in when they do.

  Done correctly, mirroring can create a more relaxed atmosphere. The psychological reason for this is that the person feels that you are "just like them"; therefore, it can be a small part of opening the door for earning their trust.

  Putting a person at ease with this method is legitimate if you are doing it to eliminate any social barriers or to create a receptive environment for discussing the benefits of certain proposals and recommendations—in other words, to effectively overcome the natural "sales resistance" we all sometimes have. However, using postural echo—or any other influence technique—for manipulative advantage is *not* cool.

Building Immediate Rapport with "LAVA"

In order to *warm up* a conversation and get it *flowing*, use "LAVA."

It might seem counterintuitive, but in almost any dialogue, the person who talks the least usually controls the conversation. *Listening* is critical to rapport building. (Your parents were right when they said, "You have two ears and one mouth for a reason.") Asking questions is the sure way to allow your companion to talk more.

"LAVA" is an acronym to help you remember *four* key areas to touch on in an initial conversation—thus equipping you for getting to know someone in a comfortable manner. *Notice* you will *not* ask about their career first—even though the typical first question one asks when meeting someone for the first time is, "What do you do?" Rather, these questions are designed to allow you to get to know something about the "whole person," such as origins, family heritage, etc., before you ask about their line of work.

Here are the four areas with suggested accompanying questions.

Preface the first question with a simple, "I'm just curious . . ." (Try saying this while at the same time bringing one hand from your upper chest/neck area slowly down toward your subject, out in front of you with your palm up. Do it naturally in one motion.)

- **Locations:** "Where are you from originally?" If the answer is "From here," then follow with, "Have you lived here all your life?" If *not* from here, ask, "Oh, what brought you here?"

  You can also ask, "Did you go to school here/there also?" (Alma maters are very important to most people.)

- **Associations:** "Do you have a family?" (If no, you can ask, "Any pets?") "Do you know anyone at this meeting/in town, etc.?"

- **Vocations:** "How do you spend most of your time?" "Have you always been in this profession?"

  "What did you want to be when you were growing up?" (This question focuses their thoughts and takes them back to a simpler time. *Nostalgia* really builds rapport!)

- **Avocations:** "How do you spend your free time?" (Opens up the conversation to hobbies and interests.)

  Always be aware of the tone of your voice throughout and lace the discourse with, "Tell me more . . ." This simple approach will always give you plenty to talk about, and it is a rapport-building gem. Try it with a big smile, and see what great things will happen!

RAPPORT AND LIKABILITY OBSERVATIONS:[15]

- In customer service settings, you can foster rapport by repeating customers' words back to them, regardless of whether those articulations are in the form of questions, complaints, or requests. (E.g., "So, you're saying you'd like to purchase ten units now with the possibility of increasing that to twenty units in May.")
- The lack of personal contact between negotiating parties in an electronic format such as e-mail can be a roadblock to a successful outcome. Research indicated this clearly in an experiment in which MBA students negotiated with one another either face to face or via e-mail. Those who negotiated through e-mail exchanged far less of the kind of personal information that helps people establish better rapport. (It is more difficult to use influence techniques in a text or e-mail.)

- Researcher Don Moore and his colleagues asked: What if, before a negotiation, the parties engaged in some form of mutual self-disclosure? In other words, they could get to know a little bit about one another's background in addition to schmoozing for a few minutes on topics unrelated to the negotiation before the negotiation takes place. To test this idea, the researchers paired up students enrolled at two elite US business schools and had them negotiate a deal. Whereas half were simply given the instructions to negotiate, the other half were provided with a photograph of the negotiating partner, some brief biographical information about the partner (e.g., undergraduate alma mater, interests), and instructions to spend some time before the negotiation getting to know one another. When participants were given no additional information, 29 percent of the pairs came to an impasse, failing to agree to a deal. Only 6 percent of the more "personalized" pairs came to an impasse. The negotiated prices were also 18 percent higher with the "personalized" groups.

While these techniques for building rapport are primarily in a context of initial encounters with people, the best time to develop rapport with those you need to influence is *before* you need them. Develop an attitude and posture of graciousness and thoughtful interaction that is an ongoing aspect of who you are, and you will find that most of the features of rapport we have identified will come naturally.

Influence Technique Two: Reciprocity

The Rule of Reciprocation is overpowering. *Reciprocity* exceeds rapport and likability in its capacity to persuade. In civilized society, it obligates us to repay others for what we receive and is an essential function for promoting fairness and equity in social and business interactions. We are raised to understand that a favor deserves repayment—typically "in kind." This is known as "the honored network of obligation."[16] Reciprocity is the glue that allows people to cooperate.[17] There is a general societal disdain for those who choose to take without giving back.

Another aspect of this Rule of Reciprocation comes from its ability to create an unpleasant feeling of indebtedness. It makes us say yes when the more logical response is no. This happens even when small favors are designed to get large commitments. Or when we accept a nice favor knowing we will feel obligated to pay it back. It is hard to resist.

The most subtle use of the power of reciprocity comes when it is used within the context of a concession. After making a larger request of someone—one that is likely to be turned down—a smaller request is made, which is the one desired in the first place. This comes across as a concession and is reciprocated with an agreement to the second request. (This comes naturally in negotiations for a car or a house.)

One key in this technique is to not make the initial request so large that it is seen as too extreme, because the tactic will then backfire. Done correctly, the initial exaggerated position allows a series of reciprocal concessions. This is known as the "rejection-then-retreat" technique of compliance.[18] One of the most famous examples comes from the Oval Office.

In 1972, the Nixon White House fell into a scandal known as Watergate. G. Gordon Liddy, who was in charge of intelligence gathering for the Committee to Re-elect the President, proposed a break-in of the Democratic National Committee headquarters at the Watergate office building. The plan involved using ten men.

This ill-advised scheme was inexplicably approved by higher-ups in the White House. But how? Especially given that victory for Nixon seemed like a lock for a second term. (He won by a landslide in the general election with 520 electoral votes to George McGovern's seventeen.) It was a classic rejection-then-retreat scenario.

The cost of the proposed operation was a pricey $250,000 in cash, which could not be traced. So it was not only risky but also expensive. But the $250,000 plan was not Liddy's first proposal. The first plan had a $1 million price tag. When this proposal was rejected, he retreated to $500,000. After this amount was also rejected, a "bare bones" plan was presented for $250,000. This one was approved. The rest is American history.

It is easier to resist at the beginning than at the end.

—Leonardo da Vinci

Not all reciprocity techniques have to be big enough to turn the fate of a nation. Small favors, seemingly as insignificant as offering a cold drink to a potential customer on a hot day, can still be defined as using this technique. Favors such as dinner coupons, tickets to the theatre, or a ride home from the airport might be used to elicit bigger favors or purchases in return. And, in most cases where it is not abused, our culture generally deems this all to be acceptable behavior.

But just be aware that your best defense against the illegitimate use of reciprocity is to ascertain the reason for a request that is put before you. If a request is truly a favor offered to you, then accept graciously—thus complying with social norms. But if you recognize a request as a trick designed to take advantage of your good manners, then you should not feel obligated.

Influence Technique Three: Authority

"We have it on good *authority* . . ." Why is this authority "good"? Because authority evokes thoughts of sound judgment and knowledge or expertise that we don't possess personally. There are many ways *authority* comes into play as a persuasion technique. Two in particular are ever present and effective.

Titles come with authority. Professional development or academic degrees carry the weight of authority. It's a given that a PhD degree holder is going to influence us with his or her opinions more than someone with only a high school diploma. Likewise, position titles in business, government, or any organizational structure make it clear who has more authority. Oftentimes, these titles are used to take advantage of others.

Attire, such as military uniforms, signifies various levels of authority. Military insignias make it easy for subordinates to show proper respect. In the corporate world, the same holds true in a more subtle way. Professionals "dress for success" partly in an effort to gain credibility—or authority—within their hierarchy or with customers. Doctors who wear a tie and a white lab coat are likely to be trusted more than those who dress more casually. Yet what doctors wear should have no bearing on our appraisal of their abilities. Even in something as inconsequential as attire for a football game, supporters "wear their colors" to simultaneously intimidate the opponent and support their own team.

Where are we vulnerable to authority in these areas? Someone who is well dressed, well credentialed, and well spoken has a lethal combination, as these people most often exude an air of confidence. Yet we must not equate confidence with *competence*. Always ask, "Is this person really an expert? Why should I believe this person's opinions?"

Here are three considerations:

First, there is a common error known as "the fallacy of the expert witness."[19] There is nothing wrong with appealing to authority, but it must be done in the right way. We must dig deeper. In a trial, the expert witness is always cross-examined. Credentials alone are not enough to certify his testimony; he must convince a jury that his reasons are adequate. Even eyewitnesses get it wrong—often. "Mistaken eyewitness identifications, and their confident presentation to the jury, are the main cause of over 75 percent of wrongful convictions that are later overturned by DNA evidence. A criminal conviction based entirely on a 'confident' eyewitness identification has a 30 percent chance of being erroneous."[20]

If this is the case with eyewitnesses, imagine how vulnerable we are to influence techniques. Juries have been wrongly swayed when the "appeal to authority" has been employed. That is why all appeals to authority must ultimately rest on the *evidence*.

Second, sometimes one's conclusion is already determined by one's starting point. People might be tempted to abuse their credentials (authority) to get their way or win an argument—thus supporting their predisposition. There is also a temptation to simply "count noses," as if the winning majority vote on a topic is the affirming basis for its validity. This "might makes right" proxy is extremely dangerous and must be recognized.

Third, another subtle yet effective kind of authority is simple *repetition*. "A reliable way to make people believe in falsehoods is frequent repetition, because *familiarity is not easily distinguished from truth.* Authoritarian institutions and marketers have always known this fact."[21] Often, when people do not have the credentials themselves or can't assemble experts to back their position, they will influence through repetition—and sometimes volume (as in raising their voice).

Adolph Hitler went even further in his 1925 autobiography, *Mein Kampf.* He not only used repetition to promote lies but, with the following, took this influence technique to another level:

> In the *big lie* there is always a certain force of credibility; because the broad masses of a nation are always more easily corrupted in the deeper strata of their emotional nature than consciously or voluntarily; and thus in the primitive simplicity of their minds they more readily fall victim to the big lie than the small lie, since they themselves often tell small lies in little matters but would be ashamed to resort to large-scale falsehoods. It would never come to their heads to fabricate colossal untruths, and they would not believe that others could have the impudence to distort the truth so infamously. Even though the facts which prove this to be so may be brought clearly to their minds, they will still doubt and waver and continue to think there may be some other explanation.

Extraordinary, isn't it? Joseph Goebbels, Hitler's Minister of Propaganda, made this notorious statement: "Tell a lie enough times, and it becomes the truth." As Daniel Kahneman explains, "System I understands sentences by trying to make them true."[22] Our natural inclination to want to believe people leads effectively to our gullibility. This unfortunate example shows how devastating influence techniques can be when used for evil purposes.

When seeking to establish authority for yourself or your cause, finding reliable authority—citing research, quoting experts, or acquiring the expertise yourself—will all help you to be more persuasive, but be prepared to defend your position without relying solely on authority.

Influence Technique Four: Consensus (Social Proof)

If you are looking to gain *consensus*, you are trying to get everyone "on the same page" or, to use a power phrase from chapter 2, to get them "fully aligned." But the persuasion concept of *consensus* deals with using "the principle of social proof." In other words, "What do others think about this? What are other people doing?" We like to make good decisions, and relying on consensus gives us confidence that we are.[23]

We tend to look to others more frequently when facing decisions in gray areas. Often, "the wisdom of crowds," as James Suroweiki's book by this title suggests, can be quite reliable. But what else can happen when everyone is looking to others in the same way for the correct answer? And nobody really knows? This phenomenon is known as "pluralistic ignorance,"[24] and it can get us into trouble.

How do we use consensus to convince or influence in a positive way and also defend against its malevolent use? Effective leaders know that by convincing a portion of a group, the rest can easily follow. This "herd mentality" is well known. If we are able to recognize the technique, we can form a defense against it when necessary and confirm its legitimate use as well. Here are some examples.

In recent years, hotels have been diligent about placing small cards in bathrooms encouraging the reuse of towels for the benefit of the environment. This has been found to be effective, as most guests do actually recycle at some point during their hotel stay. Social psychologist Robert Cialdini and his research colleagues decided to tweak this concept to see if an increase in participation could be gained by simply informing other guests of this fact. In some rooms, they placed the original signs. In others, they placed signs that also told the guest that most other guests were participating in the towel recycle program. By simply adding a few words of social proof (consensus) to the appeal, participation increased by 26 percent.

Then, they took the experiment a step further. They changed the recycle sign to indicate that the majority of the people who had stayed in their *particular* room before them had participated in the program. The participation increased by 33 percent over the standard appeal.[25]

What happened here was essentially a mini-testimonial. Even though the previous guests' identities and appearances were unknown, an anonymous "testimonial" implied consensus. This recycling example demonstrates a positive impact of the use of consensus. What about poor uses?

In Arizona's Petrified Forest National Park, there is prominent signage that states, "Your heritage is being vandalized every day by theft losses of petrified wood of fourteen tons a year, mostly a small piece at a time." This is an example of negative and unintentional social proof that many people think it is acceptable to steal rocks from the park.

Cialdini and friends once again changed the signage or *removed* it on some paths. The result? Where no signs were present, 2.92 percent of the pieces were stolen. Where signs remained, 7.92 percent were stolen. The unintended consequence of the signage had *tripled* the theft rate.[26]

News in My Back Yard

Consensus is often gained by citing a few *seemingly* related events that are geographically—and sometimes chronologically—*distant* from the party or group that is the target of the consensus influence technique. Those faraway, anecdotal occurrences are characterized as a *trend*—even when evidence is presented to expose the event(s) as anomalous. Why is this technique so powerful, and thus prevalent?

In his book *Innumeracy*, John Allen Paulos explains: "International news is usually worse than national news, which in turn is usually worse than state news, which is worse than local news, which is worse than the news in your particular neighborhood. Especially for the innumerate [loosely defined as someone who generally does not understand the meaning of statistics], a few vivid predictions or coincidences often carry more weight than much more conclusive but less striking statistical evidence."

In other words, even though things are good in your own locale most of the time, you might tend to extrapolate bad things (or good) that are happening elsewhere as having a direct effect on you when, in fact, they don't.

Yet, this is how single news stories can effectively gain momentum. They are looking for a consensus that there is a problem based on single or rare events. Now you know.

Finally, there is a consensus that *more expensive equals better quality.* While this is generally held as true, we must be careful that we are not fooled by someone pushing poor quality goods and services by abusing this principle.

Interestingly, research shows that in highly competitive situations, such as auctions, starting with *lower* initial prices can actually lead to *higher* final sales prices.[27]

Here's how:

- Lower prices gain more people who can participate.
- Lower prices create more actual bids, giving an impression of many interested parties.
- More bids per person (to get to the eventual purchase price) means more time and emotional capital spent in the process and thus a greater commitment to a good final result.

The more bidders you have, the more successful the "lower starting price strategy" can be. It is least effective when there are only two bidders. So, in a low-to-no bidder situation, the consensus of "higher price equals better quality" remains.

While there are many other examples that could be cited for consensus, these make you aware of its power for and against you.

Influence Technique Five: Commitment & Consistency

Commitment is the third word on our Power Words list from chapter 2. It connotes concepts such as "offering assurance," "dependable," "forthright," and "sincere." Commitment also involves *consistency*, another word on our list.

This influence technique involves helping people commit by getting them to make a choice, which they then will consistently find a need to justify. This need can be driven by peer pressure or self-induced.

Our need to be and look consistent in our actions can, at times, cause us to act in ways that are contrary to our own self-interests.[28] That's because we are making these consistency decisions (commitments) largely in System I, "without thinking." As we've seen, this can result in poor decisions.

This demands that our automatic responses are "well informed." In other words, your deeply held values will be largely responsible for your automatic, System I decisions. This speaks first to your upbringing and then to your ongoing character development.

Understanding your own level of commitment and consistency allows you to better influence and persuade others to comply with your requests. As we have seen already, assessing consistency is straightforward; do your actions match your words?

Here is an example of the power of getting even a minor *verbal* commitment:

> . . . one restaurant owner greatly reduced the percentage of no-shows (people who booked a table but didn't honor the reservation and didn't call to cancel it) by having his receptionist change what she said when taking a reservation from, "Please call if you have to cancel," to, "Will you please call if you have to cancel?" Of course, nearly all customers committed themselves to calling by saying "yes" to that question. More important, they then felt the need to be consistent with their commitment: The no-show rate dropped from 30 percent to 10 percent.[29]

Note that this example of a verbal commitment involved a *public* commitment, even though it was "public" only to the one person on the phone, whom the callers likely did not know personally. Imagine how powerful the public verbal commitment becomes when it is given to A) someone you know and respect and/or B) to multiple people or a large audience.

While verbal commitments are strong and often effective, when you get something *in writing*, the obligation is ramped up even further. This builds again on the power of the written word. Just as research has shown that children who write things down learn better, a written commitment also improves the likelihood that it will be honored.

Here is an example of a common, seemingly innocuous written commitment: "Retailers find that customers are less likely to cancel the agreement if the customers themselves, rather than the salesperson, fill out the application form."[30]

More research on writing

A research study had subjects make decisions among various choices:

Group A was asked to "remember their decision."

Group B was asked to "write their decisions on a magic slate and then pull the sheet up, erasing their decision."

Group C was asked to "write down their decisions on paper with ink and hand them in to the researchers."

Which group stuck with their decisions?

Group C stuck with their decisions more than 75 percent of the time. **Group B** kept their decisions half the time, and **Group A** tended to change their minds.[31]

"Get it in writing" is also a well-known refrain when it comes to more important commitments, such as enforceable contracts. Besides the legal obligation, it also involves a psychological effect when you sign an agreement for a new car, house, or marriage license.

One of the most powerful aspects of commitment comes into play when it's written in your *own hand*. No two people have the same handwriting. It is the fingerprint of communication. The personal nature of your own handwriting makes it much more difficult to go back on your word because the words *you* wrote are there for the whole world to see.

Once a pledge is made—whether verbal or written—there is *internal* pressure to bring one's self-image into line with one's actions. From the *outside*, the pressure is to adjust our self-image to match the way others perceive us.[32]

The *inside* pressure has a particularly important role to play in our commitments. You can use external pressure such as threats or bribes (as with children) to effect certain actions, but to truly get a commitment that is meaningful and lasting, you must appeal to their inner sense of personal responsibility and authenticity.

Whether verbal (in public), a signed document, or—best of all—in their own handwriting, *getting a commitment* is a useful and foundational persuasion tool.

Influence Technique Six: Exclusivity & Scarcity

What compels you to answer your cell phone when a call comes in—even when you are in a face-to-face conversation with a valued relationship? Scarcity. The chance that the caller might be unavailable later sometimes causes you to rudely interrupt the person who is right in front of you.

Exclusivity and scarcity are cousins. They play in the sandbox of the supply and demand principle of economics. When something is unique, difficult to obtain, or available for a limited time, its value increases. This is true with cars, houses, and club memberships.

In America, our attitude is generally "the more choices, the better" (even though too many options can cause "paralysis by analysis"). But when fewer options are offered—or a thing we want becomes scarce—our desire for it can increase to the point that we become anxious and make quick judgments that create regret. If you are aware of this behavioral tendency, you can avoid being taken advantage of.

Exclusivity and scarcity affect not only products and services but also information. Taking an inconvenient phone call exhibits a fear of missing out on information (from the caller). Speakers at investment seminars for retirees might give the impression that their methodologies (information) are little known and not widely disseminated and thus that they are letting the attendees "in on the secret." Often, salespeople will try to create an atmosphere of exclusivity to evoke a feeling of urgency (before someone else gets it) or appeal to your pride (a club membership).

Here is a prime example of both the scarcity and exclusivity techniques being employed.[33] A beef-importing company had its salespeople phone customers and ask for a purchase in three different ways:

- One group heard standard order requests—nothing new.
- A second group was given the same standard talk, but also told that a shortage of beef was expected in upcoming months (this was true).
- The third group was told of the shortage and also that not everyone was aware of this fact (also true).

What happened? The second group bought more than *twice* as much as the first group. Scarcity had a definite effect. But the *exclusivity* technique employed on the third set of customers caused them to purchase *six times* the amount of the first group. It was a veritable "double whammy" of persuasion.

In order to avoid the panic that tempts you when faced with situations of *scarcity* or with the pride that accompanies *exclusivity*, you must slow down and collect your thoughts, relying on wisdom to rule the day. "Haste makes waste" is not just something your grandmother told you. It's true. Good decisions are not routinely made quickly—especially long-term decisions.

EXPERTS OF INFLUENCE:

Two young professionals stood before the audience. Both were "dressed for success" in the latest business fashion. They were nothing short of immaculate in their appearance. (Authority) Neither the gentleman nor the lady were hard on the eyes (Rapport), and, based on their attire and poise, they seemed to be well adjusted and well educated. (Authority)

They were from out of town, but, as he opened the greeting in a smooth, baritone cadence, the gentleman proved to be well versed in the sites and history of the region and offered several authentic compliments for the mostly local group before him. (Rapport)

His partner then politely asked in her hospitable tone if the attendees had enjoyed lunch (which had been provided at no charge) and if they were happy to be here today in this wonderful venue. (Reciprocity) *The audience members all nodded and clapped enthusiastically.* (Consensus)

The gentleman continued his welcoming remarks, explaining that what the audience was about to learn had been thoroughly researched and recommended by the most qualified experts. (Authority) *He also said they "regretted" having to turn so many people away, but the information was limited to a qualified group.* (Scarcity & Exclusivity)

Finally, she closed the opening remarks by asking "just one small favor" of the attendees: "Please take good notes in the booklets which you received as you came in. These notes will not only help you gain a better understanding of the outstanding services we will be introducing but will also remind you of any questions you might have at the end of our time together." (Commitment & Consistency)

Within three minutes, the presenters had used each of the six persuasion techniques at least once. Given their acumen for using influence and persuasion techniques, can you imagine how many more attempts would be made to sway this audience over the next ninety minutes?

Fifteen Influence Phrases

Now that you have ready recall, words that WOW!, and the six major influence and persuasion techniques at your disposal, let's look at some phrases that help you understand the power of these techniques even more.

These phrases are technically referred to as *hypnotic language patterns*.[34] They are effective primarily because of a foundational concept known as *presupposition*.

For example, if I say, "It's probably your ability to speak well that has led to your rapid rise in the company," the presupposition is that something has led to your promotions; it must be because you're eloquent. Presuppositions are powerfully hypnotic because they are often accepted subconsciously and therefore without much scrutiny.

Here's another example: "Before you work on that special report, let's grab a quick bite to eat, OK?" This presupposes that the person will, in fact, work on that "special report." Did you notice the "OK" at the end? That's a leading technique, and it is usually accompanied by a nodding motion of the head as it's asked. Many times, the other person will easily comply with your request.[35]

Hypnotists know that there are many methods at their disposal to get people to imagine the outcome they want. By using their methods, you, too, can get people to buy your product or service, vote for your candidate, volunteer for your cause, etc. They will also provide you a defense against unscrupulous applications of these methods *against you.*

In their book *Covert Persuasion*, Kevin Hogan and James Speakman discuss a list of influence phrases that are scientifically proven to yield amazing results. They help you persuade others to come to a conclusion that is all but predetermined.

NOTE: With each of the fifteen phrases, we will provide examples and coaching on their usage and the association clue from the *classroom memory palace* [in brackets]. While these phrases will eventually come naturally to you with usage, I recommend that you continue to use the memory palace to get them into your System I thinking.

While the authors admit that many of these might not be considered grammatically correct, they are still so powerful that the authors recommend caution when using them. The examples provided relate to sales of a health club membership and a house.

1. **"You might want to _____ now."**

   (Fill in the blank with, e.g., "renew your membership" or "buy this beautiful house.") Using the word "might" is a soft way of saying, "You *would*."

   [It takes *might* to lift the *whiteboard* (number *one*)—it's heavy!]

2. **"Have you ever seen _____?"**

   (E.g., "our family membership plan" or "this beautiful neighborhood.") Notice that "seen" in this context educes "imagine," which is our number-one Power Word.

   > [After turning on the *light switch* (number *two*), you've *seen* what's in the classroom.]

   NOTE: Don't say, "Help me understand." There is a big difference between "wondering" or being "curious" about something versus "trying to understand" it. Wonder and curiosity are more open, are ready for surprises, and seek permission. Although "help me understand" is commonly used today, you run the risk of implying that you are superior—which might make you look resentful about having to make the effort.

3. **"If you could choose . . ."**

   (E.g., " . . . between a summer membership and a year-round membership" or " . . . between the house with the bigger lot or the one with more trees.") By limiting the choices to as few as possible—preferably only two or three—you will eliminate other options a person might have in mind. Also, if the second item is different from the first, we tend to see it as *more* different than it actually is. Generally, the "middle" option is the one chosen most often out of three choices.

   [The things to *choose* between are on the *carpet* (number *three*).]

4. **"I'm wondering if . . ." (or "I'm curious . . .")**

   (E.g., " . . . you should go ahead and get the full family membership" or ". . . the bigger lot is not the best house for your family.") These phrases are another way to convey that you are thinking about their best solution as you "wonder." This phrase is a great way to ask a question without doing so directly—thus taking the edge off.

[Sitting in your *chair* (number *four*), you are pensively *wondering*. (I like to ingrain this one further by thinking of Yoda doing the wondering and saying it in his distinctive voice.)]

DANIEL WEBSTER (1782–1852) was a leading American senator and statesman and a master at using influence phrases.

"[He] was one of the most successful advocates who ever pleaded a case, he ushered in his most powerful arguments with such friendly remarks as: 'It will be for the jury to consider,' 'This may, perhaps, be worth thinking of,' 'Here are some facts that I trust you will not lose sight of,' or 'You, with your knowledge of human nature, will easily see the significance of these facts.' No bulldozing. No high-pressure methods. No attempt to force his opinions on others. Webster used the soft-spoken, quiet, friendly approach, and it helped to make him famous."[36]

5. **"Can I show you _____?"**

(E.g., "our revised membership schedule" or "my favorite house in this neighborhood.") You are asking permission, which is both polite and effective.

[*Can I show you* something in this *book* (number *five*)? (Picture a book sitting opened on top of a can.)]

6. **"Would you be surprised to know that . . . ?"**

(E.g., " . . . our membership privileges have expanded" or " . . . this beautiful house was just remodeled last year.") The word "surprised" focuses attention on the next thing you will say.

[*Surprises* often come on the *telephone* (number *six*), which, in this case, is made of wood (*would*).]

7. **"What if I could show you a way to . . . ?"**

(E.g., " . . . renew your membership and save money, too" or " . . . buy this beautiful house with no down payment.") This is a perfect pre-closing question. You wouldn't ask it unless you *could* show him, so now you get the yes response, and then you close after you show him.

["*If I could show you a way . . . ?*" The *way* is through this *door* (number *seven*).]

8. **"I don't know if . . ."**

(E.g., " . . . you want to renew your membership today or wait" or " . . . buy this beautiful house.") You actually *do* believe you know, but you are being gentle.

[*I don't know if* you should jump out of that *window* (number *eight*)! It will hurt!]

9. **"Would you like to see (or have) . . . ?"**

(E.g., " . . . a list of membership privileges" or " . . . a list of amenities for this beautiful house.") This question allows you to get to the *specifics* of your proposal.

[Join me at this *table* (number *nine*), and tell me what you would *like to see/have.*]

10. **"Don't you think (or feel) that . . . ?"**

(E.g., " . . . you should renew now" or " . . . this is the right house for your family.") It is difficult to say "no" to anything that follows this question.

[If you drink what's in this *bottle* (number *ten*), you might not *think or feel* anything.]

11. **"You don't have to . . ."**

(E.g., " . . . renew your membership today" or " . . . buy this beautiful house today.") The effect here is that when you tell someone they "don't have to," they tend to think, "I can if I want to!"

[*You don't have to* use the stinky *dry-erase marker* (number *eleven*) if you don't want to.]

12. "Are you interested in . . . ?"

(E.g., " . . . renewing your membership today" or " . . . seeing this beautiful house today.") This question implies that they *should* be interested.

[*Are you interested in* what I have in this *file cabinet* (number *twelve*)?]

13. "You're right, and _____."

(E.g., "renewing your membership will afford you the health you deserve" or "buying this beautiful house will only make your family more comfortable.") People always want to be told they are right. The word "and" then allows you the bridge you need to move on to your main point.

[*You're right.* This *light* (number *thirteen*) is bright.]

14. "Imagine what would happen if . . ."

(E.g., " . . . you renewed your membership today" or " . . . you buy this beautiful house with interest rates still so low.") This goes for the close with direct usage of "imagine."

[*Imagine what would happen if* these *fourteen*-foot-high *drapes* (number *fourteen*) fell!]

15. "Some people . . ."

(E.g., "put their membership on auto-draft, and then they get the discount" or "hesitate on a house this beautiful, and then it's gone.") This is an unabashed appeal to consensus.

[*Some people* watch too many movies on the *projector* (number *fifteen*).]

SEVEN BONUS TIPS FOR INFLUENCE AND PERSUASION

Here are a few other tips and techniques to be aware of in the realm of influence and persuasion:

1. **Whisper.** When you lower your voice—or even whisper—people will lean in to hear what comes next. It is a good technique to regain someone's attention

or make an important point. A soft answer can also be effective at diffusing tension in emotionally heightened situations."

2. **Sequencing.** You can be biased about an individual either positively or negatively simply by the order in which good or bad adjectives describing that person are received.

"The sequence in which we observe characteristics of a person is often determined by chance. Sequence matters, however, because the 'halo effect' increases the weight of first impressions, sometimes to the point that subsequent information is mostly wasted.

In an enduring classic of psychology, Solomon Asch presented descriptions of two people and asked for comments on their personality. What do you think of Alan and Ben?

Alan:

intelligent—industrious—impulsive—critical—stubborn—envious

Ben:

envious—stubborn—critical—impulsive—industrious—intelligent

If you are like most of us, you viewed Alan much more favorably than Ben. The initial traits in the list change the very meaning of the traits that appear later. The stubbornness of an intelligent person is seen as likely to be justified and might actually evoke respect, but intelligence in an envious and stubborn person makes him more dangerous."[37]

3. **The McDonald's strategy.** Kevin Hogan and James Speakman, in their book *Covert Persuasion*, write: "Add on a smaller purchase to the existing order by asking a question. McDonald's does it with, 'Would you like fries with that?' The question added millions to the bottom line by slightly increasing the size of each sale. It's a much better question than, 'Will that be all?' (Which adds nothing.)

"Once a man has bought the suit, he will have no problem buying the comparatively inexpensive tie. Having bought the car, adding the stereo system is pennies on the dollar. Find out what your 'fries' are and build a question around them. You'll be adding dollars directly to the bottom line and increasing your customer's total satisfaction at the same time."[38]

4. **Don't ask why.** We tell our children never to ask "why." First of all, it can be taken as an indictment of a person's stance and immediately put that person in a defensive mode. But also, because people often *don't know why* they do things, they have a hard time answering that question. A less threatening option is to use "what." "What are you hoping to accomplish?" Or, "What are you looking to do?"

5. **Home court advantage.** Would you get on one knee and ask your girlfriend to marry you at the local 7-Eleven? *Geography matters* when setting the stage for an important meeting. A quiet restaurant versus a noisy one; a bright meeting room instead of a dim one; a spicy meal versus a tasty but mild one. These are examples of factors that will affect outcomes in interviews, negotiations, and sales opportunities. Thoughtfully choose the right environment, and you will increase your chances of a positive result.

6. **The feel, felt, found technique.** From Hogan and Speakman's *Covert Persuasion* again: "This persuasion technique has applications in every single area of life. It works on a couple of different levels. Here's an example of this technique at work:

> *I understand how you feel about that, many of my customers once felt the very same way, but when they looked closer, they found . . .*

"There are several reasons this technique is so valuable. First, it works at the level of *empathy*. This is an emotional connection to [people that] often completely bypasses the critical side of their brains (System II).

When it's stated with sincere empathy, it works. If you fake it, you will fail. Next, the technique goes on to say that many similar others have felt the same way. This lets them know that they're not alone. People like to know that other people just like them have done the same thing. This is a simple and direct way of providing 'social proof' [consensus] that others have done this also. This takes risk away. It makes [people] feel more comfortable.

"Finally, you help them share in the discovery of the solution. When you say, 'but when they looked closer, they found,' you allow them to save face. This is a critical step because it makes it okay to make a decision in your favor based on this new fact."[39]

7. **The fear of loss motivates more than the thrill of gain.** This is an important concept to remember for any product or service. This "loss aversion" motivation allows you to show the absolute risk of loss if someone "does not take action *now*." The pleasure your product or service brings after it helps avoid a loss is a bonus.

CONCLUSION

As we have seen, many factors influence our thinking and thus our actions. Usages of the six persuasion techniques, fifteen influence phrases, and various other topics discussed in this chapter are everyday occurrences. The tendency to make decisions automatically with your System I brain can put you in a vulnerable state—especially when you are under stress, rushed, distracted, or tired. You tend to default to the easiest way to make a decision. You can now recognize these compliance techniques when employed against you.

Finally, always remember that the power to persuade and influence using these methods carries a great responsibility. Wield your influence wisely to benefit others.

The next stop on your journey to developing the Old School Advantage involves a roadrunner, a hero, and a world-famous detective.

Turn the page, and let's get to work!

CHAPTER 4
Reason

A fool may talk, but a wise man speaks.

—BEN JONSON

WHAT DOES IT MEAN TO REASON?

Without reason, there is no effective argumentation or examination. There are many definitions for *reason*. The following are most applicable to our discussion:[1]

- To think or argue in a logical manner.
- To form conclusions, judgments, or inferences from facts or premises.
- To urge reasons that should determine belief or action.

Forming conclusions, logical arguments, establishing reasons for your beliefs—all of these aid in your ability to be an authentic leader within your sphere of influence. The ability to reason and to see through illogical arguments is a skill that will cast you into the fray of ideas well equipped to persuade others with wisdom well beyond your years, regardless of your age.

Sound reasoning begets sound argumentation. I use the term "argumentation" in a formal sense—not to mean quarreling, but, rather, debating or arguing in an effort to find *truth*. The study of Reason is the detection and dissemination of truth. In other words, we are pursuing a civilized, calm, and logical discussion of what is right and reliable through honest examination.

> We learn something every day, and lots of times it's that what we learned the day before was wrong.
>
> —Bill Vaughan

In the mid-nineteenth century, John Stuart Mill wrote *On Liberty*. His treatise "Of Liberty of Thought and Discussion" in chapter 2 is enormously instructive. He explains the great benefit that is lost without the examination and subsequent argumentation of ideas:

> If the opinion is right, they are deprived of the opportunity of exchanging error for truth: if wrong, they lose, what is almost as great a benefit, the clearer perception and livelier impression of truth, produced by its collision with error.
>
> To refuse a hearing to an opinion, because they are sure that it is false, is to assume that their certainty is the same thing as absolute certainty. All silencing of discussion is an assumption of infallibility.

You always believe that the view you hold on any particular issue is the correct one. Otherwise, why would you hold it? You have the *right* to be wrong—yet, like everyone, you want to be right. Civil argument in the arena of ideas either corrects a wrong view or substantiates a correct one. If there is a point you haven't thought about, then your attitude should be that you would be thankful if it were brought to your attention. Perhaps it would even be an opportunity to correct your wrong position before you make a serious mistake. There is nothing to fear when truth is objectively sought with pure motives. Mill goes on:

> Wrong opinions and practices gradually yield to fact and argument: but facts and arguments, to produce any effect on the mind, *must be brought before it*. Very few facts are able to tell their own story, without comments to bring out their meaning. The only way in which a human

being can make some approach to knowing the whole of a subject is by hearing what can be said about it by persons of every variety of opinion, and studying all modes in which it can be looked at by every character of mind. *No wise man ever acquired his wisdom in any mode but this; nor is it in the nature of human intellect to become wise in any other manner.*

If wisdom is what you seek, then seeking truth through examination and argumentation is paramount.

The key to understanding *what truth is* involves understanding the characteristics that truth exhibits. Consider the following:[2]

- If something is true, it is true for all people and in all places. (2+2=4)
- All truth claims are absolute, narrow, and exclusive.
- All truths exclude their opposites.

Furthermore:

- Truth is *discovered*—and it is independent of anyone's awareness of it. (Like gravity.)
- Truth is unchanging even if our beliefs change. (The Earth was still round when it was thought to be flat.)
- Beliefs cannot change facts—regardless of how sincerely they are held. (The Earth was still round.)
- Truth is not affected by the attitude of the person professing it. (Neither confidence nor arrogance affirms or annuls truth.)
- Contrary *beliefs* are possible. (This includes personal preferences.) Contrary *truths* are not. (Unfortunately, oftentimes people are not seeking truth—they are seeking excuses to justify their personal beliefs.)

While this brief study will provide you instruction in the tools and techniques of argumentation and examination (asking probing questions), you should not forget that the real mission is to unashamedly seek what is true—having confidence that *truth always survives scrutiny*. Therefore, your job is to develop the intellectual ability to analyze the arguments of others and also to formulate your own.

This study will contain five components:

1. The "Road Runner Tactic" for Self-Defeating Statements
2. The Three Most Important Questions
3. Argumentation
4. Figures of Speech
5. Public Speaking

Once you have a good idea of how to use these tools, you will understand how powerful your newfound Old School Advantage in this area can be.

Let's get to work!

THE "ROAD RUNNER TACTIC" FOR SELF-DEFEATING STATEMENTS[3]

If you could be equipped with only one weapon of reasoning, how to detect self-defeating statements should be it.

Given the characteristics of truth we just reflected upon, consider these statements:

1. "I can't speak a word of English."
2. "My brother is an only child."
3. "I will now draw a square circle."

Simple examination of these statements yields that they *cannot* be true. They are self-defeating. But the following statements are a bit more complex and are quite common:

1. "There is no such thing as absolute truth." (Is that absolutely true?)
2. "All truth is relative." (Is that statement relative?)
3. "That might be true for you, but it's not true for me." (Is that statement true for just you or for everyone?)

The simple follow-up questions in parentheses amount to an obvious rhetorical refutation of these self-defeating statements. Yet, in our culture, broadbrush statements such as these are typically accepted without serious challenge. Identifying and exposing statements such as these with a simple logical question is known as using the *Road Runner Tactic*. The Road Runner Tactic was named after the cartoon characters Road Runner and Wile E. Coyote. The Road Runner was always too fast and too cunning. Wile E. fell to his demise time and again because he "had nothing to stand on."[4] (This technique is also known as *"playing back the tape."*[5])

While it is not available in every argument, the Road Runner Tactic—examining, identifying, and quickly challenging self-defeating statements—is your first weapon of argumentation when you are discussing divergent opinions.

EXAMINATION OF TRUTH THROUGH QUESTIONS

The power of questioning goes back millennia. The Greek philosopher Socrates is famous for the Socratic method, which is simply a form of inquiry and discussion between individuals based on asking and answering questions to promote critical thinking and clarify ideas. The Socratic method is designed to eliminate ideas that have no viable hypothesis. In a bit of wry humor, Socrates said his practice of philosophy could be defined as "reflection on propositions emerging from unreflective thought."[6]

Successful people understand that if they ask better questions, they get better answers. Good questions uncover the perceived truths that people carry within their minds and hearts. Furthermore, people come to understand how much *you* know and care by the quality of your questions. Asking the right questions at the right time places you in the exclusive group of those who optimize their personal influence. And to find better answers, you must not only ask better questions—you must ask as many questions as possible.

The three questions I am about to teach you might be the most important questions you could ever learn. They will allow you to go on the offensive in an *in*offensive way. Greg Koukl, author of *Tactics*, developed the technique he calls *the Columbo tactic*—named after the seemingly bumbling but actually brilliant detective played by Peter Falk in the TV series *Columbo*, which ran intermittently for twenty-four years between 1968 and 2003.

Lieutenant Columbo famously used an "Oh, by the way . . ." approach as he was leaving each crime scene or suspect's lair. The key to his success in apprehending the perpetrator was to *never make a statement when a question would do*. Here are four distinct advantages to using questions:[7]

1. **Sincere questions are friendly and flattering.** They invite congenial interaction on something the other person cares a lot about: his or her own ideas.

2. **You'll get an education.** You'll leave a conversation knowing more than you did when you arrived. Sometimes, that information will be just what you need to make a difference.

3. **Questions allow you to make progress on a point without being pushy.** Since questions are largely neutral, or at least seem that way, they don't sound "preachy." When you ask a question, you aren't necessarily stating your own view. There's a further benefit here: if you are not pressing a point, you have nothing to prove and therefore nothing to defend. The pressure is off. You can relax and enjoy the conversation while you wait for an easy opening.

4. **Finally, and most importantly, carefully placed questions put you in the driver's seat.** Being an asker allows you a control of situations that statement-makers rarely achieve.

With these four considerations in mind, let's take a look at our first question.

> ## Warning:
>
> *Tone of voice* sparks more conflicts in conversation than any other factor. (You will learn more about the proper use of tone in chapter 5 on Storytelling.) If your first reaction to someone's comment is anger, take a deep breath, count to ten (seriously), and wait for your second reaction. If you detect an adverse reaction coming on from your fellow conversationalist, soften your tone. Even if you have to fake it, this will let the temperature cool. If it doesn't, then postpone the dialogue for another day.

QUESTION #1: "WHAT DO YOU MEAN BY THAT?"

Practically speaking, meanings are not in *words* per se. Meanings are in the minds of the *people* using the words. Words are simply the triggers for the meanings that are buried in the mind.[8]

Socrates valued words and encouraged using them with great care. That also meant *defining* them. He would always ask someone to begin by defining their words, saying, "For it is when you begin to study definitions accurately that you start plumbing the depth of ignorance."[9]

Essentially, this first question is saying, "Please define your term (or terms) for me."

In addition to defining terms, there are multiple purposes for beginning with this question:

A. It is a natural way to *bridge to a more extended conversation*—an opener, if you will.

B. Perhaps you really don't know what the other persons are getting at, so you simply want to *gather more information*. Maybe they are experts in their field and you have no clear idea what they are trying to convey. Question #1 can allow them to break down their argument into concepts you can understand.

C. It *helps you know what these people think or know*. You genuinely don't want to misunderstand or misinterpret the meaning of their statements, which could lead to you addressing an issue they did not intend. Also, you want to *make sure they know what they are talking about* and are not just arguing as pseudo-intellectuals on the topic.

D. It *buys you more time* to formulate a cogent response to their answer.

In many situations, you might not want to ask the question exactly as it is presented here. You can imagine that if you asked the question by placing the emphasis too heavily on a particular word—for instance, "that," as in, "What do you mean by *that*?"—it could come across as abrasive or challenging. By using variations of the same question, you can accomplish the effect you need. Here are some examples of variation of Question #1:

- "That's interesting. Can you tell me more?"
- "Please expand on that a little more for me."
- "You don't have to go into detail, but I am curious what you mean by _____."

Did you notice the influence phrases? These are all forms of the question that soften up the conversation and move it forward in a constructive manner. Sometimes, you can use the original question ("What do you mean by that?") first and then use the softer forms for subsequent clarification or usage.

Use Question #1 often, and it will keep you in control of the conversation without offending the other persons—and, at the same time, keep the pressure on them to defend their position. The "illusion of knowledge"[10] is powerful. But many an argument has seemed cogent before collapsing under the weight of just one instance of this simple first question: "What do you mean by that?"

We are all under the impression that we know more than we actually do. Even experts can eventually run out of answers to this "tell me more" line of questioning. Use this query skill thoughtfully to determine if your discussion partners are well versed in their position or if they are simply parroting a line or idea they heard from someone else . . . as is so often the case.

QUESTION #2: "HOW DID YOU COME TO THAT CONCLUSION?"

If people are able to successfully answer your multiple queries in Question #1, they have generally proven that they know *what* they are talking about and have more than a cursory understanding of the issue and their position. But that does *not* mean they have the truth on the matter. They must now navigate through the choppy waters of Question #2—"How did you come to that conclusion?"

In order to help you avoid confrontation and be as winsome as possible in a discussion, these variations also work well:

- "Would you mind telling me more about the evidence you found that supports your belief?"
- "Please share with me more about your reasons for believing that."
- "I'm wondering . . . What makes that so compelling for you?"

In whatever form it takes, Koukl calls this second question the "burden of proof" question. "Whoever makes the claim bears the burden [of proof]."[11] It is about answering the *why* for their position. Too many times, we put ourselves in a defensive position when it is not our duty to defend anything because we did not make the claim. The one who makes the assertion is responsible for giving a cogent argument once they make a claim.[12]

Question #2 gives the person the benefit of the doubt in terms of presuming that he or she did adequate research or investigation into the subject matter. If the person did not, you will soon expose this fact.

Many who have not done their homework will try and forgo providing proof with a simple and weak, "I just believe it. I just know that's the way it is." This does not work in the realm of serious discussion. They must give *reasons* for the position they are espousing—just as they have the right to expect the same from you. You are testing them for reliability. While sincerity can certainly be considered a virtue, it is not *evidence*.

WHAT HAPPENS WHEN YOU FEEL STUMPED?

Remember, you can always buy time with questions whenever you feel that you are losing control of the situation. When stumped, Koukl recommends refraining from presenting your own case and instead saying something like this:

> "It sounds like you know a lot more about this than I do, and you have some interesting ideas. The problem is, this is all new information for me. I wonder if you could do me a favor. I really want to understand your points, but you need to slow down so I can get them right. Would you take a moment to carefully explain your view and also your reasons for it to help me understand better?"[13]

He explains that this line of dialogue demonstrates that you are taking them seriously and gives you valuable time to think. When all your questions have been answered, he recommends ending the conversation by saying these magic words: "Let me think about it. Maybe we can talk more later."

This sentence frees you from any further obligation to respond at the moment. There is no more pressure because you have pleaded ignorance. You move on to argue another day.

QUESTION #3: "HAVE YOU EVER CONSIDERED . . . ?"

Questions #1 and #2 are largely intended to impress upon your conversation partners that you are someone who is agreeable and interested in what they have to say. You have not committed to any type of agreement with their point of view—but you have been very *agreeable*.

If you have assessed their position honestly and still feel you are correct in your beliefs, then by threshing out the first two questions thoroughly, you have placed yourself in a position to more easily turn their perspective toward your own. Koukl provides a third and final question. (Keep in mind, this third question is not always needed, nor arrived at in every discourse.)

The question "Have you ever considered . . ." is what is known as a *leading question*. Unlike the negative connotation this type of question can have in a court of law, where a witness is presumably being led to answer in a way that might unwittingly bolster the questioning counsel's case, this leading question should be asked in an honest attempt to lead your discussion partner to the truth of the matter at hand.

If one of the three questions is going to offend, it will be this third one. Variations of "Have you ever considered . . . ?" are easy to construct with the influence phrases from chapter 3. In fact, *all fifteen* of them would work! Here are three examples:

- "Would you be surprised to know that . . . ?"
- "If I could show you a way to . . . ?"
- "Imagine what would happen if . . . ?"

You then simply fill in the dots with your own argument—which, again, is softened in the form of a question. You are showing great respect while at the same time showing your openness to discussing the matter.

In a case where you are faced with a moment of great importance or substantial resistance, a more direct question could be used here: *"What if you are wrong?"* This is a *rhetorical* question and therefore elicits an immediate assessment of their position with the implication of potentially serious consequences.

If ultimately you must disagree, you can say something like this:[14]

- "It's my understanding that . . ."
- "This is the way it seems to me . . ."
- "Let me suggest an alternative, and tell me if you think it's an improvement."

> NOTE: *Rhetorical questions* are asked solely to produce an effect or to make an assertion, not to elicit a reply. They are *the* most powerful form of question because a statement put in the form of a rhetorical question produces a *personal* reaction. Although not asked to gain an answer to the specific question, they are asked to raise a point or start a discussion, and, in this way, they require some sort of response. The attention is moved from you, the questioner, to them, the answerer.

DEFENDING AGAINST QUESTIONS

If you can employ the Columbo tactic, so can your opponent. Koukl stresses that you must remember that you are in control of your side of the conversation. When someone tries to use leading questions with you in an abusive way, simply refuse to answer and politely say something like this:

> "Before we go further, let me say something. My sense is that you want to explain your point by using questions. That confuses me a bit because I'm not sure how I should respond. I think I'd rather you just state your own view directly then let me chew on it for a while and see what I think. Would that be all right with you?"[15]

You have made it clear that you are not going to comply with the request to answer his or her questions, leaving you in full control.

THE GENETIC FALLACY

Koukl also teaches that when people are feeling a lack of confidence in their argument, they will often resort to attacking you—or your source. The common approach is for them to say something like "Who are you to say?" or "What does he know?"

When this occurs, they are using what is known as the *genetic fallacy* or the *fallacy of origins*. By attacking you—or those you are citing as the source—they seek to discredit the assertion you put forth.

For example, they might say, "I don't believe what John Stuart Mill says about liberty because he was British and not an American." Obviously, one's national origin has no effect on one's ability to hold particular beliefs on any subject. This attempt to disqualify a position based on an unrelated factor is fallacious.

Conversely, they might also use the genetic fallacy as an *offensive* tactic. They will cite their own source as "an expert on the subject with a PhD," and therefore they must know what they are talking about.

It is important to remind them that any human arguments must stand or fall based on their own merits. Truth (or falsehood) does not depend on the source (speaker/author) of it.

You can measure the size of a person by what makes him or her angry.

—Bits & Pieces

The Steamroller

Changing minds is a difficult task. It should be. We can't live a life in which what we know and believe is tossed to and fro like a rowboat in the Pacific. That is what argumentation and examination are designed to do—slowly but surely mold our views toward truth. But why don't people accept good arguments? Frankly, *emotion* and *prejudice* are the main culprits. We all have to deal with these cousins of confusion, and when they are in full force, discussion can get dicey.

Emotional arguments often cause people to become very defensive and try to "steamroll" you and your position. Steamrollers use various tactics; they interrupt, ask questions so quickly you can't answer them, or change the subject—all in an effort to keep you off balance.[16] You can see this tactic played out almost any day of the week by watching any political talk show on television.

Wouldn't it be great to have a phrase that would stop the steamroller, eliminate ill feeling, and make him listen respectfully? Here is one:

"I don't blame you one bit for feeling as you do. If I were you I would feel the same way. However . . ." (then gently repeat your perspective on the matter and wind down the conversation for another time).

This approach can soften the most difficult argument. What's more, you can say it and be sincere, because if you *were* the other person, you, of course, would feel just as he does.[17]

Yet, there are times when trying to courteously bow out is not an option. For those times, you need a way to cope with the situation.

Koukl offers these three steps to take to stop the steamroller:[18]

1. **Stop him.** Politely ask for the courtesy of continuing your point without interruption. Raising your hand slightly and saying, "Excuse me. I am

not quite finished," or, "May I answer your first question before we go to another?" might help. Getting a *verbal* consent to this request is important. Stay calm and confident. (Think of a grandfather clock during a thunderstorm; calm and consistent.)

2. **Shame him.** This step involves getting more aggressive and saying something on the order of "May I ask a quick question? Do you really want to hear my response?" or "Can I ask you a favor, John? I'd love to respond, but you keep interrupting me." *Using his name* might soften this blow a bit.

3. **Leave him.** If a steamroller persists, then he is not interested in finding truth. Once he is finished, drop the subject and give him the last word. Graciously bowing out does not come naturally for most of us. But it conveys confidence in your own position and can be very effective in the long run.

COLUMBO: YOUR NEW BEST FRIEND

The great advantage of using the three questions (the Columbo tactic) is that *you no longer need to make assertions* in order to convince others. You are removing the burden of proof from yourself, and you can use questions to achieve your goal in a much more powerful way.[19] Ultimately, if you come to an impasse, it is OK to let the conversation die out. You have made your points, and rarely is it feasible to win someone to your point of view in one sitting. There will be other opportunities.

My mother always told me, "You can get what you want easier with honey than you can with vinegar." When you argue, think and act like an envoy representing truth while at the same time remaining *constantly curious*. After all, you can learn truth in the most unexpected ways from the most unlikely sources. A full frontal assault will usually only lead to an impasse—and perhaps escalate into an emotional confrontation.

Also remember that even though the argument is directly with your partner in the discussion, those easiest to convince are often those third-party individuals who might be observing the dialogue.[20] They might be softer targets with whom you can make headway more easily.

You can be confident in any conversation, no matter the topic, if you can remember what Detective Columbo loved to ask: "Do you mind if I ask you a question?" Then proceed to Question #1 . . .

ARGUMENTATION

Throughout this book, I have emphasized the importance of using the Old School Advantage tools for noble purposes. One of the greatest ancient teachers of rhetoric, Quintilian, called the ideal orator "a good man speaking well." Unfortunately, one who "speaks well" can also manipulate for evil. That is why the "good man" aspect is imperative. In this section, you will learn more about the effective use of language in your effort to reason—and thus argue—well.

An argument should not be a fight. Fighting is about dominating your opponent, which only elicits revenge and animosity. Argumentation involves persuasion and influence with the goal of either changing someone's point of view or coming to a greater personal understanding. Fighting is about *winning*. Arguing is about arriving at an *agreement*.

Two of the best books on argumentation and rhetoric are *Thank You for Arguing* and *Word Hero*, both written by Jay Heinrichs. These are excellent resources for students who wish to delve deeper into the subject, and they provide much of the guidance highlighted in the following section.

PAST, PRESENT, FUTURE

Blame, *values*, and *choice* are the three core issues in any kind of argumentation.
- Who stole my watch? *Blame.*
- Should Bob and Susan split up? *Values.*
- Shall we go out for dinner? *Choice.*

Heinrichs also points out that:

- *Blame* lies in the *past.*
- *Values* are in the *present.*
- *Choice* is in the *future.*

Why is this important?

When an argument is headed in the wrong direction, you can change tenses to get it back on track. For example, a disagreement with your spouse rarely ends well if you are both dwelling in the past (blame). Bringing it back to the present allows you to talk about what is important (values), but you must not stay there too long, or one of you might get "preachy." Casting the discussion into the future allows a conciliatory "I'll do better next time" or "How can we avoid this in the future?" (choice).

In a business discussion in which agreement is elusive in the present tense, try saying, "You're all making some good points, but how are we going to proceed?" This will quickly get things moving into the future again.

Aristotle's Argument Tools

Aristotle maintained that the three most powerful tools of argument were:

1. Argument by character, or *ethos.*
2. Argument by logic, or *logos.*
3. Argument by emotion, or *pathos.*

Ethos deals with personality, reputation, and trustworthiness. As Aristotle's contemporary Isocrates once said, "The argument which is made by a man's life is of more weight than that which is furnished by his words." (*It's who you are, not just what you do.* Remember?)

Your ethos can be improved with the use of humor, which calms people down and also sets you above the fray. But, as Heinrichs explains, "it is perfectly awful at motivating anyone into any sort of action."[21] (P.S. Beware of using humor in e-mails!)

Logos uses logic to persuade. However, the all-too-common ignorance of logic makes way for nasty political ads and dishonest salespeople. In the same way that "it is not what you say, it is what people hear,"[22] "the opinion of your audience is as good as what it knows, and what it *thinks* is true counts the same as the truth."[23] Formal logic starts with truth, moves to another truth, and then assumes you must reach a conclusion that is also true. This is known as a syllogism.

The first two truths—or statements—are called premises, the truth of which implies the truth of a third statement, known as a conclusion. The term for deriving a conclusion from something known or assumed is "deduce." In a good deductive argument, if the premises are true, then the conclusion must be true.

1. Aristotle is a man.
2. All men are mortal.
3. Therefore, Aristotle is mortal.

Now consider this simple story, which shows how logic can fool us:

"From a jar of fleas before him, the celebrated experimenter Van Dumholtz carefully removes a single flea, gently pulls off its back legs, and in a loud voice commands it to jump. He notes that it doesn't move and tries the same thing with a different flea. When he's finished, he compiles statistics and concludes confidently that a flea's ears are in its back legs. Absurd perhaps, but variants of this explanation in less transparent contexts might carry considerable force for people with strong enough preconceptions."[24]

Error Types

There are two types of logical errors we make:

- A *Type I error* occurs when a *true* hypothesis is *rejected*.
- A *Type II error* occurs when a *false* hypothesis is *accepted*.[25]

Pathos, the argumentation tool in the realm of emotion (to remember, think *patho*logical), can take an agreement and turn it into a commitment. Short and simple words evoke more emotion, and pathos tends to work well *after* ethos and logos have been employed. Aristotle taught that a speech before a large crowd was a good environment for pathos, while ethos and logos worked better one-on-one.

> Where there is much desire to learn, there of necessity will be much arguing . . . for opinion in good men is but knowledge in the making.
>
> —John Milton

ARGUMENTATION TIPS AND TECHNIQUES

Simply scoring points for debate purposes is not the reason you should argue. You are trying to achieve understanding for both you and your hearers. The following twelve techniques provide additional insight into argumentation tools that allow effective dialogue and examination:[26]

1. **Effective argumentation—order of tactics:**
    A. Use facts first.
    B. Redefine your opponents' terms (if theirs are faulty).
    C. Claim the discussion is "irrelevant" (if, in fact, it is).

2. **Paralipsis.** You mention something by saying you aren't going to mention it. "I won't mention the fact that you snore like Fred Flintstone."

3. **Use "and."** Used instead of "um" or "you know," "and" gives oral continuity. It also sounds more authoritative (this use is common in scripture).

4. **Avoid repeating terms that hurt your argument.** If you say, "I am not a crook," all people hear is the word "crook."

5. **"It's a joke."** If you have to say this, you're likely in trouble because your remark was not received as a joke. Be careful. A sarcastic or caustic comment can be remembered for a lifetime.

6. **Emphasize high standards.** Saying "I fell short of my own expectations" emphasizes high standards and increases your ethos (character) in an audience's mind.

7. **Speak last if possible.** Research shows that the last speaker has a persuasive advantage because he or she can restate the earlier speakers' positions and persuade a vulnerable audience. (This is why debates switch the speaker order in each stage.)

8. **E-mail is best suited to logos.** This means pathos is a bad idea, usually because the reader cannot decipher your tone or see your face or body language.

9. **Text messages are all *ethos*.** They are valuable *in the present*, just like a two-way radio.

10. **Note length matters.** The longer the written note, the more *logos* (because it is full of details or specifics). Short notes convey ethos (like text messages). If you want to gain ethos through your notes, make them shorter with people at your level or below. (Higher-ups write shorter notes, figuring they do not need to justify their decisions.)

11. **Telephone is *logos* (provides facts) only.** It is not the best place to create or express *ethos* (values) or *pathos* (emotion—no facial expressions or body language).

12. **Conference rooms can alienate.** Don't meet in a conference room unless all can attend in person. Otherwise, set up a teleconference where members call in from their private offices so that the meeting can be kept in logos. (Absent members can sense the exclusion from the group.)

Figures of Speech

Now that you have several new rhetorical tools in your belt, it is time to have some fun and spice up your argumentation skills with figures of speech. *Word Hero* provides many options. Here are my favorite twelve. (Please note: While I did not offer the memory palace cues here, I am assuming that by now you feel comfortable applying their usage in areas where you feel they would be helpful. E.g., if you write a great deal, then having these tools memorized and in your System I thinking would be beneficial.)

1. **Contraster.** This figure allows you to change a concept by putting another next to it to make it seem better or worse.

   Common: "He has an excellent sense of direction; I have none at all."

   Contraster: "After one day in a foreign city, he can move about as thoughtlessly as a butterfly. I have to ask directions to get from my office to home."

2. **Feigned precision.** Giving an exact-sounding number when exaggerating. Best used for humorous effect.

   Common: "They have a million kids!"

   Feigned Precision: "I think they must have twenty-seven kids."

3. **Kindergarten imperative:** Instead of issuing a command, you state your own need.

Example 1, with a child: "Danny, I need you to put down that rock."

Example 2, on an airplane: "I need all seat backs and tray tables in the upright position."

4. **Mirror image.** A stylish device that states the reverse of a phrase, clause, or sentence. Also called a *chiasmus*, it is common in everyday literature and conversation.

Example 1: "She looked for trouble, and trouble found her."

Example 2: "Ask not what your country can do for you; ask what you can do for your country."

Example 3: "School might get old at times, but, in these times, you must get old school."

5. **Multiple synonyms.** The cataloguing of words with the same meaning to pile on a key concept for amplification of your point. Boil down your point to one key word, and then simply take out your thesaurus. Often used humorously.

Example (for a dead dog): "Rover has bought the farm, checked out, defunct and dearly departed. He's gone to meet his maker; a bygone bloodhound whose doggie due date has expired."

6. **Portmanteau.** Marries two stand-alone words or names to make a fun new word.

Examples: Billary, Brangelina, Obamanation, podcasts, spork, villianaire.

7. **Reductio ad absurdum.** Often used to reduce an opponent's position to absurdity. (This can be an ethically questionable rhetorical approach, so use with caution, and be aware if it is used against you.)

>Example 1: "I guess you want to childproof the entire country." (For the nanny state.)

>Example 2: "You want to stuff vegetables into our gas tanks." (For bio fuels.)

>Example 3: "I suppose you would outlaw chocolate chip cookies." (For mandating healthy menus in schools.)

8. **Sound repeaters.** Employing the same sound either at the beginning, middle, or end of a word. *Rhyming* is the ultimate example. *Alliteration* is also a form.

>Rhyming examples: "Heroes and zeroes." "Rings and things."

>Alliteration examples: "Lugubrious lamentation." "Sell sizzle, not steak." "A slippery, sly, smarmy pseudo friend." "Nattering nabobs of negativism."

9. **Understatement.** Exaggeration is often dismissed by audiences. In some situations, understatement can actually have the effect of exaggeration, without the dismissal.

>Example 1: "Nothing in life is so exhilarating as to be shot at without result." —Winston Churchill

>Example 2: "The report of my death was an exaggeration."
>—Mark Twain

10. Verbing. This device takes a noun and makes it a verb.

Examples: Chair a meeting, workshop, Google.

11. Word origins. Relaying the origin of a word for your audience is effective in several ways. *First*, it brings a certain level of sophistication to the discussion and shows you did your homework. *Second*, it almost always enhances your own understanding of the word and expands your comments on the topic at hand. *Third*, it is an "interrupter" in the message that can help focus attention back on your speech if anyone in the audience has wandered.

Example: *res ipsa loquitur.* Latin for "the thing speaks for itself." (I.e., it's obvious.)

12. Word repeater. Repetition technique that is useful in speeches or any other time you want an emotional effect. Coaches and politicians use this one often.

Example 1: "Dream more, learn more, do more, and become more."

Example 2: "We practiced together, we sweated together, we lost together, and we won together. We—TOGETHER—are a team."

Public Speaking

A critical underlying component of any argument—especially in a public setting—is *kairos,* which means doing *all the right things* rhetorically at *just the right time.* Seizing those fleeting opportunities is essential to successful persuasion through argumentation. Arguments can die based on timing alone.[27]

The great Roman orator Cicero believed that we should be prepared to argue both sides of a case. This means knowing your opponent's position as thoroughly as possible. After this preparation, "essentially it comes down to this rule of thumb: Ethos first. Then logos. Then pathos."[28]

Through ethos, you expose your common sense, your character (who you are), your empathy for the audience, and so on. After this is accomplished, then your audience is ready for you to establish the facts and logic of your argument—logos. Finally, "firing up" your audience with emotional appeals—pathos—allows you to end with a crescendo that leads to action.

Heinrichs suggests the following classical outline structure for a speech:[29]

Introduction: Use ethos to create goodwill with your audience. (E.g., cite common knowledge or understanding of their community or culture.)

Narration (state facts): Include the history of the topic, facts and figures, etc. (logos)

Division: Make your case against an opponent's viewpoint, whether your opponent is actually presenting or not. Redefine terms in your favor here if needed—and if they are legitimate.

Proof: Present your actual argument with examples. Now that your facts are out there, make sure you get to the future tense as soon as possible.

Refutation: Extinguish the opposing argument now that your audience has heard both sides (from your perspective). Remember: if your opponent wants to stay in the past or the present, call your opponent on it.

Conclusion: Restate your most powerful points and play on emotion (pathos).

NOTE: What if you sense that the audience is against you? Use the "Reluctant Conclusion technique."[30] All of your conclusions should be arrived at reluctantly in a sense—*if* you have vetted the questions thoroughly and honestly.

While this outline provides a valuable overview for preparing a great speech, don't dwell on making it perfect. As you ponder the techniques and principles introduced in this discussion, think about delivering the perfect *one line*.[31] One sentence can make a memorable speech and provide the launching pad you need for greater dialogue.

Furthermore, that one key line can be used in what Jay Heinrichs calls the Pith Method. Start with a key line of your message, then try and make it a headline. Your other thoughts can then stem from this. In preparing a speech, a few key lines can bloom into your outline, making it easier to give without notes (especially since you have memory palaces!).

Perhaps you have heard me speak and know that my message is built on this one line:

> School might get old at times, but in these times, you must get old school.

From there, I can go many places. But you will know after I have finished that I believe undeniably that there is no school like the Old School . . . because it's better! (I just snuck another line in.)

Speaker Tips

Always take advantage of every public speaking opportunity you are offered. It will not only make you a better speaker each time you do so, but—more importantly—it allows you the chance to clarify your ideas for *yourself* as much as for your audience.

Here are my ten favorite speakers tips gleaned from among those offered by Harvey Mackay, author of *Swim with the Sharks without Being Eaten Alive* and one of America's foremost speaking coaches:[32]

1. **Room size.** If a hundred people are going to attend, the room size should hold seventy-five. If five hundred people are coming, the room should hold four hundred. You want the excitement of a standing-room only, bumper-to-bumper crowd.

2. **Turn the lights up full blast,** unless you are showing slides. Studies show that people remember more and laugh more in brightness. Dim the screen area, but light up the audience. Now you can still have excellent eye contact with your audience.

3. **Have a real pro introduce you** . . . not a poor speaker who is being given the honor because of status in the organization. Introducers are critical. The stage must be set.

4. **Never end with a question-and-answer session.** You cannot control the agenda or the quality of the questions, and the fireworks of your topic can end with a fizzle. Start the Q&A five minutes before the end of your talk, and then transition from one of your answers to a real climax.

5. **During Q&A:** Most people are shy about asking the first question; therefore, you might get stymied by an awkward silence. Break the ice by stating that problem and then saying, "OK, we'll start with the second question!"

6. **Never mispronounce a proper name.** If you're not sure, check with the sponsor. Then double check.

7. **Do not go over your allotted time,** whether it's ten minutes or ten hours. This puts additional pressure on all concerned.

8. **If you don't have a smashing "opener" and "closer,"** go back to the drawing board. And don't step up to the microphone until you do.

9. **Debrief yourself within twenty-four hours of a speech,** and take ten minutes to write down what you could do better the next time. The amount to be learned is infinite.

10. **Try something new every time you speak,** and you'll never become stale.

Old School Presentation Tips:

As you learned in chapter 1, obtaining the *ready recall* memory skill enables you to make a connection with your audience because you can look them directly in the eye as you speak. Eliminating technological crutches such as PowerPoint slides can provide you with this connection opportunity. However, in many situations, pictures and charts are either needed or wanted to optimize your presentation. Here are three Old School tips for making the greatest impact with and without technology aids:

1. If you can effectively give the entire presentation orally and/or using a flip chart or white board on which you write the information as you say it, then do it. This maximizes your impression, showcases your talents, and minimizes distractions.

2. When technology is needed—e.g., PowerPoint—then use a blackout option on your laptop, which keeps the information on the next slide hidden until you are ready to reveal it. A common "build" feature in the PowerPoint program can do the same thing intra-slide. This technique allows you to still recite from memory the points you want to make *before* they are revealed on the screen. This gives the accurate impression that you know the material by heart and it is information that falls well within your area of expertise.

3. If you really want to go for a great impression and you are confidently prepared, then preview your entire presentation *before* launching into it. Expound on as much of the information as you feasibly can without stealing your own impact statements, surprises, or punch lines. This allows you to follow the age-old public speaking advice of "Tell them what you are going to tell them, tell them, and then tell them what you just told them." However, in your case, it is even more powerful. By giving them as much as you can *before* even starting the presentation, you will be doubly reinforcing that you *know your stuff*.

Where we are wrong, make us willing to change; where we are right, make us easy to live with.

—Peter Marshall

CONCLUSION

In this chapter, you have seen many thought-provoking ideas and techniques that will enable you to achieve a level of comfort in any discussion scenario, be it with a significant other, a child, a customer, a supervisor, a coworker, a friend, a stranger, an antagonist, or a large audience. As a result of this instruction, you should feel not just equipped but also *inspired* to make a difference in your sphere of influence. Become a "champion of reason," and always surround yourself with learned and honest people who will argue with you.

You are now ready to study the fifth core skill in the Old School Advantage program. And as important as good arguments are, reason is still no match for the most powerful communication tool ever devised: *a good story*.

CHAPTER 6
Storytelling

If a picture is worth a thousand words, a story is worth a thousand pictures.

Here is one of the most important questions you can ever ask yourself:

"What one skill, if I developed and performed it in an excellent fashion, would have the greatest positive impact on my career?"[1]

The answer is *storytelling*. And the good news is that it is a learnable skill. You can become a master.

But before we get into the specifics, let's consider an important concept that is germane to this discussion. It regards hemispheres. Not global ones, but those within your skull. In *A Whole New Mind*, author Daniel Pink points out several pertinent facts concerning the inner workings of our thinking processes.

Generally, the left hemisphere of our brain is sequential—A, B, C, D, etc.—while our "right brain" interprets many things simultaneously. The left hemisphere *analyzes* the details, and the right hemisphere *synthesizes* them. The left hemisphere is the "thousand words," and the right hemisphere is the "picture," if you will. While the left brain specializes in *text*, the right brain specializes in *context*.[2]

As I mentioned in the introduction, the challenges we face in this technological age are numerous. We are inundated with so many facts that trying to keep up with all of them is futile. However, placing myriad facts in a *story* format provides an avenue of greater understanding and delivers the facts with an *emotional* impact.[3]

Our culture is dominated by the left brain, especially in academia and business. But tools such as standardized testing of left brain knowledge are inadequate to measure the worth of a person to an organization. We need something more. We need to become more right brained in our thinking. Why is this important?

As Pink discusses, in the last century, "machines proved they could replace human backs. This century, new technologies are proving they can replace human left-brains." Will technology eliminate all left-brain jobs? No. But it will "destroy many and reshape the rest."[4]

Because of "big data," jobs that can be replaced by a set of rules or repeatable steps are in danger of extinction. Computers and left-brain workers overseas are doing things cheaper and faster each day. The technology that created so many jobs in the last three decades could eventually *replace* them as well.

You can protect your career opportunities by developing your right-brain capabilities. In this generation, being "brain-balanced" reduces the chances that you will be replaced by a foreign competitor or by an algorithm. You must not only survive—you must thrive. *Storytelling* is the highest level of interpersonal communication. *It is your secret weapon.*

Regardless of your current station in life, if you have ideas that could change the world (and you do!), stories make it happen. Even in the left-brain-laden technology field, "a new profession has emerged in recent years, the 'data scientist,' which combines the skills of the statistician, software programmer, infographics designer, and storyteller."[5]

By making storytelling one of your key skills, you are enhancing your leadership potential immensely. And what is leadership? Leadership is *winning hearts and minds.* We have already equipped you with ready recall, fit words, influence techniques, and argumentation principles. By adding the capstone of storytelling, you will be well suited for the task of leading at any level.

In this chapter, we will delve into the following areas:

1. Story's *Real* Power
2. Becoming a Master Storyteller
3. Seven Types of Stories
4. BIG Concepts in Little Stories

Let's get to work!

Story's Real Power

Storytelling is the oldest tool of influence, and *everyone* loves a good story. This is why we read books and go to the movie theatre (besides the popcorn). Story is the way humans have always communicated best and most. In every culture throughout history, survival and success depended on the younger generations learning stories from their elders. Conversely, when stories cease, nations fall.

> When an old person dies, a library burns to the ground.
>
> —African proverb

If you want to encourage someone, tell that person a story. In doing so, you enable the person to experience "what it would be like if . . ." (i.e., "*Imagine . . .*"). Stories work for humor, romance, drama, or tragedy. Storytelling works well for any subject matter because our brains are simply wired to learn through anecdotes. There is no walk of human life that escapes the influence of stories.

As you read the following story, consider the broad yet deep lessons it teaches about life.

Once upon a time, there was a farmer in the central region of China. He didn't have a lot of money and, instead of a tractor, he used an old horse to plow his field.

One afternoon, while working in the field, the horse dropped dead. Everyone in the village said, "Oh, what a horrible thing to happen!" The farmer said simply, "We'll see." He was so at peace and so calm that everyone in the village got together and, admiring his attitude, gave him a new horse as a gift.

Everyone's reaction now was, "What a lucky man." And the farmer said, "We'll see."

A couple days later, the new horse jumped a fence and ran away. Everyone in the village shook their heads and said, "What a poor fellow!"

The farmer smiled and said, "We'll see."

Eventually, the horse found his way home, and everyone again said, "What a fortunate man."

The farmer said, "We'll see."

Later in the year, the farmer's young boy went out riding on the horse and fell and broke his leg. Everyone in the village said, "What a shame for the poor boy."

The farmer said, "We'll see."

Two days later, the army came into the village to draft new recruits. When they saw that the farmer's son had a broken leg, they decided not to recruit him.

Everyone said, "What a fortunate young man."

The farmer smiled again and said, "We'll see."

—Author Unknown

Lesson 1: Most people in this world react (or overreact) to every event as though it is the last event that will ever occur. They are tossed to and fro by the news of the day.

Lesson 2: The farmer faced adversity with calm resolve and even with a smile.

Lesson 3: Many times, what looks like a setback might actually be a gift in disguise.

Lesson 4: All events and circumstances can be gifts that we can learn valuable lessons from *if* we have the tools and abilities of discernment.

Lesson 5: This Chinese farmer personifies a gentleman we all should aspire to emulate: One who has lived and seen. One who understands. One who has wisdom ever at his side.

***This* is the power of story.** Each of these lessons, which convey powerful teachings, has filled many tomes of instruction through the centuries. Yet the sheer economy of words and the context—which only stories can provide—benefit the listener each time they are repeated. And, with a good story, the right brain is ignited with meaning that imbeds remembrance.

Consider another simple example:[6]

> Fact: "The queen died and the king died."
>
> Story: "The queen died and the king died of a broken heart."

This one-line story shows the components of a good story.[7] Namely:

- Challenge
- Struggle
- Resolution

The challenge was clearly the queen's death, and the struggle was the king's grief from which he, too, died. The phrase "of a broken heart" in the second version gives context and elicits an entire story of romance and tragedy in the lives of this ruling couple. What was the resolution? Perhaps it was the king reuniting with the queen in the next life. This one line does not say. But there is likely a prince or princess waiting in the wings to carry on their legacy.

The stories that surround us are inescapable.

In politics: Former president Bill Clinton once said that politics is "about giving people better stories." Clinton was a relatively unknown, small-state governor from Arkansas when he rose to power, defeating an incumbent president in 1992. How did he do it?

Clinton is the consummate rapport builder. He is legendary for making you feel like the only person in the room when he speaks with you. And he is a master storyteller. In the 1992 presidential debates, it was easy to see how well he connected with the hearts of the studio audience (and thus the audience at home). President Bush and third-party candidate Ross Perot seemed to be more interested in the time of day (Bush actually looked at his wristwatch during the live debate) and line charts (which Perot became known for). The politicians who get personal and tell the best stories usually win. Charts, graphs, and big, impersonal numbers are for second (or third) place.

In art and music: As you observed in chapter 1, the story behind the painting, or perhaps the artist's personal story, causes collectors to relish their purchases. And when they share the art with others, they enjoy the backstory as well. The *story* is what makes the art valuable.

How many are familiar with the story of Wolfgang Amadeus Mozart, set in Vienna, Austria, during the latter half of the eighteenth century? Specifically, a contemporary composer of his—Antonio Salieri—while recognizing the genius of Mozart, tried to thwart him due to pride and envy. This story, whether witnessed in book form or in the motion picture *Amadeus,* is compelling and causes us all to engage in self-refection. Nothing can do that like a story.

In sports and popular entertainment: We have watched many shows in the world of sports that profile the human side of our athletic heroes. Oftentimes, the more tragic or pathetic (*pathos* again) the profile, the higher the ratings.

News shows like *60 Minutes* and *20/20* are classics, offering stories that are mostly out of the mainstream because they offer a compelling real-life plot line. (And reality always seems to be stranger and more interesting than fiction.)

In our homes: Perhaps the most frequent use of stories through the years has occurred at the hearth and the dinner table. Most of us have stories from parents and grandparents. The home is a natural place for teaching through storytelling to take place. May it always be so.

In every aspect of life, stories pull us in. They have tremendous influence on us, as our elected officials and grandmothers know all too well. Here are more characteristic effects of stories that show the tremendous advantage they provide to both the teller and the hearer.

TEN EFFECTS OF STORYTELLING:

1. **Relaxes and grabs attention.**

When you say the words, "Let me tell you a story," good things happen. I have seen it again and again in staff meetings, with my children, and at public speaking events. It is like magic. People adjust their seating and almost always lean forward or open their eyes wider. Most can't hide a smile, even though they have no idea what is coming next. The thought of a tale takes us back to our childhood, when stories were used so often to instruct.

Research has also documented that engaging stories lower blood pressure and slow the heart rate. The left brain, which has built walls around itself for protection, is powerless as stories circumvent its defenses.[8]

2. **Simplifies.**

We are amazed at the volume of information that is available in our technological age. When we ponder the amount of material students today must master in order to complete their course work, it is mind-boggling.

Stories have the unique property of simplifying and concentrating concepts more efficiently. The economy of words that is inherent in stories affords us the leverage we need to synthesize and simplify the vast amount of information that inundates our lives. Here is one practical example of the effects of storytelling concerning a common workplace issue:[9]

One study compared the effectiveness of four different methods to persuade a group of M.B.A. students of an unlikely hypothesis: that a company really practiced a policy of avoiding layoffs.

In one method, there was just a story.

In the second, the researchers provided statistical data.

In the third, they used statistical data and a story.

In the fourth, they offered the policy statement made by a senior company executive.

The most effective method of all turned out to be the first alternative: presenting the story alone.

3. **Engages the imagination.**

You already know the power of the *word* "imagine," whether in your questioning or when using influence phrases. Stories actually get the listener to go where the imagining takes place—and in living color.

One of the clearest examples of why and how stories work so effectively is the power of chronology in spectator sports. Every play, every shot, every touchdown is a new event in a story timeline where the outcome is in doubt. And while we don't do it often anymore, when you do have the occasion to listen to a game on the radio, you know how your mind's eye can take you right to the stadium and the middle of the action.

The imagination of your listener acts in this same way when they hear your stories. It is the powerful ally that directs them to the place where you want to take them. The key is to do so subtly and skillfully.

4. **Facts vs. Plot lines.**

As mentioned, facts are left brain and stories are right brain in nature—text vs. context. You also learned in chapter 4 that in order to substantiate your argument, you should use these tactics in this order:

A. Use facts first.

B. Challenge your opponent's definition of the item in dispute.

C. Declare your opponent's points "irrelevant" (if they are).

And now we add . . .

D. Tell a story.

Remember, you should be seeking truth. In and of themselves, facts are not the whole truth. They need context. Mark Twain famously wrote in his autobiography, "There are three kinds of lies: lies, damned lies, and statistics." (Twain was quoting Disraeli.) The story around the facts or statistics is what should reflect reality.

For instance, Barack Obama won the 2012 presidential election by approximately 5 million votes. Thus, it is said that he was elected by a "majority."

Yet only 32 percent of voting-age Americans voted for him. The additional context of how many voters stayed home might be relevant for many hearing this story. (Both Republican and Democratic presidents have been elected with similar numbers, not just Obama.)

If your product provides "23 percent more efficiency," what does that mean? Put names, places, and dates in story form to talk about the advantages of that extra productivity, and now you have something powerful to tell. The effectiveness of your claim now takes on an exponential property because people can imagine and understand the benefits. From a defensive standpoint, you must also understand how facts or statistics can be outlined to deceive you.

Facts and figures can help frame a situation, but clarity and action comes when those facts are linked with events—real or even imagined.

5. Softens difficult situations.

Ironically, when discussions stay on the level of facts and figures, there is a greater chance of an adversarial environment as people defend their positions. Stories give you a way up and a way out—if needed.

Facts live in the realm of *push*. Stories *pull*, or draw in. When you make your case in the form of a story, you create curiosity, build interest, and encourage participation. People are likely to feel more comfortable because they can think for themselves.[10]

This sets up an atmosphere of cooperation rather than drawing a line in the sand with left-brain positions. Even if you don't succeed, a story gives you the opportunity to diplomatically bow out. Therefore, it is particularly handy in a high-risk situation where disagreement is very possible. Storytelling is less direct and, therefore, more gracious—prompting less resistance.[11]

6. Packed with tact.

In chapter 4, you learned the argumentation technique known as *paralipsis.* You mention something by saying you aren't going to mention it. ("I won't mention the fact that you snore like Fred Flintstone, dear.")

The same can be achieved through story—only with tact. You can tell a story when confidentiality or decorum dictates that the *kairos* (time and place) is not right for an awkward question or statement. Stories let you communicate in "gray areas" when you need to say it without really saying it.

My favorite example is a diet ad that shows a "before and after" picture. The advertiser of the weight loss program or exercise product is practically shouting through the television, "Hey, you are *really* unhealthy, like this guy in the 'before' photo! And everybody knows it! Why don't you get off your couch, pick up the phone, and get yourself in shape?" The "subtlety" of the pictures does all that screaming for them.

7. **Better than a promise.**

Stories show the benefits of a product or service better than a promise.[12] People can see themselves engaged in the use of a product or service as you tell them how well it has worked for a "recent customer" (consensus).

Simply suggesting or describing how something works provides far more persuasion to the sales effort. (You don't have to actually sell products or services to use this technique. It might be just describing how much fun it would be to go to the baseball game this Saturday night in order to "sell" your companion on the idea.)

8. **Attributes wisdom to the storyteller.**

When you tell a powerful story, you are connecting people to what is important to them and helping them make sense of the world. When this happens, an incredible and valuable thing occurs—the listener attributes the wisdom and intelligence of the story to *you*.[13] It makes no difference whether or not you deserve this kind of respect—you get it anyway.

Consider the power of this storytelling characteristic: If you tell an inspiring story about Mother Teresa, the audience will likely attribute some of her good qualities to you. Why? Because you "must be like her if you are telling us about her in such a complimentary and sincere way."

This is especially good news if you are a student or young professional who might have trouble garnering respect simply because of your age or lack of experience.

9. Retells *itself* again and again.

You can't influence people long term if they cannot remember your message. Stories combat poor memories. Because stories tend to evoke emotional (pathos) reactions in hearers, they are far easier to remember than facts and figures (which tend to disappear very quickly).

The fact that listeners are creating their own images as you tell your story allows them to replay their own version, which they obviously remember better. (This imagination effect is why we are usually disappointed by a movie after we have read the book. Even Steven Spielberg sometimes has a hard time meeting the expectations we have conjured up in our imaginations.)

Another factor that helps the chances of your story being remembered is *specificity*. It is counterintuitive, but good storytellers try to be specific because it actually creates more connections with the listener. For example, if you specifically describe your mother, the listeners will not envision your mother alone. They will go to their own childhood and see their own mother in their mind. This is done effortlessly.[14]

10. Provides massive return on investment (ROI).

Telling stories costs almost nothing. Therefore, its ROI is almost unlimited. This also spills over into other areas of the financial realm. If you and your organization are communicating through stories, it usually means you are processing ideas more efficiently. This lowers staff costs (fewer hours), among other savings, and provides more revenue through increased sales opportunities (higher closing ratios).

In fact, storytelling is so important to the bottom line that I routinely advise and assist corporate clients in creating a proprietary *Story Vault*— where a company catalogs stories for corporate situations. These stories then become ubiquitous throughout the organization.

This would include both macro stories (e.g., "Yes, Bank of America is proud of our heritage of providing funds to build American icons like the Golden Gate Bridge and Disneyland . . .") and micro stories that might pertain to anyone from the management team to customer service teams to account executives. These stories become important instruments for success both internally with teammates and externally with customers.

Telling your own stories and hearing new ones helps you figure out how the world around you works.

The Story Vault

Two of the most notable champions of the Story Vault (although they certainly did not use that term) were the Brothers Grimm. "In 1807, the Grimm brothers began collecting folk tales that had, up until that point, never been written down. In 1812, they published a collection of 86 tales under the title *Children's and Household Stories.* By the seventh edition, the last published in their lifetime, the collection had grown to 211 tales. If not for the work of the Brothers Grimm, we might never have heard such stories as Rumpelstiltskin, Snow White, Sleeping Beauty, Rapunzel, Cinderella, Hansel and Gretel, Little Red Riding Hood, and the Frog Prince."[15]

When you document your own stories, you are also saving stories for posterity—even if only for your family or organization.

BECOMING A MASTER STORYTELLER

Let me tell you a story . . .

I had a marketing professor in graduate school who told us about his first scuba diving experience. He was naturally excited to apply what he had just learned from his cursory training at a resort hotel. The first time he submerged in the crystal clear waters of the Caribbean, what did he see? A wall of barracuda!

While he had never faced this menacing scene, he knew enough about barracuda to know that they are among the most frightening creatures in the sea. My professor explained how his bulging eyes filled his goggles as his breaths became short and shallow with fear.

Within a few moments, however, he was pleasantly surprised to realize they were not going to do anything but stare back at him. Even so, he tugged firmly on the line attached to the boat above and cautiously paddled the few meters to the surface to frantically tell his instructor about the confrontation.

He was informed that there was no need to be alarmed. Barracuda don't act in concert like the dreaded piranha in the Amazon. In fact, barracuda are scavengers and might mistake snorkelers for large predators, only following them in hopes of eating the remains of their prey. Swimmers have rarely reported being bitten by barracuda, and such incidents might be caused by poor visibility more than anything else. What my professor was really facing was a wall of *individual* fish, not a dangerous gang of fish seeking to make him their lunch.

He recalled that story to teach his students this important lesson:

> When you speak to an audience, you are speaking to individuals—not a group.

This precept has stayed with me. You must keep this overarching principle of individuality in mind as you learn ways to become a master storyteller. This will cause people to repeat your story to others one-on-one because they felt a connection—even if they were members of a large audience.

THREE ESSENTIAL ELEMENTS OF A GOOD STORY

1. **Surprise!** In the barracuda story, the moment my professor faced the perceived danger in front of his face, you felt his fear for just a moment. The surprise element in this short story was that there was really no danger to

speak of. A story without a surprise is a dud from the start. The essence of story is to tell people *something they do not know*. By definition, this is a surprise—be it a mild one or one that is more intense and thrilling.

2. **Targets the heart.** Storytelling is such a dynamic tool for influence because it gives people space to think for themselves. Stories grow in the mind of your listener. More specifically, they grow in the *heart* of your listener. This keeps ideas alive without you even being there.[16] The listeners keep telling it again and again in their minds (and to others), thus ingraining the story deep into their hearts with each recollection.

    The difference in humans and animals is the ability to consider who we are *now* in relation to who we can be in the *future*. The ability to tell a story that speaks to the heart provides an effective way of building a bridge from what is to what could or *should* be.

3. **Leads to wisdom.** Your goal should be to "awaken sleeping wisdom" in the listener, rather than provide a convincing portrayal of your argument. If you can accomplish this, "right" decisions can flow.[17] This is true because of the following equation:

Intelligence + Knowledge (Facts) x Experience = Wisdom

Synthesizing facts into a good story is tantamount to converting knowledge into wisdom—through experience. The problem is that all of our lives are limited by time. Furthermore, we have all overestimated our abilities, especially in youth. The wisest among us learn from the experiences of others. In junior high, I started collecting a recipe box full of three-by-five index cards, on which I wrote quotes and sayings. One that I still remember said, "Learn from the mistakes of others—you can't live long enough to make them all yourself." This is what storytelling does, even small storytelling. It allows you to teach values from your own perspective as well as from others who have gone before.

A new story—whether from your own experience or someone else's (like my professor's)—provides a new perspective. After all, any new facts that you might provide are usually placed into a listener's current story (perspective). Facts are neutral, and if you add new ones, people will continue to slot them into their own story. But if you can provide a new story, then the same facts will be interpreted differently—presumably with more wisdom.

The Story Circle

The basic components of a story are best pictured in a circular fashion.

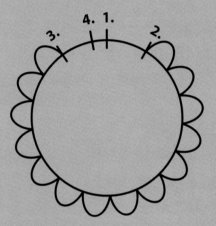

The Story Circle has *four stages*:

1. State of perfection.
2. Adversity.
3. Adversity is overcome.
4. Return to a state of perfection.

The state of perfection in stage 1 is a relative state. There is no time in life when everything is perfect. Life is like a railroad track on which bad things are occurring on one rail while, on the other rail, good things are happening.[18]

When adversity occurs in stage 2, it usually is the result of an antagonist—a villain or circumstance of some sort. This throws the "state of perfection" into chaos. Note that this stage might last for a prolonged time and have many tangential "ups and downs" (and subplots) along the way.

In stage 3, the adversity is typically overcome as the result of a hero or heroine arriving to "save the day."

Stage 4 returns to the "state of perfection," which oftentimes is an even *better* state than was originally present.

Every Academy Award–winning motion picture or literary classic has this same simple structure. Heroes are sympathetic and universally recognizable characters, and the drama of this fundamental plot gets the story moving. And the "aha!" usually follows.[19]

This four-part formula works well because A) an unexpected challenge or question will get your audience's attention, B) the emotional experience (pathos) found in the narration of a struggle is compelling, and C) once the problem is overcome, the resolution is a call to action for the listener as well.

With this simple approach, you will show your audience that *every challenge is truly an opportunity.* They begin to see themselves as the hero, not the victim. Transform their thinking (their story), and you will transform their actions.

Fundamentals of Storytelling

Story is the rich soil into which you can plant the Old School acorns of recall, words, influence, and reason. These techniques are constantly growing into mighty oaks that help you not only discover truth but convey it in an effective manner as well. As a rule, none of us change our minds quickly. Nor would we want to. Incremental acquisition of new information and applied wisdom leads to a satisfying and productive life that will be characterized not by perfection but by the constant pursuit of it.

Yet, you might still be reluctant to tell a story because you are afraid of looking silly or unprofessional. You might hold back because you don't want to come off as manipulative, or perhaps you fear damage to your credibility. So you keep everything logical and rational—on the left side of your brain, where the facts keep you safe.

But if you want to have real influence, you must take chances. Not foolish chances, but those that will make a difference in people's lives. You have to affect them on an emotional level. You must get to their *pathos*. Always staying in a guarded, "professional" mode will never allow you to show your humanity and touch hearts.

Preparation builds confidence. Here are the *fundamentals* of good storytelling:

1. **Listen first.** Good storytelling is about listening and then telling. A good listener not only learns stories to repeat, but also builds rapport and gains additional insights, which naturally result in better storytelling. Avoid "bottom lining" someone—or asking for the same. Although this seems more efficient, ironically, it actually can delay decisions because the full story is never told. And often, when people are indecisive, it is simply a result of needing more information in order to move forward. So even though it might take a bit longer to hear or tell the whole story, in the long run, it leads to faster and better decisions.

2. **Try starting with a compelling question.** "Good orators will often pose compelling questions at the beginning of their presentations to get the audience thinking about a subject, switching them from content absorption mode to content consideration mode. These orators make listeners participants in the speech, not observers. Similarly, good parents often phrase their parental instructions in the form of questions: 'If everyone else was jumping off a bridge, would you?'"[20]

3. **There are always three conversations at once.** Anytime a communication takes place, there are three conversations going on: 1) the actual discourse

(or presentation), 2) the conversation the speaker has in her own mind ("Are they listening? What should I say next?"), and 3) the conversation in the mind of the listener. ("What is she saying? I can't wait to respond.")

Stephen Denning explains why this is significant:

> You proceed on the basis that the relationship between you and your listeners is symmetrical. You talk as if the listeners could take the next turn in the conversation.
>
> For each member of the audience, there are two listeners: the physical person you see in front of you and a second listener known as "the little voice in the head." And if you're asking yourself, "What on earth do you mean by 'the little voice in the head'?" that is exactly the little voice that I mean! The little voice may be distracting the listener from paying real attention to what you're saying.
>
> The conventional view of communications is to ignore the little voice in the head and hope that the message will somehow get through. Unfortunately, the little voice often doesn't stay quiet. Often the listener is getting a new and possibly unwelcome perspective on what the speaker is talking about.
>
> So you do something different. You don't ignore the little voice in the head. Instead you work in harmony with it. You engage it by giving it something to do. You tell a story in a way that elicits a second story from the little voice in the head. When this occurs, the little voice is already racing ahead to figure out how to implement the change idea. And because the listeners have created the idea, they like it. It's their own wonderful idea! The result is personalized coherence across large numbers of people.[21]

4. **It's not just oral.** People are not strictly evaluating what you say. Your appearance and movements are all part of "your story." In fact, you are telling this story even when you are silent. We might not want to judge a book by

its cover, but we do. "Even when you tell a story about who you are, people filter your story through their interpretations of what they see and hear as you speak."[22]

Body language speeds up a story even more. Annette Simmons warns that we should not place too much emphasis on conventional interpretations of body language. "Don't buy someone else's theory about what body language says. Crossed arms don't always mean the same thing. Presentation courses that preach a cookie-cutter posture only churn out people who are trying to look like something they are not."[23]

Even a subtle gesture can be very persuasive. "A modest use of gestures can add meaning to your story, intensify your message, and create a stage upon which your story is played. You can use your hands to create props, to draw scenery, to increase the intensity of an emotion, to intentionally send an incongruent message, or just to have a bit of fun."[24]

5. **Facial expressions transcend borders and cultures.** We all understand how to communicate emotional content without using words. A smile equals happiness, and a frown means anger or disagreement. "Actors don't study the anatomy of which muscles paint joy on their face. They study how to conjure up joy in their mind and body because they know that when they feel joy, it will show on their face." One expression can replace multiple sentences and speed up your story.[25]

6. **Timing, pauses, and silence.** These add variety to your story—often bringing more power than the words can. Pauses give listeners the opportunity to participate in and process the story.[26] Have you ever noticed how well comedians do this? They provide pauses, giving you ample time to "get it" and also laugh. They don't want the next punch line lost in residual laughter. (They also use facial expressions and body language masterfully during these "time outs.") On the contrary, if you listen to an audio book, how often must you pause the recording so that you can grasp the thought just articulated? This exemplifies how frustrated your listener can get if you do not use pauses

wisely. Silence can also provide you with the opportunity to command more attention just when you need it.

7. **Tone is the most important oral communication tool.** It can ultimately override every other aspect of your communication. But the trick is not to work on your tone; work on your *feelings*. As with the actors' expressions, the right tone will follow if the feeling is right. Faking it will result in severely weakening your message. We have all seen people try too hard and fall flat on their storytelling face. They come across as needy—even desperate. This is why authenticity in storytelling is vital.[27]

8. **Lose the notes.** Without using your notes, your story might not include every detail you wanted to include. But telling an imperfect story while looking directly into their eyes is much better than including every detail and looking at the podium. And guess what helps you do this easily? Your memory palace!

9. **Avoid your curriculum vitae.** You can't tell an audience that you are honest and trustworthy or what your GPA was in college. They must come to the conclusion on their own that you are a credible and reliable person. The best way to accomplish this is to share a story from your life that relates this clearly. You are a one-of-a-kind person. No one has had the experiences you have had. No one has met the people you have met or read the books you have read. Telling them about the turning points in your life lets them live inside of you for a short time. This is the power of story and personal testimony.

10. **Get the audience's attention with *their* problems.** Start with the issues that you know are keeping your audience awake at night, and present them more starkly than your audience has ever heard them articulated. Needless to say, this captures their attention quickly. Once they are riveted (and they will be), go into your springboard story. A softer way of doing this can be a

more indirect story of how you or someone else is dealing with a situation you know the audience is also dealing with. Other ways of getting attention include questions, an arresting metaphor, admitting vulnerability, or an unexpected exercise. The key thing to remember is to get the emotional connection *before* the reasons are presented, so they will reinforce the decision the audience needs to make.[28]

11. **Don't name the value in your story.** For example, avoid stating, "Here is a story about courage . . ." Your audience might see a sermon coming and turn you off before you get started. You also run the risk of telegraphing the punch line or the moral of the story. Also, don't end with "And that is what I have learned . . ." or "That is why I made this decision." Remember: storytelling is intended to allow people to come to the conclusion they should come to—on their own. Don't make it for them.[29]

12. **Bad news first.** Even though they don't elicit action, sometimes you have to deliver negative messages. Never tell a negative story without a positive follow-up. That is why the bad news must always come first. When you take this approach to storytelling (and life in general), then you can actually live a life where there is "no bad news." In other words, always having a follow-up of positive news indicates that the solution is always already on its way. Yes, something bad might have occurred, but we must always go back to one of our earlier important concepts: "Challenges are opportunities in disguise." This is a good way to communicate. It's the best way to live.

13. **Avoid hypotheticals.** First of all, real stories are more interesting. They also add credibility. But scientifically, hypotheticals only speak to a small part of the brain, while real stories are "whole brain" (think "healthier"). And, no disrespect to college professors, but by and large, they live in the world of hypotheticals. And they can be pretty boring.[30]

14. **Use direct quotes rather than summary.** When your story involves other people (most do), bring them in the room with you.[31] Hear the difference:

    A. He said, "I don't think I am going to make it, man."

    B. He didn't think he was going to make it.

This is a subtle yet significant difference in tone and urgency. The fact that direct dialogue in storytelling (as in example A) is not often used today presents another excellent opportunity for you to wax old school.

15. **Practice daily. It's easy.** Once you take an interest in becoming a master storyteller, a daily dose will come naturally. Athletes practice their craft every day. You should, too. Stories are everywhere, so become a story scavenger hunter. Reading articles or books and watching movies will take on a new level of enjoyment for you.

Use "LAVA" in Your Public Speaking

Addressing an audience in a public speaking opportunity is the perfect time to use the LAVA technique you learned in chapter 3. Remember: like the barracuda in the story about my scuba-diving professor, each person sitting before you is observing you as an individual. Therefore, you should address them *personally*.

By using the LAVA technique in your casual interaction *before* you approach the podium, you can collect valuable information from audience members—or information about the unique characteristics of the place or institution where you are speaking.

Finding topics or interests through which you can connect personally will impact your listeners emotionally, thus creating instant rapport with the group. You could do this by elaborating on a favorable quality of the organization or on one or more of the members with whom you have just visited. Doing your homework on the individual members *before*

---

you arrive at the engagement—days in advance, if possible—is also a way to help make them feel comfortable with you early on.

At minimum, research the history of the geographical region or find an interesting feature of it, or find a common story to share with the group. This will allow you a warm reception into the group and access to the values they share—and thus to their hearts.

STORY TYPES

Now consider seven different types of stories and their proper usage. In her excellent book *The Story Factor*, Annette Simmons categorizes the first six for us:[32]

1. "Who Am I?" Story

As Simmons explains, "Personal stories let others see 'who we are' better than any other form of communication. Ultimately, people trust your judgment and your words based on subjective evidence. Objective data doesn't go deep enough to engender trust." (This supports the mantra of "it's hearts, not charts," which I repeat often.)

The question "Is this guy boring?" is the first thing audiences ask themselves when the speaker appears. "Public speakers who start with a genuinely funny joke [or story] answer this easily anticipated question: 'Once you make me laugh I conclude for myself that at the very least you aren't boring, so I relax and listen.'"[33]

Telling a story about "Grampy," "Nana," or any other beloved person in your life is another way to connect with almost any audience because it takes the listener to a (usually) pleasant place of familiarity. You can tell an audience "who you are" by telling a story about someone you loved or admired. It could also be a mentor, friend, or hero.

My boyhood hero was legendary college basketball coach John Wooden. If you are old enough to know about his success, humility, integrity, and high character traits, you could reasonably attribute many of his valuable characteristics to me as I describe my admiration for him. This is especially beneficial in circumstances in which you are unknown to the audience, in which you are considerably younger, or in which you have far less experience than those you are addressing (this goes for one-on-one conversations as well).

2. **"Why I Am Here?" Story**

"Who are you, and why are you here?" That is what people seeing you for the first time want to know. Simmons says, "When you focus all your communication on showing your listeners what they might gain, you come across as hiding your gain. Your message begins to seem incongruent, insincere, or worse, deceitful."[34] Here is an example of a story Simmons relates that avoids these pitfalls. It is about a gentleman who is soliciting funds for a worthy charitable cause:

> He tells them that when he was in the Holy Land, someone explained the difference between the Dead Sea and the very much alive Sea of Galilee. The Dead Sea has no outlet. Both are fed by the same source but the Dead Sea can only receive an inward flow. The Dead Sea is prevented from flowing outward and the accumulation of salt has killed it. The Sea of Galilee is alive only because what flows in can also flow out.

NOTE: You can take this metaphor and catalog it in your Story Vault. Once everyone in your community understands this story, its meaning will bring a much fuller context to the conversation.

This metaphor demonstrated that, for him, "giving is a necessary function of thriving and feeling alive. His message not only explained 'why I am here' to the person he was visiting, but it begins to give a glimpse of his 'vision' of how alive we feel when we give to others and let our wealth flow both in and out."[35]

3. "Vision" ("Future") Story

There is no question that we all constantly tell stories to ourselves and others about the future. We are creative beings by nature, and that means we are thinking about what comes *next*.

Leadership in any organization is inextricably tied to the future, and those who are best at identifying and imagining the greatest opportunities are usually the most successful. When the leader of a business organization announces, "We are going to be a billion-dollar company in five years," the troops pay homage to the noble thought, but it is likely they don't care much about it after the meeting is over. Vision stories help people get out of the past, which is set in concrete (and where *blame* lives), break away from the present (*status quo*), and move into the future (where *hope* resides).

As stated earlier, details in stories create more connections that make them easier to remember. But, as Stephen Denning explains, vision or future stories that contain *too* much detail (like a specific number within a specific timeframe) could undermine the very power the leader is seeking to employ. "The more detail the story includes, the greater the likelihood there is of error [or failure]—and hence loss of credibility."[36] This is why leaders must use vision stories to accompany stated quantitative goals.

Denning cites famous examples such as Winston Churchill and Martin Luther King, who both refrained from giving any details in their most famous orations (Churchill in his "We will fight them on the beaches" speech and King's "I have a dream" speech). Ronald Reagan's exhortation at the Brandenburg Gate in 1987—"Mr. Gorbachev, tear down this wall!"—had no dates or deadlines, but we still remember it as the most famous line of his presidency.

All three of these memorable refrains were short on details but long on poetic and general principles that inspired us. "Evocative future stories that are told and retold become part of the common mind. It's the unified expression of many voices playing on the same theme. A successful vision is a dream, but it's a dream with a twist: it's a dream that is *shared*. When we share the same dream, we all begin to participate in it."[37]

Of all the types of stories, the vision or future story is the "most likely to sound corny on paper, but might get you a standing ovation when delivered in person and with authenticity. Vision stories are very easily taken out of context. One of the difficulties in telling an authentic vision story is the fear that detractors can take it out of context and make us sound sappy, or 'out there.' Vision takes courage."[38]

Here is an example of a good Vision Story: "A man came upon a construction site where three people were working. He asked the first, 'What are you doing?' and the man answered, 'I am laying bricks.' He asked the second, 'What are you doing?' and the man answered, 'I am constructing a wall.' He walked up to the third man, who was humming a tune as he worked, and asked, 'What are you doing?' and the man stood up and smiled and said, 'I am building a cathedral.' If you want to influence others in a big way, you need to give them a vision story that will become their *cathedral*."[39]

4. "Teaching" Story

It doesn't matter what you are teaching—a skill, a classroom subject, or a life principle—stories do it better.

For example: "Telling your new receptionist where the hold, transfer, and extension buttons are on the console is not going to teach her how to be a great receptionist. However, telling her about the best receptionist you ever knew, Mrs. Ardi, who was from Bangladesh and could simultaneously calm an angry customer, locate your wandering CEO, and smile warmly at the UPS man, gives a much more clear-cut picture of the skills that you want her to display. Later, under stress, her brain is better equipped to handle complex situations if she can ask herself, 'What would Mrs. Ardi do?' instead of, 'Where is the hold button?'"[40]

Stories are not only compelling and easier to remember; another great advantage is that they considerably reduce the time needed to convey an idea. This is the "economy of words" that stories inherently provide. In chapter 7, you will be given a list of metaphors/short stories that can fill the first file in any story vault.

5. **"Values in Action" Story**

Children, subordinates, and peers learn by our example. This is the best way to teach, and one that comes with great responsibility. But when you can't teach by example, storytelling makes a good substitute. "Stories allow you to impart values which keep people thinking for themselves," Annette Simmons writes.[41] She continues: "If you can convince them they are on a hero's journey, they can begin to see obstacles as challenges, and choose behaviors more befitting a hero than a victim. Change their story and you change their behavior."[42]

Here is an example cited in *The Story Factor* that addresses being the first to market a great idea:

> "I hear people talk about the 'early bird gets the worm,' but something that is just as true—and people don't talk about this as much—is that it is the second mouse that gets the cheese! The first mouse gets his head squished. I don't want to be the first mouse. I want to be the second mouse. The people out there on the cutting edge of technology are actually on the *bleeding* edge of technology. I want our company to be smart about where we put our resources. Let someone else be first; second is where the money is."

This story didn't dictate to anyone, but it influenced some design engineers to think in a new way. "They could decide to change their behavior and spend more time supporting current products and less time chasing new technology. Again, here is a very short story that proves that even in a fast-paced world, stories work."[43]

6. **"I Know What You Are Thinking" Story**

It is a tough and competitive world. Sometimes, people will try to discredit you or your message. Simmons suggests telling a subtle "I Know What You're Thinking" story in order to counteract without acting counter.

"A speaker I heard recently started his speech with 'I am a statistician and this will be the most boring one hour of your life.' He then told some silly story about how his last group needed resuscitation. We loved it. He read our minds, zeroed in on our major fear—'this is going to be boring'—and dispelled that fear with a story."[44]

If you know there is likely to be some resistance to your story, preempting that doubt or cynicism can prove a valuable way to defuse a situation and clear the minds of your listeners so that you may have a fair hearing. But be careful. There is some risk. You don't want to bias an audience that was not even thinking what you are trying to preempt.

7. **"The Springboard" Story**

The final story type is explained by Stephen Denning in his book *The Leader's Guide to Storytelling*. He explains that the Springboard Story might be the most important for a leader or an organization to use because it most effectively communicates multifaceted ideas in order to inspire action.

A springboard story is based on an *actual* event, preferably recent enough to seem relevant. It has a single protagonist with whom members of the target audience can identify. And it has an authentically happy ending, in which a change has at least in part been implemented successfully. (It also has an implicit alternate ending—an unhappy one that would have resulted had the change not occurred.) The story has enough detail to be intelligible and credible but—and this is key—not so much texture that the audience becomes completely wrapped up in it. If that happens, people won't have the mental space to create an analogous scenario for change in their own organization.

Who is the hero or heroine of your story? It's not a group, not a team, not a company, not a country. You are looking for a *single individual*—perhaps an anonymous individual who carries out or facilitates implementation of the change idea.

Here you are plugging into an archetypal narrative pattern—the hero's journey [story circle]. You are taking your audience on the journey of someone who set out to accomplish something that is difficult, someone who met obstacles along the way but finally triumphed. Ta-dah! Everyone has heard this kind of story thousands of times. Sound corny? But it works. This kind of story has deep roots in the human psyche. All of us tend to see our own life as a journey with goals and obstacles that get in the way of attaining those goals. So when we hear a story in the form of a hero's journey, we respond from the deepest reaches of our psyche.

It's a good idea to link the date, the place, and the single protagonist at the start of your story. The specificity for the place and time might seem trivial, but it is critical because it shows that the story is true. [It replaces telling someone, "This is a true story," which can cause pushback.] In this way, the listeners, who are likely to be searching for someone to identify with, will be grateful. They will understand that here is a storyteller who understands their need for a protagonist. If you introduce the protagonist further on in the story, after you've laid the scene for instance, the audience will be wondering all along, Who is this story about? Where is it heading? Who's the hero?

Denning gives this example:

As you know, Global Consulting aspires to become the leading provider of consulting services in its field. So we're trying to implement lots of changes to make that happen. Let me tell you about one recent example of how this is working out.

It's about James Truscott, who works for us in London. A few months ago he heard about an invitation to bid on a large consulting engagement for one of the biggest industrial firms in the U.K.— British Engines. What had been happening even as recently as a couple of months ago is that we weren't winning many of those big consulting engagements because our staff from different countries would compete among themselves for the same engagement and end up totally confusing the client.

What James did in this case, when he heard about the invitation to bid for this worldwide account, was that he contacted all the people in Global around the world who deal with British Engines. He brought them all together as a team and together they developed Global's pitch to British as a global team.

As it turned out, a competitor undercut us with a lower price, but James went back to British as a global team. He didn't lower the price. Instead he went back to British with other experts from the firm to explain why we were more expensive, so that in fact British could see that they were getting a better deal.

And guess what? We won that multimillion-pound engagement with British. It was a huge thing. It showed to us the power of acting together as a global organization, rather than acting from individual country perspectives. Just think what a company Global could be if all of us would join together and think about the client from a global perspective, so that we could serve the client better as a whole. Just imagine the impact that would have!

When a change has been successfully implemented, at least in part, either in your organization or somewhere else, it becomes a great springboard story from which to drive even greater positive change.[45]

Using Humor

Humor can be employed in any kind of story. It is the side of life that endears and allows us to tolerate even the most difficult situations. (Funny stories are even told about the dearly departed at most funerals.) Obviously, a humorous story out of context can be hurtful or embarrassing. However, levity allows you to recall painful events in a way that demonstrates that you have mastered the experience instead of allowing it to master you.

Leaders understand that humor allows us to deal with the difference between the way things are and the way they ought to be. This is why it is such a valuable tool. When used adeptly, humor can expose folly, increase understanding, and create trust through the humility that it reveals.

> Humor lets a leader win small battles in order to make larger ones unnecessary.
>
> —Booker T. Washington

The most effective managers use humor *twice as often* as middle-of-the-pack managers.[46] Even Abraham Lincoln—a serious man by any measure—knew that humor and storytelling could influence better than humiliation and shame. He was often attacked for his leniency on his enemies. When one woman told him that he should destroy his enemies, he answered, "Isn't that what I do when I make them friends?" His is the storyteller's style of influence—seeking not to win but to erase the lines that divide.[47]

Here is an example of using humor to teach that, while four people can have the same set of facts, they can arrive at four different conclusions.

There are four people on a train en route from Paris to Barcelona—a beautiful young girl traveling with her elderly grandmother, and a stately general traveling with his aide, a young, handsome second lieutenant. The foursome is sitting in silence as the train enters a tunnel in the Pyrenees, the mountain range on the border between France and Spain.

It is pitch-dark in the tunnel. Suddenly there's the sound of a loud kiss, followed by a second sound, that of a loud, hard smack. Upon exiting the tunnel, the four people remain silent, with no one acknowledging the incident.

The young girl thinks to herself, *Boy, that was a swell kiss that good-looking lieutenant gave me, and I really enjoyed it. What a shame my grandmother slapped him, because he must have thought I did it. That's too bad, because when we get to the next tunnel, he won't kiss me again.*

The grandmother thinks, *That fresh young man kissed my granddaughter. But fortunately I brought her up to be a lady, so she slapped him real good. I'm glad because now he'll stay away from her when we get to the next tunnel.*

The general thinks to himself, *I can't believe what just happened. I personally handpicked him to be my aide, and I thought he was a real gentleman. But in the dark, he took advantage of that young girl and kissed her. But she must have thought it was I who kissed her, since I was the one she slapped.*

Meanwhile, the young lieutenant is thinking, *Boy, that was wonderful. How often do you get to kiss a beautiful girl and slap your boss at the same time?*[48]

FINAL KEY: AUTHENTICITY

Stephen Denning says, "Just as DNA is a sample which contains all of the genetic code of your physical body, so too a brief, well-chosen story is the DNA of your character. [Stories] can reveal the DNA of your whole biological person. A brief, well-chosen story can shed light on your entire life history. A story you tell about an apparently trivial incident can expose the entire fabric of your [being]."[49]

To consider that a seemingly inconsequential story from your past can have such an impact is both valuable and scary. After all, who you are—your character—is not based on a single incident, but on the entirety of your life experiences. Right?

This shines a light on the importance of *authenticity. It is not just what you do; it is who you are.* And that "who you are" *cuts both ways.*

Consider this quintessential and infamous example of counterfeit authenticity: "I now pray to God that he will bless in the years to come our work, our deeds, our foresight, our resolve; that the Almighty may protect us from both arrogance and cowardly servility, that he may help us find the right way, which he has laid down for [our] people and that he may always give us courage to do the right thing and never to falter or weaken before any power or any danger."

Who said this? Jefferson? Washington? Lincoln? Billy Graham?

These words were spoken in 1938 by Adolph Hitler and helped influence a nation to genocide.[50]

On a brighter note, authentic storytelling on a personal level is beneficial in a variety of situations:

- **A first introduction.** You can use the LAVA technique you learned in chapter 3 to *warm up* the conversation and get it *flowing*. It creates a natural atmosphere that elicits personal stories.
- **Tense situations.** Perhaps a difficult topic or decision has to be made. Often, suspicions run high in these circumstances.
- **Giving advice.** When you need to provide coaching or counsel.

Authenticity works well in these scenarios because it builds trust like nothing else. Don't be afraid to be vulnerable and tell stories about yourself or people you care about. Remember, when you tell stories about people whom you regard highly, their character is a reflection of who you are. You are revealing your values and innermost feelings through theirs. Your authenticity also equips you to deal with more difficult people and situations.

For example, in circumstances where you face a *cynical listener* and your competence or sincerity is in question, you need to deliver compelling evidence of your character, and you need to do it quickly. Since cynical people don't care about good intentions, an evidence-based story helps to convince them. Since they don't know you, firsthand experience is not available. The right story can deliver a vicarious "firsthand" experience, which can overcome their doubts.[51]

Secondly, if *irrational emotions* are in play, you need to highlight the "big picture" to make their situation seem smaller. Jealousy commonly exists within an individual's small story. Give a larger and broader story perspective to reframe shared interests.[52]

Finally, when you are authentic and open up to others, you can *provide hope* through stories about the turning points in your life. Turning points provide fertile ground for telling stories of perseverance and overcoming adversity. They encourage and allow people to relate to you like nothing else can.[53]

BIG Concepts in Little Stories

Here is a sampling of short story examples that show how big concepts can be portrayed in a very efficient and enjoyable manner. (Note: In chapter 7, we will provide an additional list of words and phrases that provide this same economy of concepts.)

THE STARFISH

A little girl finds starfish stranded on the beach by the low tide, and she tosses them back into the ocean. A passerby, seeing the thousands of starfish left stranded, tells the girl that her task is hopeless. How can she possibly make a difference? She replies, "It made a difference to that one," as she tosses another one back into the water.

Big Concept: Mother Teresa said, "If I look at the masses, I will never act. If I look at the one, I will." Anecdotes are inherently more persuasive than statistics. Every good deed we do has an immediate impact on those around us. The ripples continue outward as we influence others and as they, in turn, influence those in their circles.[54]

THE STICKY NOTE

The story of the invention of the sticky note has become legendary:

"It took five years from the time Dr. Spence Silver invented the peculiar substance—an adhesive that didn't stick very much—to the time a new-product development researcher named Art Fry came up with the concept that turned into the Post-It note. Recalling his frustration at trying to keep his place in his church choir hymnal, Fry realized that Silver's 'failed' adhesive could make for a wonderfully reliable bookmark."[55]

Big Concept: Be aware of serendipitous opportunities. Some inventions come from unexpected or peripheral sources. Sticky notes are a perfect example.

I, PENCIL

A small essay written in 1958 by entrepreneur Leonard Read taught a big lesson. "I, Pencil" presented the origins and manufacturing of "an ordinary wooden pencil," which required what Read called "innumerable antecedents"—which required millions of people in dozens of countries to perfect and perform the tasks necessary to create it.

The story starts first with the cedar tree harvested from northern California. Then there are the saws and trucks and ropes and other equipment, all built in different places; the mill in San Leandro, California; the trains to transport the wood; the processing plant with kiln and tinting; the electricity from the dam to power the plant; the millions of dollars in equipment used to build the pencils; the graphite from Sri Lanka, mixed with clay from Mississippi and chemicals from who knows where; the wax from Mexico and beyond; the yellow lacquer with castor oil; the brass to hold the eraser, forged with metals from mines around the world; the eraser, made with factice from Indonesia and pumice from Italy.

Finally, there are the trucks that deliver the pencils and the stores that sell pencils to the public for about ten cents each. All of this and much more is needed to make one yellow pencil. There are at least three marvels here.

First, few who contributed to the pencil meant to make a pencil. The miner in Sri Lanka probably doesn't know that the graphite he's mining will end up as a pencil, and the miners who mined the copper to make brass probably don't know that the little metal thingy on pencils is even made of brass.

Second, as the pencil in Read's tale explains, "Not a single person on the face of this earth knows how to make me." That knowledge isn't stored in any one place; it is dispersed among millions of different people.

Third, no (human) mastermind oversees the process. It's all coordinated by people working freely in specialized jobs following the price of countless goods and services. This is one of the greatest wonders in the universe, but it's gotten the worst press. If we didn't see its effects after the fact, we would never believe it.

Most of us believe pencils exist, even if we don't know how they're made. Imagine if Leonard Read had written the essay today and chosen an Apple iPad rather than a pencil. I have an iPad. I love it. I haven't the slightest idea what makes the darn thing go, let alone how to make one from scratch. No surprise there. But the fact is, no one does.

Big Concept: The miracle of free markets in the economic system of capitalism enables us to do something together that no one can do alone—regardless of any one individual's resources or talents.

THE STORY OF PYRRHUS, KING OF EPIRUS

Pyrrhus, the king of Epirus, a region of Greece, is planning an attack on Rome. His trusted adviser, Cineas, thinks it's a bad idea. Cineas is an impressive guy, a brilliant wordsmith and negotiator whom the king often uses as a representative. But even though he has the trust and ear of the king, it's usually not a great idea to tell the king he's making a mistake, even when you're a favorite of his, so Cineas takes a roundabout approach. Here's how Cineas begins in Plutarch's version of the story in *Lives*:

"The Romans, sir, are reported to be great warriors and conquerors of many warlike nations; if God permits us to overcome them, how should we use our victory?"

"Well," says Pyrrhus, "once we conquer Rome, we'll be able to subdue all of Italy."

"And then what?" asks Cineas.

"Sicily would be conquered next."

"And then what?" asks Cineas.

"Libya and Carthage would be next to fall."

"And then what?" asks Cineas.

"Then all of Greece," says the king.

"And what shall we do then?" asks Cineas.

Pyrrhus, smiling, answers, "We will live at our ease, my dear friend, and drink all day, and divert ourselves with pleasant conversation."

Then Cineas brings down the hammer on the king:

"And what hinders Your Majesty from doing so now?"

Big Concept: "We have all the tools of contentment at hand already. You don't have to conquer Italy to enjoy the fundamental pleasures of life. Life is a journey to savor and enjoy. Ambition—the relentless desire for more—can eat you up. Plutarch's *Lives* was written about two thousand years ago. Plutarch was telling a story from maybe three hundred years earlier. That money doesn't make you happy is an *old* story."[56]

ACHIEVEMENT

In 1954, Roger Bannister did something everyone said was impossible. He ran a mile in under four minutes—breaking the barrier by only six-tenths of a second. No one in all of recorded human history had ever run a mile in under four minutes. But soon afterward (just forty-six days later), a man named John Landy broke Bannister's record. To date, well over one thousand different people have recorded a sub-four-minute mile. No official consensus on the exact number of times the record has been broken seems to exist now that so many people have done it so often.

Big Concept: When the bar for human achievement is raised in any particular arena, human beings rise to the occasion. When the bar is lowered, human beings simply exert less effort.

TRUTH

"Truth, naked and cold, had been turned away from every door in the village. Her nakedness frightened the people. When Parable found her she was huddled in a corner, shivering and hungry. Taking pity on her, Parable gathered her up and took her home. There, she dressed Truth in story, warmed her and sent her out again. Clothed in story, Truth knocked again at the villagers' doors and was readily welcomed into the people's houses. They invited her to eat at their table and warm herself by their fire." —Jewish Teaching Story

Big Concept: "Concepts don't get any bigger than a story about *truth* itself. This story has been told and retold since the eleventh century. When a story has been told for almost a thousand years, it must have something useful to say. Clothing truth in story is a powerful way to get people to open the doors of their minds to you and the truth you carry."[57]

SONGS & POEMS

Stories are also ever present in music and poetry. Here are a few examples:

RUDOLPH

There is perhaps no more beloved or well-known Christmas fable than that of Rudolph the Red-Nosed Reindeer. It is based on the 1939 poem by Robert May. His brother-in-law, Johnny Marks, put the poem to music, and it became an overnight hit, culminating in an animated television special by the same name in 1964. I know the tune is already playing in your head as you read this. Now read the lyrics from the perspective of understanding the underlying message:

> Rudolph the red-nosed reindeer
> had a very shiny nose.
> And if you ever saw him,
> you would even say it glows.
>
> All of the other reindeer
> used to laugh and call him names.
> They never let poor Rudolph
> join in any reindeer games.

Then one foggy Christmas Eve
Santa came to say:
"Rudolph, with your nose so bright,
won't you guide my sleigh tonight?"
Then all the reindeer loved him
as they shouted out with glee,
Rudolph the red-nosed reindeer,
you'll go down in history!

Big Concept: Turning a liability into an asset. This is a story of social rejection based solely on a visible physical characteristic. And yet, what happened? When a situation arose that required his special talent, Rudolph saved the day and was not only accepted by his peers but also took on hero status for saving Christmas![58]

THE ROAD NOT TAKEN

This is my personal favorite poem, which I committed to memory years ago. Read it slowly and hear the story Robert Frost tells. *Your* story . . .

Two roads diverged in a yellow wood,
And sorry I could not travel both
And be one traveler, long I stood
And looked down one as far as I could
To where it bent in the undergrowth;

Then took the other, as just as fair,
And having perhaps the better claim,
Because it was grassy and wanted wear;
Though as for that the passing there
Had worn them really about the same,

And both that morning equally lay

In leaves no step had trodden black.

Oh, I kept the first for another day!

Yet knowing how way leads on to way,

I doubted if I should ever come back.

I shall be telling this with a sigh

Somewhere ages and ages hence:

Two roads diverged in a wood, and I—

I took the one less traveled by,

And that has made all the difference.

Big Concept: Most paths laid before us in life are easier and more predictable. They are the way of the crowd or majority. Others are unknown and often more difficult—but more likely to be full of greater opportunities and excitement. This poem falls firmly in the "nothing ventured, nothing gained" category. This is shown by the two paths described—one has been used more often, the other has not. By taking the path less traveled, in the long run, it turns out better for the traveler. Also, the big life choices we make are largely irreversible. So when exercising your freedom of choice (another underlying concept), do so wisely.

NORMAL DAY

I heard the first stanza of this poem by Mary Jean Irion quoted in a speech when I was just beginning my professional career, and it stuck with me. It is not as well known, but it is packed with an important message.

Normal day, let me be aware of the treasure you are.

Let me learn from you, love you, bless you before you depart.

Let me not pass you by in quest of some rare and perfect tomorrow.

Let me hold you while I may, for it may not always be so.

Big Concept: Live in the present, for that is the only place life is. The past is set in stone—and thus unchangeable. The future never comes. Make the most of your time, and treasure those days that make up the overwhelming majority of your lifetime—"normal days."

Conclusion

Being a master storyteller is an engaging and compelling way to live. Once you truly understand the leverage that stories offer you to overcome problems and effect good, it brings confidence and peace of mind. Life becomes more meaningful as time expands to make each moment part of an overall story.

Becoming a better storyteller *and* story listener allows you to make more sense out of events—both wonderful and tragic. They can be interpreted within the context of *your* story. By telling and listening to new stories each day, riches are found. Once this is established as a habit, wisdom builds upon that which cannot be gained from a book, a mentor, or any other secondhand form of learning. Intellectual learning is too superficial. Storytelling leads to real influence with deeper meaning.[59] And with the continual acquisition of greater wisdom comes the glorious discovery of more *truth*.

It's time now to take your complete Old School Advantage skill set and see how it applies in the real world!

CHAPTER 6

Impress

You never get a second chance to make a good first impression.

—Will Rogers

You have, at most, five to seven seconds to make a first impression. One New York University study says you have less than one second![1] Either way, that's a short amount of time people take to evaluate you. Along similar lines, any ideas you offer will be assessed within about thirty seconds. "If your first impression is powerful enough, people will never forget it. If not, they will [forget it]—and *you* as well."[2]

Because the initial encounter with a person is so critical, we need to make applications of the Old School Advantage skills in a practical way for live interactive situations, both formal and informal. There are situations where it is obvious that a formal interview is taking place, such as for college entrance, a job, or a promotion; there are also those situations where we don't perceive that an interview is taking place when that is exactly what is happening. These "interviews" can include a date or social occasion, first introductions (whether formal or casual), and public speaking. But make no mistake—you are *always* interviewing.

In all of these scenarios, you are being closely observed. People note whether or not you make eye contact and use appropriate words, along with your demeanor, body language, and tone. They also assess *who you are* based on the content of your stories. Given this, every interpersonal communication has at stake the opportunity of making a lasting and favorable impression.

Here is what you will learn in this chapter:

1. Remembering Names and Faces

2. Interview Dos and Don'ts

3. Answering the Most-Asked Interview Questions

4. The Reverse Interview

5. Leaving an Unforgettable Impression

Let's get to work!

Remembering Names and Faces

Southwest Airlines finished its forty-second straight year of profitability in 2014. This is an extraordinary achievement in any industry and particularly among air carriers. There is no arguing that the co-founder and longtime CEO, Herb Kelleher, had much to do with the company's success. Kelleher was not only a larger-than-life and beloved figure amongst his employees, but he had a characteristic that many great leaders have—a great memory for names and faces. Kelleher had an engaging style that inspired a full-page ad from his sixteen thousand employees in *USA Today* on Bosses Day, 1994. The first on the list of eleven reasons they thanked Herb was "for remembering every one of [their] names."[3]

William Shakespeare once said: "There is no sound so sweet as the sound of one's own name." There is a magic contained in one's name that arises from the fact that it is the only thing wholly and completely owned by this person and no one else. Therefore, it is natural that people feel special when you say their name. It makes them feel connected to you. But if you are like me, remembering names is easier said than done. (I've even forgotten someone's name within three seconds of hearing it!) I am not sure what Herb's secret was—but here are some techniques that will enable you to achieve success in this area.

Nine Tips to Remember Names and Faces:[4]

1. **Attitude and empathy.** It can be motivating to approach all introductions as opportunities to be polite and likable. Also remember that no one—including you—likes to be forgotten.

2. **Listen and focus.** Often we are nervous when an introduction is made, if for no other reason than we are afraid we will forget the name or we are worried about the impression we are making. Focus on *the other person*, not yourself.

3. **If you didn't hear the name clearly—*ask again.*** You won't be held responsible for remembering a name you could not hear because of room noise or another distraction. The key is to say, "I'm sorry, I didn't catch the name," or something similar. But do so *immediately*. This is key. Don't wait. This signals to the person that the name needs to be repeated clearly or slowly. Listen well this time! This is also acceptable to do if you were just nervous. It is also OK to ask for a spelling if the name is unusual. They will appreciate the effort to get it right.

4. **Repeat the name back.** By *repeating* the name right back to the person, slowly and clearly, while smiling and maintaining eye contact, you show that you're genuinely pleased to meet him or her. Then use the name early in the conversation, such as at the end of a statement or question. For example, say, "Do you live in this area, Bob?" Say the name *three times* in your first conversation, and you will have it. Also, for good measure, say the name again when saying goodbye. This will ingrain it in your memory for the next time you cross paths.

5. **Use *associations* with *other people.*** This should come easily for you after our ready recall discussion in chapter 1. Maybe they look like someone else you know with the same name. Perhaps they look like a celebrity. Use mental pictures of them together such as, "Ben is an attorney who looks like Ben Affleck," or "Jenny reminds me of Jennifer Aniston."

6. **Use *associations* with *objects or animals.*** There are several methods that you can employ here:
    - Find an animal or object with the *same letter* as the person. Some examples: "Kimberly-Kitten," "Billy-Boat."

- If it's a name that can naturally be associated with *something visual*, then make use of this connection. For example, names like House, Gold, Wood, Briar, Paris, Bree, etc., can all be linked to visual images of those things to help you recall the name.
- Associate the name with a word that it *rhymes* with, for example, "Terry Berry."
- Associate the name with something of *similar meaning*, for example, "Cliff-Mountain."
- Associate the name with *what it sounds like*, such as Mr. Siegel becoming Mr. Seagull.
- *Substitute words for names* that you can't associate with visual images. For example, Alyssa Freiburg could become "Alyssa fries burgers."

7. **Use the face or other distinctive features.** Try to examine the person's face, hair, or other characteristics when you're talking, and find something that is easy to remember—nice teeth, bushy eyebrows, deep wrinkles, dapper dress, or anything unusual or distinguishing. You can associate the name with this feature, so that you will remember next time. An example: "Jenny with the crooked smile." Selecting the most outstanding feature is the easiest to remember.

8. **Write it down.** As soon as possible, make a note of the new friend's name. (Napoleon III, 1808–1873, nephew of Bonaparte, wrote down the name right after he met a person.) I keep a five-by-seven recipe card file box filled with index cards. I staple the new friend's business card (if available) to the upper corner and then write the date and occasion where I made their acquaintance. I also write as much as I can remember about them on the card so that I can make associations in order to recall not just their names but other information about them as well. If you have used the LAVA technique in your conversation, it works perfectly as an aid to remembering names because it "paints" a picture of their life that gives you many aspects by which you

can remember that person. You then have the luxury of waiting until after the occasion to make a note of their information. You can also keep a small notebook or use apps like Nameorize or Namerick for iPhone/Android to write down the names of new people you meet. Don't write anything down when you're talking to them or in their presence. Wait until you are done talking, then go somewhere discreet and write a fast entry down in your notebook or phone app if it's convenient.

9. **If you forget again *later*, ask again.** It is completely acceptable to admit that you have forgotten a person's name. You can say: "I'm terribly sorry, but I've forgotten your name. Would you mind telling me what it is again?" Smile, treat it lightly, and move on. The alternative—failing to remember the person's name next time and ignoring him or her—is *far worse* than any momentary admission of a short-term memory loss.

> Good manners are made up of petty sacrifices.
>
> —Ralph Waldo Emerson

ANDREW CARNEGIE (1835–1919) was a Scottish-American industrialist who led the enormous expansion of the American steel industry in the late nineteenth century. He was also one of the highest-profile philanthropists of his era; by the time of his death, he had given about $350 million (in 2016 dollars, $4.76 billion) away to charities and foundations—almost 90 percent of his fortune.

"What was the reason for Andrew Carnegie's success?

He was called the Steel King; yet he himself knew little about the manufacture of steel. He had hundreds of people working for him who knew far more about steel than he did. But he knew how to handle people, and that is what made him rich. Early in life, he showed a flair for organization, a genius for leadership. By the time he was ten, he too had discovered the astounding importance people place on their own name. And he used that discovery to win cooperation. To illustrate: When he was a boy back in Scotland, he got hold of a rabbit, a mother rabbit. Presto! He soon had a whole nest of little rabbits—and nothing to feed them. But he had a brilliant idea. He told the boys and girls in the neighborhood that if they would go out and pull enough clover and dandelions to feed the rabbits, he would name the bunnies in their honor.

The plan worked like magic, and Carnegie never forgot it.

Years later, he made millions by using the same psychology in business. For example, he wanted to sell steel rails to the Pennsylvania Railroad. J. Edgar Thomson was the president of the Pennsylvania Railroad then. So Andrew Carnegie built a huge steel mill in Pittsburgh and called it the 'Edgar Thomson Steel Works.'"[5]

THE JOB INTERVIEW

There are essentially three vocational orientations: A *job*, which earns you a paycheck; a *career*, which entails a deeper investment in your work; and a *calling*, which is a passionate commitment to a cause bigger than oneself.[6] Regardless of where you are on this vocational continuum, the interview process—no matter how formal or casual it might be—will be of great importance to your success.

The following section will first list the dos and don'ts of a face-to-face interviewing situation. Then, a list of ten common interview questions will be presented. You will see examples of both poor and great answers, as well as commentary for each.[7] Be sure to notice the fit words and phrases throughout the dialogue.

The first objective here is to avoid any answers that would cause the interviewer to cut your interview short. In fact, not only do we want the interview to keep going, we want you to pile up favorable impressions along the way. This will create a "halo effect," which occurs when one or more positive characteristics of a person dominate the way that person is initially viewed by others. An interview is also a glimpse into the future in that it provides information into who you are as a person based on your description of past achievements and experience.

INTERVIEW DOS AND DON'TS

From the moment you arrive, employers are analyzing your potential fit for their organization. Qualities related to this potential fit are exhibited at every stage in the interview process. This starts in the reception area (and maybe even in the parking lot, if they can see you).[8]

What To Do in an Interview:

- *Always* do your homework and learn about the organization and the open position. Review the website of the firm as thoroughly as you can, including their mission statement and core values. You might subtly use some of the terms from their website that align with your own values in your conversation. Remember—the company chose those key words and concepts very carefully before posting them for the whole world to see.

- *Always* review your personal online postings. Today, one of the first thing employers do is peruse your social media accounts to assess your standing in your community—and thus your character. We all make mistakes, especially when we are young and less wise. Make sure yours are not on parade.

- *Always* introduce yourself to everyone you meet at the interview location and *smile*—making eye contact—when meeting *any* associate. (The receptionist talks to the interviewer about you later.) This conveys confidence and shows you to be personable. The expression on your face is more important than even the clothes on your back. And remember: smiles are contagious, and "the eyes are the window to the soul."

- *Always* have the *top button* of your jacket buttoned the first time you meet someone. As you are seated, you may unbutton it for comfort.

- *Always* have a firm handshake, but don't crush the person's hand. It is best to wait for the interviewer to offer a hand first.

- *Always* say the name out loud while still shaking the person's hand and looking into his or her eyes. A simple "Nice to meet you, Ms. Jones" gets the job done. Because you might be a little nervous at first, this will reduce the possibility that you will forget her name.

- *Always* say "Ms. Jones" (or Mr. Jones) if the perceived age difference between you and the interviewer is ten years or more, even if she introduces herself with her first name. If she wants you to be more familiar and use her first name, she will tell you so the second or third time you use her surname. This practice goes a long way in establishing your old-school credentials.

- *Always* wear a wristwatch to the interview. (Borrow one if you have to.) It will make you stand out in our smartphone age, and it screams "old school" and the positive things that are associated with it.

- *Always* consider whether to wear clothing that conceals tattoos for this particular work environment. In most cases, you will want to.

- *Always* carry a nice padfolio (preferably leather) and a nice writing instrument (preferably a nice ballpoint pen).

- *Always* let yourself be relaxed and friendly. Personal but professional conversation is encouraged.

- *Always* nod to show that you are listening. (Just don't overdo it.)

- *Always* be honest with all of your answers. "Let the chips fall where they may."

- *Always* feel comfortable asking questions of the interviewer along the way and especially when you need clarification.

What to Wear for an Interview

How you dress for an interview might not get you the job—but it *can* eliminate you from contention. Therefore, there is no reason to take chances in this area. Your attire in the first interaction speaks to your manners, your self-image, and the seriousness with which you are approaching the opportunity before you.

Blue is one of the best colors to wear to a job interview because it exudes trust and confidence. Lisa Johnson Mandell at AOL Jobs writes: "Studies show that navy blue is the best color for a suit to wear to a job interview, because it inspires confidence. You are more likely to get the job when you wear navy blue to an interview than any other color."[9]

Neckties and scarves should be conservative colors as well. Dark red and blue—solid or with stripes—will nearly always suffice. Avoid ties or scarves with polka dots, animals, or other distracting things on them. A white, cream, or light blue shirt or blouse works well. Don't wear anything that would distract from your countenance. You are selling *you*—not your taste in contemporary fashion (or lack thereof).

What Not To Do in an Interview:

- *Never* arrive late or call the interviewer to ask where the office is located on the day of the interview. (Calling a few days ahead is OK, as it shows thoroughness.)
- *Never* use your electronic devices while waiting for the interview in the reception area (unless it is an emergency). This shows focus and the level of seriousness you place on the opportunity. You are, in effect, saying, "I am concentrating on this great opportunity and want no distractions right now."
- *Never* make requests to staff members (e.g., "Get me a coffee.").
- *Never* make jokes or insults about the people you have (or haven't) met during your interview.

- *Never* say negative things about your previous workplace, your coworkers, or even your friends, family, or the stranger that cut you off on your way to the interview. Employers do not want people who are negative and complain, even if it is justified.

- *Never* criticize a work strategy employed by the company. It might have been your interviewer's "pet project."

- *Never* wear heavy cologne or perfume. Some people have allergies.

- *Never* have an engagement after the interview that might require you to leave early. If there is a potential conflict, schedule the interview on a different day or earlier.

- *Never* discuss salary, benefits, or vacation during your interview unless brought up by the interviewer.

- *Never* indicate that you are planning to leave the job to go back to graduate school, move, or start your own company any time in the future. The interviewer obviously knows that you can quit any job at any time, but during the interview is not the time to divulge or even allude to such plans. After all, you might be there your entire career.

- *Never* answer a question with a simple yes or no. Expand on your answers appropriately. (More on this below.)

- *Never* wear open-toed shoes. They generally are too casual for a first impression.

Concerning Other Courtesies in an Interview:

There are a few words and clichés that often cause people to tune out, perhaps making them completely miss the message you are trying to convey.

- **"Have a nice day."** This phrase is well intentioned, but trite because of its overuse. *"Thank you for visiting with me today. I really appreciate the opportunity."* These are more authentic words for your departure. They show your insight into proper social etiquette.

- **"No problem."** The word "problem" is, in itself, a negative word. When you unpack "No problem," what people are saying is, "I can do what you've asked because it will not unduly burden me." It is better to simply say, *"You're welcome,"* or, even better, *"It is my pleasure."* Both of these convey the appropriate politeness for the occasion.

- **"Like," "so," and "you know."** These are the verbal ticks of our time. They will sink your first-impression ship like a torpedo.

Remember that most résumés talk about *what* you have accomplished. You want to focus generally on relaying *how* you did those things and, in some cases, *why* you did them. If you are successful in answering these overarching questions, then *who* you are will come out. And remember, that is what counts most. This will separate you from the rest of the pack.

Thinking of the first interview like a first date will also serve you well. Keep things polite and guard against getting too casual. Now that you have your Old School Advantage credentials, you should be so well prepared that your answers will come to you as second nature (System I thinking). This allows you to have a dialogue that shows you are an authentic, "can-do" employee who will take personal responsibility and relentlessly pursue perfection. You will have them simply saying, "Wow!"

Scrubbing Your Résumé

There are myriad books concerning what to *include* on your résumé, but the following words are *not fit* résumé words in today's business climate. Make sure they disappear from yours so you will get the chance to apply the interview techniques you are about to learn.[10]

"Results-oriented." This term is one of the worst, HR experts say. "People use this term in lieu of giving me specifics," says Liz D'Aloia, founder of HR Virtuoso. Analyst Carl Forrest says, "It implies that the reader should just take your claim at face-value."

"High technical aptitude." Wes Lieser, marketing recruiter at Versique Search and Consulting, says, "This is comparable to a baseball pitcher telling someone that he or she can throw a baseball. It goes without saying." Instead, talk about the specific programs and applications you excel at using.

"Assisted." If you "assisted the CEO," what did you do for her? Use specifics to describe your experience.

"Strong work ethic." Kimberli Taylor, office manager for Conover & Grebe, says this phrase will not impress her. "I hate this because it is not a skill or an asset. It is an expectation of any employee. Listing it as a skill tells me that the candidate believes work ethic is optional for some jobs." Frequently, "strong work ethic" is simply a space-filler on résumés for people with no other skills to list.

"Disruptive," "cutting-edge" and other trendy adjectives. Stick to plain English when describing your accomplishments, says Dennis Tupper, corporate recruiter at Eliassen Group. "You are not reinventing the wheel, but chances are you are accomplishing some great things. Keep it simple."

"Self-starter." You might think this term makes you look like a productive, eager employee, but it doesn't necessarily come across that way. "'Self-starter' is generic, and as an adult if we have to motivate you then you are probably not someone we want to bring into our organization," Tupper says. Instead, list projects that show your leadership or initiative.

"Detail-oriented." This is another term that should be thrown out, Tupper says. "We expect all people we hire to pay attention to detail," he says.

Ten Common Job Interview Questions and Answers

Before the first question is asked, you can break the ice by saying,

"Thank you for seeing me today. I am very excited to be here. I don't know what you had in mind for today, and I don't know if you had a chance to look at my résumé, but I am happy to begin by answering any questions you might have, or I can start out by telling you a little bit about myself."

Almost no one will say "no" to this. You are meeting these people specifically so they can find out more about you, and you just made their job easier with this opening offer. You also are showing a lot of confidence in a situation where the recruiters are used to seeing passive fish waiting for them to take control. It is human nature to sit back and listen—but you are going to let your old-school confidence show!

NOTE: Be sure to have your padfolio open and your pen in hand and ready once the first question is asked. This shows the interviewer that she has your undivided attention and that you believe there is going to be important information given to you that will need to be written down. Do *not* look at the pad when answering questions. Making eye contact is also important at this moment. You are ready for new and important information, and your attentiveness puts you in control of the engagement whether the interviewer realizes this or not.

I would rather hire a man with enthusiasm than a man who knows everything.

—John Rockefeller

Below are ten likely questions you will be asked. Question 1 is presented in more detail since it sets the tone for the rest of the interview. Questions 2 through 10 are formatted to give you examples and coaching [in brackets] from actual interview situations.

Let's get to work!

Q1: INTERVIEWER: "How would you describe yourself?" or "Tell me a little about yourself."

> [Note: Q1 is also the same question you offered to answer in your "break the ice" opening.]

These are common forms of a first formal interview question. A well-delivered response right up front gives you confidence for the rest of the interview and creates the "halo effect" for the rest of the meeting.

The best way to prepare for this question is to find five or six words or phrases that describe *who you are*. And a good place to find those descriptors is from our list of words and phrases in chapter 2. For example:

"I believe it is important to be *consistent* . . ."

"I have been described as *determined* . . ."

"I think I have a lot of *common sense* . . ."

"I don't like people who make *excuses* . . ."

"To me, *nothing is more important than* . . ."

Find the words that best describe you, then write out your thoughts on paper *before* the interview. Injecting these descriptive words and phrases into your own *LAVA profile* makes for a perfect outline for describing who you are in sufficient depth and in a short period of time.

In this "elevator pitch," or "story of you," you want to convey reasons why they should hire you, what you enjoy doing, and some of your strengths—and weaknesses (yes, weaknesses too).

This "Tell me about yourself" question is probably asked 80 to 90 percent of the time in an interview, and having your answer perfectly rehearsed (it won't sound rehearsed) and ready to go means you can sell yourself early and often. If done properly, it will also serve as a template from which to answer other questions that might come throughout the course of the interview.

Q2: INTERVIEWER: "How did you find out about this position?"

[This question might be nothing more than a survey of their recruiting methods. It could also be a test of initiative.]

POOR ANSWER: "So I saw your ad online, and then it was kind of crazy—I walked past your building that same day and thought, 'This is a coincidence!' So basically it was by chance I guess. I am really glad it worked out."

[There are several words here that are less than appropriate in a first interview setting. Starting an answer with "So" is normal these days, but given an opportunity, more formal speech is akin to overdressing for a party—it is better than *under*dressing. Finding the opportunity "by chance" is far less compelling than "doing your research." Avoid the word

NOTE: By spending some time researching before the interview, you can usually find aspects of the company that you find impressive, and then you can mention them in an authentic way. But don't just go to the company's website. Search for news about the company on other news sites. In particular, look for history and characteristics of the company that might not be all that well known. By doing this, you might uncover a valuable tidbit your interviewers were not aware of. But even if they are, it shows you went beyond the obvious sources to get to know more about the company. Knowing something about the philosophy driving the company, including interviews given by and biographies about key people in the firm (past and present), is impressive.

"basically." It adds nothing to the explanation and is an unnecessary add-on word.]

OLD SCHOOL ANSWER: "Well, the *simple truth* is that I have been a fan of your company and your *exceptional* products for a long time now. But I also saw that your company was involved at a charity event and it seems that your team is *united* for a worthy cause. And I can tell there is an energetic *corporate culture* here as well. Given that, I did some additional research and it seemed pretty apparent to me that I should pursue this opportunity."

[The hint of nostalgia in the phrase "simple truth" is a small indication of someone who was raised with solid values. *Exceptional* is not a common word—especially for younger people. It would get the attention of the interviewer in a positive, yet subtle, way. The fact that the candidate took notice of the company's charitable inclinations gives a clue as to his community awareness and involvement. This is also reinforced by his use of the words *united* and *corporate culture.*]

You have to be able to describe even the most complex of ideas in four minutes or less. If you can't, you'll miss out on some big opportunities.

—T. Boone Pickens

Q3: INTERVIEWER: "What is your current/most recent position and company?" and "Why did you leave?" or "Why do you want to leave?"

[This is a multifaceted question. It will give the interviewer some insight as to your level of satisfaction at your current job. It will attempt to assess your current opportunities. Finally, it is designed to determine your timetable for leaving and how serious you are about leaving. This question obviously will not be asked of students just entering the workforce.]

POOR ANSWER: "I am currently [fill in the position]. I am looking to leave because my manager won't give me a raise. I have the most seniority, and I haven't had a raise in two years. I always show up on time. The company doesn't treat their employees right. I have seen layoff after layoff, and I want to find another position before anything happens."

[This answer raises the specter of someone who is mostly concerned about the financial aspects of the opportunity and would be a high risk of leaving for an extra dollar if given the chance. Entitlement, low expectations ("I always show up on time" is no big contribution), and fear of a layoff might indicate he knows he is next on the list to be asked to leave.]

OLD SCHOOL ANSWER: "I am simply looking for a change at this point in my career. I have been with ABC for ten years, and I love the company and the people there, but I feel that I have not reached my personal development potential there and I need a new *challenge* and more *opportunities* to grow. I want to work for a *performance-driven* company that is *people centered*. The *bold* approach you take here seems to be *fully aligned* with the *passion* I have for this industry. I have talked to the owner of my current company, and she understands and wants me to *pursue my dream* because she knows this opportunity could be *life changing* for me. She knows your company is very strong in my specialty, and I want to work with a team that I can make stronger and that will make me better at the same time. I feel honored to have a current employer that supports me like that. It will be difficult to leave."

[The candidate touches on several fit words and phrases, but the main thing is his *authenticity*. He understands that challenges and opportunities are directly correlated. He is not shy about expressing how he knows this is a great opportunity for him both personally and professionally. Yet he also fully acknowledges the positive characteristics of the company he wants to work for, which reinforces the "fully aligned" comment that he made. He is also gracious and complimentary concerning his current employer. They will hate to lose him—which means this company would likely love to have him.]

"Old School" Interview Questions

If you think *you* have faced tough interview questions, consider these. They are from 1892.

- What is the trait you most deplore in yourself?
- What is your idea of perfect happiness?
- What do you regard as the lowest depth of misery?
- Who are your favorite poets?
- What is your current state of mind?
- How would you like to die?
- What is your greatest fear?
- Which words or phrases do you most overuse?
- What or who is the greatest love of your life?
- What do you consider the most overrated virtue?
- What is the trait you most deplore in others?
- On what occasion do you lie?

Q4: INTERVIEWER: "If I were to interview your coworkers (or those closest to you), what would they tell me about your weaknesses?"

[Notice that the assumption here is that you do *have* some weaknesses. Everyone does.]

POOR ANSWER: "I don't really know that many computer programs, and I wish I had more self-discipline, you know. I also tend to procrastinate, and I have a weakness for chocolate. I hate public speaking."

[This is a pivotal interview question. While the interviewer might be listening for any weaknesses that could be a "red flag," she will also be assessing your approach to answering this question. The interviewer is probing to see if you are humble in admitting to any shortcomings you have and determining what you are doing to improve (*pursuit of perfection*). So tone is important, as you learned in chapter 5. The "you know" is out of place because the interviewer knew nothing about it. It is another nervous verbal habit.]

OLD SCHOOL ANSWER: "That is a good question. [Pause for a few seconds.] Let me see. I would have to say *time management* is the biggest continual challenge that I wrestle with in my work life. But I am working to improve. I recently took a class that taught me some valuable techniques.

"One technique involves always reviewing my schedule *on paper* the night before. I learned how this reduces stress because it allows me not to wonder all night about what I have to do the next day. It also allows my subconscious to actually work on challenges I am facing while I sleep. I occasionally wake up with an idea that I had not considered before. Another tip I learned was to schedule in "time blocks." At work, if I have three hours before my next meeting, I can simply break this into one-hour segments and work on certain tasks during this timeframe. I set the timer on my phone and then set it aside, also ignoring my e-mail, until the block is complete. I am then free to check on my texts, voicemails, and e-mail later. It is amazing how much more efficient I have become with this simple method."

[The pause and admission early in her answer showed that the candidate was humble and thoughtful about her weaknesses. She also had taken steps (the workshop) to improve. This showed her to be old school in the areas of *initiative, accountability, personal responsibility*, and *determination*—not to mention *continuous improvement*. Notice that you do not have to actually *say* the words in order to evoke the concepts in the mind of the listener.

Probably the best thing about this answer is that it is foolproof because everybody has issues with managing their time well. But you need to be sincere, using your own words, so as not to sound rehearsed. The interviewer will be able to relate to the candidate easily and, as a bonus, he will get some free time management advice he was not counting on. Thus, the applicant is also building *rapport* and *likability* with this answer. Also note that the candidate did not start listing *all* her faults, which might come across as too self-deprecating. A representative fault that specifically deals with the workplace was sufficient. (I will offer more details on the time management techniques mentioned in this answer in the next chapter.)]

Q5: INTERVIEWER: "Can you describe a situation where you have had problems with a supervisor or a coworker?"

[Again, notice that the assumption is that you *have* had an issue with a coworker or teammate at some point. Saying no or "Not really" is not an option here.]

POOR ANSWER: "Yes, I had to leave my last job because they would not give me a promotion like they promised. Like, I worked there longer than all but one person. The guy that did get promoted was a jerk to everyone and always smelled like smoke."

OR

"I pretty much have gotten along with all my managers."

[In the first answer, we see excuses that might indicate an entitlement mentality and someone who is difficult to work with. The "like" verbal tick is present also. In the second answer, the interviewer might think he was either being evasive and there were big problems with former coworkers, or the applicant was saying, "I am so good I get along with everyone," which is not realistic.]

OLD SCHOOL ANSWER: "I have been fortunate to have a good working relationship with all of my managers. But I have made mistakes, and it takes effort on both sides. At my last job, I remember that I misunderstood an assignment, and, for the next week after that, my manager treated me differently. I made it a point to discuss with him what happened face-to-face, took responsibility, and then described how I was going to fix the problem. Moving forward, I started to give weekly update e-mails on what projects I was working on and where I was operating compared to the deadlines. After I started doing that, things returned to normal—and even improved."

[The OLD SCHOOL ANSWER shows that he is self-managing both in his duties and in his relationships. He comes across as sufficiently humble, but makes *no excuses* and takes *personal responsibility*. There will *always* be a coworker who is difficult to work with (sometimes, it is *you*). If you couldn't figure out how to get along at your last job, you won't figure it out at your next job. This answer provided more *likability* and an *authentic* story.]

Don't Strike Out on This Curveball Question

It is not unusual for an interviewer to ask this question, which has doomed many a candidate:

> *"What books are you currently reading?"* or *"Who is your favorite author?"*

Because the books we read tell others so much about *who we are*, this is an excellent way for a recruiter to gain insight into not only your

---

lifelong learning habits, but also your character. Always give an honest answer. If you have been in school, it is all right to say, "I have not had much time to read anything but textbooks lately, but I am looking forward to reading several books, including [name them here], as soon as I can." Otherwise, let this be a warning/reminder that *leaders are readers*. And other leaders know it. If you are not reading, get started now!

Q6: INTERVIEWER: "Describe some times when you were not very satisfied with your own performance. What did you do about it?"

POOR ANSWER: "So, I have always been pretty happy with my performance. I work hard, prepare, and it pays off. This is why I had the highest sales last quarter."

[The candidate probably feels he they nailed this one, but it fails to answer the question and doesn't give an example of when he worked hard to improve. Again, don't start a first sentence with "so."]

OLD SCHOOL ANSWER: "I am never completely satisfied with my performance. One example is at my last summer job when I worked at a golf course. When you mow greens on a golf course, you have to align the mower up *perfectly* because it is different from a regular mower. It is heavier and harder to maneuver. Also, the grass is so short that it makes it difficult to see where you mowed previously unless there was heavy dew the night before. I would get frustrated when my supervisor would criticize the job I did because I was *determined* to get it right. On a golf course, a maintenance crew is only as good as its weakest member, and I felt that I was letting the group down. It was a bit humbling, but I remedied the situation and took advice from the guys who had been there a long time. As I practiced and implemented their instruction, I finally had a *breakthrough* and had *perfect* lines over all the greens I mowed for the last half of the summer. I almost hated to go back to school."

[At first glance, this answer might seem a bit long. But this applicant clearly is "all in" with whatever job he is involved with. This applicant also does a great job in the *storytelling* department! He takes you to the golf course early in the morning when the mowers are getting revved up for the day's work and you can see the dew on the grass. The interviewer will imagine him telling stories about their great products too. *Pursuit of perfection* and *determination* are obvious in this applicant's character—as well as *commitment* to the team. He also is not afraid of hard work, as working on a golf course in the summertime is a hot and difficult job.]

Q7: INTERVIEWER: "Give me an example of an important goal you had to set, and tell me about your progress in reaching that goal. What steps did you take?"

POOR ANSWER: "I don't necessarily write my goals down, but I am always very aware of what I should be doing next. I can't really think of any examples where I had an epic fail or anything . . . you know."

[This applicant is evidently unaware of the business maxim that "a goal unwritten is simply a wish." The word "always" makes the first sentence even more pretentious. The negative term "epic fail" injected a negative tone to the answer. It also did not answer the question . . . you know.]

OLD SCHOOL ANSWER: "The most recent job I had was not technology dependent, but I knew I needed to learn some additional skills if I wanted to *optimize* my contribution to the team. I laid out a written plan so that I could learn how to use their e-mail system and signed up for a course at a local community college on Tuesday evenings. I was able to become proficient at Outlook and also Excel as a bonus. It cost a little extra money to do this, but I just viewed it as an *investment in my future*."

[By using the word *optimize*, this applicant shows that he wants to be the very best. He is *dedicated* to self-improvement and lifelong learning as evidenced by incurring a personal expense to do so. He is cognizant of this need in order to have a bright future. His answer exudes *optimism* because of this *commitment*.]

Q8: INTERVIEWER: "What are your long-range career objectives, and what steps have you taken toward obtaining them?"

POOR ANSWER: "If I am going to take a job with someone, I would pretty much want it to be with a company where I could eventually become the CEO one day. I know that by starting in the entry level and working my way up from there, I can someday run a company. I have watched my mom do it for a long time, and I know I have the skills to do it as well."

[It is one thing to be ambitious, but this applicant is at the very least overconfident; depending on the rest of his answers, he might even be delusional. There are no specifics concerning future plans. This indicates that he likely has not considered it much. This also indicates a possible flight risk when the "right thing" catches his attention. While his mom might be highly qualified to run a company, he will have to prove his capabilities.]

OLD SCHOOL ANSWER: "*First things first*: I know I have a lot to learn, and I am *committed* to *continuous improvement*. My long-term goal is to become an *expert* in my *discipline*. I enjoy taking a "*hands on*" approach to whatever I do, and when there is a problem, people know I will try to find a *lasting solution*. I don't worry about a title so much as having a *well-rounded* skill set. For me, *life is an adventure*, and I want to be with a company that is *people-centered* and *passionate* about what it does. I know it will take a lot of work, but if it were easy, anyone could do it."

[No fewer than *eleven* fit and WOW! words were chocked into this response. While not everyone can pull this off without sounding scripted, it is golden when it flows naturally. (Remember "Ninety Days to WOW!") The answer might have been short on specifics, but it is clear that the applicant had thought about the future as an exciting and adventurous proposition. He just wants to find the right team, and rest assured, the interviewer will be interested if his other answers are this good.]

Q9: INTERVIEWER: "How well do you work with people? Do you prefer working alone or in teams?"

POOR ANSWER: "Oh, I am definitely a team player. We had an awesome football team at my high school. We went 13-2 and lost by a touchdown on like the last play of the game in the state championship. Individual sports are OK, I guess, but they seem kind of boring. I still don't get why anyone would waste time, like, playing golf, for example."

[This applicant made an attempt at a story answer, but it fell flat when he seemed to forget where he was for a second as he relived his glory days. (Think Uncle Rico in *Napoleon Dynamite*.) He had also better hope the interviewer is not a golfer or an enthusiast of any other individual sports. The question asked by the interviewer was completely ignored.]

OLD SCHOOL ANSWER: "I enjoy both. I think it is important to take *personal responsibility*, but *nothing is more important than* the team if you belong to one. It just depends on where my employer's *priorities* are and where they think I can make the greatest *impact*. That is where I want to be."

[This is an example of a powerful answer that is not long yet works in the major themes through multiple fit words and phrases. It does not contain a story, and that is all right in this instance. If every answer contained a story, it could begin to look contrived, and you might lose the opportunity to ask your reverse interview questions because you run out of time.]

Q10: INTERVIEWER: "What is your typical way of dealing with conflict? Give me an example."

POOR ANSWER: "I definitely don't like conflict. So I will try to find a way to avoid it and to always keep the peace if I possibly can."

[This answer is akin to the stereotypical Miss America contestant that wants to "bring world peace" if she is only given the chance to wear the crown. It probably sounded great to the applicant, but companies don't want someone who avoids problems. They want problem *solvers*.]

OLD SCHOOL ANSWER: "There is usually a reason why the conflict is happening, so I want to find out what that is. No one likes conflict. I once had a teammate on a club soccer team who seemed to be mad at the world, and she was taking it out on the whole team. She was not always like this, so I asked her to go have a cup of coffee to see what was bothering her. I asked, "What's going on with you? You aren't your normal self, is everything OK?" It turned out that her company was having some financial problems, and she was worried about her job. After we talked, things were much better. I think she realized I was an ally and that she could come to me if she needed to talk. I think that if we try to find out what is behind the conflict, we can almost always work toward a solution."

[This is a phenomenal answer. Notice that there were not a lot of fit or WOW! words per se, but the old-school tenor was obvious throughout. The tone was *mature* as the applicant showed how she was interested in *pursuing* a *dialogue*, knowing this would likely help solve things. This shows her to be *people centered* and someone who will fight for a relationship. She provided adequate detail to explain what was going on, but she was also brief enough to not be boring.]

THE LAST QUESTION: "What question do you wish I had asked you/should I have asked you—but didn't?"

This question—or some derivative of it—is often asked at the end of an interview. It is normally a difficult question to answer because you have been laser-focused on providing answers to questions, and now you are put on the spot as the questioner. But as an Old School student, this becomes one of the easiest questions of all. How?

You have your padfolio on your lap, right? Inside, you should have the ten questions above with your detailed answers written out for you to refer to when needed. (Hopefully, you memorized them.) One or more of the ten questions were likely *not* asked during the course of the interview. When the interviewer asks, "Which question do you wish I had asked?," you simply answer with the question from the list of ten that you feel most comfortable with.

In other words, *you* get to pick the question and the answer that you know you can blow out of the water! And then the WOW! factor really kicks in.

The "What is the Old School?" Question

Your interviewer might ask, "What is the Old School Advantage training on your résumé?"

This is your chance to elaborate on your Old School training. Throughout the interview, you have been exemplifying not only *what* it is but also *how* to use it. You've been making eye contact the entire interview, and there was no question that you were well prepared. This gave you confidence, which showed throughout the process. They've noticed something about you. You use different words and phrases than most of their candidates, and your poise is obvious. They have sensed that you are "wise beyond your years," and they're also impressed with your stories and sense of humor. You come across as someone who is comfortable in your own skin—someone they want on the team. To sum up, they realize you have the rare and elusive "It factor."

So here is your answer to that question (enthusiastically!):

"I am so glad you noticed that on my résumé. I realize that this generation is inundated with technology. In fact, I think you would agree that if you had to pick a symbol of our time, it would be the smartphone. And as great as it is, I believe it has diminished our ability to communicate on a personal level as well as we should.

When I came across the Old School Advantage training, I jumped on it. They teach five fundamental skills in the areas of ready recall, words that WOW!, influence, classical argumentation, and storytelling. They then go into leadership skills and map out a personalized curriculum in their Lifelong Learning program. It took some extra effort to read the material and go through the initial workshop, but it was some of the most valuable training I have ever received."

After you have told them what the Old School Advantage training is all about, it will make perfect sense to the interviewer, and he or she will be doubly impressed. This answer will solidify you as a top candidate who brings unique skills and a great attitude to the organization.

THE REVERSE INTERVIEW

When an interview is over, it has really just begun.

Once finished with their questions, interviewers will typically ask the following, almost in passing: *"Do you have any questions for me?"* This question is seemingly harmless and straightforward. But it can either lead you astray or present your greatest opportunity of the engagement. Good recruiters deem the questions asked by candidates to be indicative of how they think, what their personalities are like, and how interested they are in the company and the position. Therefore, the most successful interviews result when a candidate actually becomes the interview*er* and asks insightful questions. It also allows you to figure out if this company and its team are a good fit for *you*. Job interviews are fact-finding missions for both parties. This being the case, here are a few things to avoid during the reverse interview, followed by the questions you need to ask.

Three mistakes to avoid:

Ask nothing at all. This could easily give an impression that you haven't given any serious thought to the possibility of working with the organization.

Ask obvious questions. Asking questions that can be answered with a simple Internet search signifies laziness and inattention to detail—two qualities that can easily disqualify you as a prime candidate.

Asking yes or no questions. In an information-seeking conversation, you should ask as many open-ended questions as possible.

The reverse interview questions you ask should fall into three categories: *Company Culture*, *Specifics about the Job*, and *Management Style*.

NOTE: Make sure your padfolio is open, indicating your readiness to record the answers forthcoming. Then say, *"Yes, I do have a few things I was wondering about."* Even though you can easily place these questions in your memory palace, by looking down at your pad, they will surmise that you have put much thought into the process and the opportunity.

[Once again, Old School Advantage coaching tips are in brackets.]

Company Culture:

1. **"What brought you to ABC Company? Why have you stayed?"**

    [The answers to these questions give you immediate insight into the culture. If the interviewer's reasons align with your own for wanting to join the company, that might be a good sign. If she responds, "Hey, it's a job," that's a red flag. These questions also provide a chance for you to build greater rapport. This is the perfect time to subtly weave in questions from the LAVA conversation technique to find out more about the interviewers by encouraging them to talk about their favorite subject—*themselves.*]

2. **"How would you describe the company's values?"**

    [First of all, this question will reveal how well the company instills and publicizes its values internally. An interviewer is a "face" of the organization, so she should know them well. Secondarily, the content of the answers reveals what is important in the corporate culture so that you may assess if you can be fully aligned. Sharing the same values as the company you join could be the most important factor of all as you consider your next employer. Finally, this question relays the message that you are a person who cares about values—a person of character.]

3. **"What are the high points of the company's five-year strategic plan?" or "What are the most important goals for the company in the next five years?"**

    [Either of these questions will provide some insight into the corporate vision—and thus the culture. They reveal what is important on a macro level and how well they have planned. If they have no five-year plan, or if the interviewer doesn't know what it is, this is a bad sign. Asking these types of questions also portrays you as someone who is thinking beyond your own job and is concerned about the company as a whole. It also implies that you are not a "job-hopper" since you are asking about the next five years.]

4. **"What's the biggest challenge your company faces right now?"**

[This question indicates that you're already thinking about how you might add value. The fact that you're already considering the job's challenges makes it easier for hiring managers to picture you in that position. You might mention some possible solutions on the spot or in a follow-up "thank you" note (handwritten). But don't overstep your bounds here. One other valuable thing about asking this question is that if the challenge described seems like something you can't or have no interest in solving, you might want to pass on the opportunity.]

5. **"Did you make your numbers last quarter?" (If no, then, "What happened?" If yes, "How were you able to accomplish this?")**

[This is a critical question that might help you uncover the firm's financial footing and cultural values. If they did not make their targets last quarter, you can probe more for other recent history to detect their financial trending and stability. If they did make the numbers they wanted, then by asking how they did it, if they say, "We had to lay off some people," you have a very important perspective you otherwise would not have received.]

Specifics about this Position:

1. **"Why is this position open?"**

   [This question might have already been covered in the course of the interview. But if not, it reveals whether the job is a newly created position. A follow-up of "Did the previous person leave, and (if so) is there an internal candidate?" is also good to ask. If it's a new position, then you might have some input into how the job is defined, if you're hired. If there's an internal candidate, then that opens up many more questions *in your mind*, such as the obvious one: "Will the internal person have an edge among the competition?" or "Will the internal candidate hold any animosity toward me if I get the job?"]

2. **"What is the most important task for the person in this position to accomplish in the next ninety days?"**

   [This gets down to the fundamentals of your job duties and hopefully some details from the hiring manager about what's most important in the position. By putting a date or timeframe in the question, it indicates that you are likely a deadline keeper, and thus organized, and that you take your duties and opportunities seriously. It also indicates that you want to get off to a fast start, if hired.]

3. **"What improvements is the company hoping a new employee can make in the available position?"**

   [This question allows the interviewer to reveal problems that might have been present with a former employee without you needing to ask specifically about them—or why this new position is being created. It also indicates that you fully expect to make improvements if you are hired.]

4. **"What two or three traits are the most important for the new employee to have?"**

[This question can give you insight into the work environment within the department you would be working in. If "team player" is one of the traits, as it often is, then you will be working with others, and independent decision making might be limited. "Self-motivated" might mean you will spend much of your time alone in your office. Whatever the answer, it is valuable information to have, and the thoughtfulness of the question continues to subconsciously raise your "stock price" in the mind of the interviewer.]

5. **"To whom do employees in this position report, and how are they assessed by their manager?" (If you think you would like to have this job at this point, personalize this question and ask, "To whom *would I be* reporting?")**

[Asking to whom you'd be reporting and how success will be measured tells them you are ambitious and not just a clock-watcher. If you're hired, knowing how achievement is measured will help you get off on the right foot. The fact that you are already asking about performance measures indicates your eagerness and an inclination to set goals and achieve them.]

Management Style

1. **"What's your management style?" and "What kind of employee do you work best with?"**

[If the interviewer is also your potential manager, this question will help you to get a feel for what he or she might be like on the job. This question shows you are ready to work with him or her.]

2. **"How will my performance be measured, and who will conduct the evaluation?"**

[Don't assume that your direct manager handles the entire evaluation process. This question also will give you more insight into what the company deems important because what they measure is typically a good indicator of what they value most.]

Last Question:

The last question you ask is an important one. Depending on your interest level in the position, there are two versions of the last question. Version A is a standard follow-up inquiry. If you are neutral about this opportunity at this point, you can ask:

A. **Where are you in the hiring process, and when and how should I follow up?"**

[This is a good closing question because it shows that you're genuinely interested in the job, while also providing essential logistical information in a comfortable request.]

However, if you *really* want this job, then go for it with this Version B:

B. **"Are there any lingering questions in your mind that would prevent you from offering me this job today?"**

[The interviewer has likely not heard this exact question before. (Note that you are stating that you really would like this job—but you are couching an otherwise bold approach in the form of a *question*.) If they like you, it could seal the deal. It is a confident approach, and they will appreciate it. If they don't hire you on the spot, don't worry. Often, they will follow up soon after the interview when a decision has been made. In any case, you can walk away with no lingering doubts, and they know for certain you want to be a part of their team. *You can also then ask Version A, above, if they are not ready to answer Version B at that time.*]

You can imagine that these particular reverse interview questions are not typically asked in this manner. But rest assured: because of *what* you asked and *how* you asked it, the interviewer will come away from the meeting with a very good feeling about *who* you are as a candidate.

Follow-Up

If a call was promised to you in three days and does not come, feel free to call on the fourth day. This will not come across as impatience and could be seen as your astuteness and enthusiasm for the opportunity. Often, the candidate that hesitates to call for fear of being a "pest" is lost in the mix. Also, *always* send a handwritten note thanking them for their time and consideration. (More on this shortly.)

The interview process—from the interview dos and don'ts to the interview script—are designed to leave a lasting positive impression. You want to leave the interviewer thinking, "I can't quite put my finger on exactly what it is about that candidate, but all I know is that she has what we want, and I want her on this team!"

The incrementally positive impression you leave with each fit word, figure of speech, short story, and reverse interview question will have its intended effect and bring you the success you desire and deserve. You will find the interview process to be a place where applying your Old School Advantage skills will really pay off. You might even find yourself greatly enjoying a process that most people dread—all because of the confidence you have garnered from your training.

THE TELEPHONE INTERVIEW

Once your résumé has made it to the "let's consider this candidate" pile, employers will often begin the process with a telephone interview before a face-to-face interview in order to save time and screen out obvious outliers. For you, this should create a comfortable situation since you will have your written notes and questions right in front of you during the call. However, there are some nuances to understand even though you have your notes.

1. *Verbal cues* showing that you are listening carefully and engaged are very important since the interviewer cannot see you. Don't interrupt the interviewer's line of questioning, but an occasional "OK," "that's interesting," or "yes" equates to positive body language in an oral form that indicates your attentiveness and thus your interest.

2. *The reverse interview questions* are even more valuable on the phone, as they indicate a level of preparation to the interviewer and allow you to dig out as much information about the opportunity as possible before committing the time to a face-to-face interview.

3. *Your only objective* is to get a face-to-face meeting.

Once the conversation is winding down and you are convinced this is an opportunity you wish to pursue, say something like this:

> "This is a very interesting opportunity, Ms. Jones. I know I could make a significant contribution to your mission. My only question now is when can we get together?"

Once the invitation is offered to meet face to face, you should ask about the actual interview procedure. In particular, inquire about the number of interviews the hiring process will require and what start date is planned for the new hire.

THE GROUP INTERVIEW

In addition to the individual vetting of candidates, it is common for companies to conduct group interviews to assess the teamwork and interpersonal skills of candidates. These group dynamics can be observed in office atmospheres as well as in more casual environments, such as a dinner engagement.

These situations can be intimidating, and their competitive atmosphere can lead to increased anxiety. However, preparation breeds confidence. The good news for you is that many of the same points of preparation you undertook for the individual interview apply here as well.

If the one-on-one interview has already occurred, then be sure and review your notes concerning the research you did on the company, the job description details, your elevator speech about your qualifications, and why you feel this is the right job for you. Here are other key aspects to consider in the group interview:

- *Arrive early.* Being early allows you extra time to meet the interviewers, take in the surroundings, and settle yourself. If others in the group arrive early as well, be sure to take the initiative and introduce yourself. This shows you're friendly and team spirited.

- *Politeness is key.* Don't be too talkative, and always be aware that there might be another candidate who is a bit invasive or even trying to psych you out. It is OK to excuse yourself from that situation by explaining that you need a few minutes to yourself before the interview starts. Simply move to another part of the room. Once the group comes together— over dinner, for example—the interviewers are watching to see how you interact with other people. A courteous demeanor toward your fellow interviewees is important.

- *Stay alert!* Group interviews are interactive. Pay attention, as you will be expected to participate, and any lack of participation or enthusiasm will be noted.

- *Listen closely.* Interviewers will often give an overview of what they are expecting as well as detailed instructions. Some group interviews involve training and exercises involving several steps. For example, you might have to perform a mock sales pitch using their company's methods to reach a successful sale.

- *Be respectful.* Interviewers are looking at your leadership skills. Don't talk over others or try to be the loudest. Instead, think as a facilitator might. This shows that you are confident and that you are willing to listen to others.

- *Give others a turn.* If a group or team exercise is assigned, show leadership by volunteering and also look for a chance to politely delegate when appropriate. Don't try to do it all yourself, because good leaders don't do that. Take detailed notes if you are allowed to do so.

- *Make eye contact with everyone.* When speaking or presenting, don't focus all your attention on one person. (This is a common habit when you are nervous.) Also, include shy people. Be considerate, and ask their opinions. This shows you are a real team player.

- *Praise other good ideas.* Be sincere, and let the chips fall. Have the attitude that you want to build up others any time they deserve it. You want the best candidate to get the job. If you aren't hired, you're still one step closer to the right place for you. (Plus, you could be complimenting a future coworker or even a boss.)

- *Be sure to say goodbye to all before you leave.* Send a handwritten follow-up note to the interviewers *and* the other candidates thanking them for their time and consideration.

MAKING AN UNFORGETTABLE IMPRESSION

In regards to any significant encounter or occasion—such as a job interview—you can make a positive and lasting impression with the quintessential old-school practice of sending a *handwritten note* as a follow-up gesture. It is one of the most impactful actions you can take because it brings out the best in you. It's true that communicating electronically is a big time saver. Yet what we gain in speed, we lose in personalization. By taking the extra time to write a card, find an address, and then mail it, you have, in effect, said, "I could have texted or e-mailed you a 'thank you' in fifteen seconds or less, but time is the most valuable thing anyone owns. I felt like it was worth giving up a few extra minutes of my time in order to make sure you know how important this communication, and our relationship, is to me." That is powerful. It makes an impact.

A letter's value almost always exceeds the writer's effort.[11]

A personal note speaks to authenticity and uniqueness like no other form of communication, and it is universally accepted in a positive way. Prominent leaders know the power of their own handwriting. Lincoln, the elder Bush, and Clinton are three presidents who come to mind who built careers on their ability to communicate. It is no coincidence that they applied the art of the handwritten note.

NOTE: When the United States Postal Service published a "Mail Moment" survey, it concluded with the bittersweet observation that "two-thirds of all consumers do not expect to receive personal mail, but when they do, it makes their day."

Your handwriting is like your fingerprint. It can't be faked, and it can't be imitated in print or voice. In spite of the technology that crowds in on us, ink on paper is the best way to express the thoughts that matter most. The act of writing helps you choose better words; this process even enters the realm of art, and art has survived technology in every age.[12]

Another advantage is that people usually do not discard handwritten missives. I have several drawers at home and at work where scores of handwritten notes reside. And a unique and intriguing characteristic of handwritten notes is that they keep on giving. Each time I reread one, it gives me the same feeling it did the first time I looked at it. By contrast, verbal compliments are typically gone in just a few minutes. (Mark Twain said two months was the longest he had seen a compliment stick around.)

In this section, you will learn *how* and *when* to use the notes you will soon be writing.

Excuses

Here are common excuses for *not* writing notes:[13]

1. **Too busy.** Writing two cards per day might take ten minutes. Do you waste that much time staring at a computer screen? Telephone calls usually last longer, and e-mails can take much longer.

2. **Nobody does this anymore.** Precisely! This is why it is such an opportunity to stand out.

3. **Bad handwriting.** You are probably out of practice—this is true. But it does not take long to regain the skill, and you are likely just self-conscious when you shouldn't be. Whenever people like you, they will like seeing your handwriting. Imperfections are usually seen as marks of individuality in this realm, not as flaws.

4. **Don't know what to say.** Unacceptable. Yes, you do.

5. **Notes are slow.** The mailbox surprise is worth the wait. It is like a gift—the anticipation when opening a handwritten note brings pleasure to the sender and the receiver, and snail mail is old school.

6. **"It's for girls," some men might say.** If US presidents, Napoleon, Einstein, and Paul the Apostle did it, so should you.

Materials Matter

First of all, take the time to consider the composition of the paper you are using. Good-quality stationary or cards are made with more cotton and linen fiber than ordinary paper, which has more wood fiber.[14]

A fountain pen is obviously the old school way to go. Use either blue ink or, if you want the "Declaration of Independence" feel, chocolate brown ink (which I prefer).

Customized Note Cards

Customized note cards are very effective. They are designed to say something about you *before* the card is even opened. Think of "your brand" or of a logo that might represent you or symbolize "who you are." Here are a few examples:

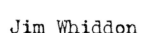

Jim Whiddon

This simple card has my name in an "old typewriter" font. No one uses typewriters like this anymore, so it is a subtle way to get attention and make a statement that I am a traditional thinker. A parchment color or brown card stock with a "heavy" feel works well with this style. It is not designed to be too fancy, but it still has a unique feel and quality. This basic design is a good standard approach to a customized card. (You can also use paper grocery bag material envelopes to evoke a nostalgic sense from the recipient.)

James N. Whiddon

This card is my personal note card. For my name, although I use a typed font, it has a "feel" as though it were written by a quill pen. With the logo, I am trying to say, "I value books, writing, and lifelong learning because I am seeking truth and wisdom so that I can pass it on." That is "my brand." I want the recipient to think of me in that way—at least subliminally.

Jim Whiddon

This third example is obviously for someone who might love horses or loves the traditional feel of the fox hunt. It sets a tone for the person's brand.

This final example is a card that could say several things about the sender—all of them positive.

The theme "Well played . . ." could certainly be a nice life philosophy. "Always do your best" or a more subtle, "job well done" meaning comes out. Or perhaps the card represents your passion or current hobby—or even a profession you would like to pursue someday. The meanings for any card can be multilayered and even offer double or triple entendres representing *who you are* and what you enjoy doing. With a little thought, you can get creative with the picture or drawing and the accompanying words.

Perhaps you are less traditional and like a more modern or contemporary feel for your brand. Whatever you portray on your customized card can effectively frame what you would like others to know about you and your message.

OTHER NOTES ON NOTE CARDS

While the personalized note cards I described work for most occasions, there are times when sending a *preprinted card* made up with your organization's logo printed on it is appropriate—for example, when you are looking to support a branding effort of your products and services to your customers.

There are also times when sending a *generic blank card*, which is easily found at any pharmacy or card store, strikes just the right tone. A blank generic card can send a message that you made a special trip to the store to get this card so you could send it today. Even if you have them on hand for this very purpose, the "you went to some trouble to send me a card" message will be clear because you had to go to the store and get them at some point.

General Note Rules[15]

- Include a date—even on a note card.
- Minimum of three sentences.
- If you greet with a first name, sign with your first name also.
- PS—Keep postscripts to one sentence.
- Use *Ms.* if you are unsure of a woman's marital status or if she has kept her own last name.
- Use postage *stamps* on handwritten notes. Commemorative stamps or customized stamps are also interesting and effective alternatives. Never use a meter.
- If you include a business card in the envelope, place it behind the card so that it may fall out when opened—almost indicating, "Oh, by the way . . ." Avoid placement inside of the card lest it signify an overanxious sales approach.

- A missing return address is likely to get the recipient to open your card immediately. Otherwise, it might be set aside if they know you well—or if they don't know you at all.
- If you really want to wax "old school," then write in cursive. Beautiful handwriting is equally scarce and striking. It will make an additional positive impression if you have that talent.
- When using a folding note card (most are), include an impactful quote or passage on the top half, with your main personal sentiment or message written on the bottom half. This adds a pleasant and effective touch to any handwritten communication.

Thank-You Cards[16]

- Send right away (after receiving a gift or favor). But also send late rather than never.
- Send in addition to a verbal thank-you.
- Mention the *specific* gift or favor.
- For emerging adults, thank-you cards demonstrate a maturity level. Send even for sleepovers and meals. It will impress!

Condolence Cards[17]

- Handwritten is critical to show sympathy. A phone call or e-mail pales in comparison and borders on inappropriate.
- Be *specific* as to what the departed person meant to *you*. This helps with healing for all parties.
- Use the deceased's *name* in the note. It's all right to use the word "death."
- Grief is a long process. Sending another card at an important date (birthday, holiday, etc.) is very thoughtful.
- Using your very best handwriting signals your respect.
- Use only blue or brown ink. No black or other color.
- Writing notes can be therapeutic for *the one who has experienced the loss* as well. Encourage them to do so.

Apology Cards[18]

- A handwritten note is the best way to say, "I'm sorry." E-mail is the worst.
- Say, "Please forgive me," or simply, "I'm sorry."
- Don't say, "Oops" or "You're probably upset about this . . ."
- Handwritten apologies save friendships. "An apology is the superglue of life. It can repair just about anything." —Lynn Johnston

With all the technological advancements in communication in the last twenty years—and with more likely to come—the power of a personal note will never be diminished. Learning the art of the handwritten note gives you one more invaluable tool to ensure your success in all of your relationships. *Write at least one every day*, and you will be astonished at the doors that will open and how well it enhances relationships already in place.

NOTE: No one saves "love e-mails." That is one more reason to send a hard copy that can be saved forever.

Several Electronic Communication Items

- If, for any reason, you realize that your message needs to be delivered faster than the US Postal Service can get it there—*send an e-mail*. (For example, a decision on the job you interviewed for today will be decided that same evening.) It is better to lose the effect of the handwritten note and get your communication delivered than to have it delivered too late.
- An *e-mail is a letter*. Be courteous and say "Dear . . ."
- Send important e-mails at lunch. Most of us multitask early and late in the day. Lunch is when we tend to catch up on e-mail.

- Try to get in the habit of *changing the subject line* in every e-mail. This will make it easier to retrieve when there is a back-and-forth exchange in a long e-mail sequence.
- A *head shot* of you in your e-mail in the signature is always a nice touch to help you connect and build rapport.
- Unless it is a family member, close friend, or associate—include *your name in all text messages.*

CONCLUSION

The applications we have offered in this chapter were meant to help you use your newfound Old School Advantage primarily in formal interview situations. But I remind you again—you are *always* interviewing for something. I suspect that, about now, you are gaining tremendous confidence in your ability to use these tools and can even see yourself getting better each day. That is exciting!

Next, you will learn a cornucopia of old-school methods that will broaden and deepen the impact you are going to have in your sphere of influence as a *leader*.

Always bear in mind that your own resolution to succeed is more important than any other.

—Abraham Lincoln

CHAPTER 7

Lead

If your actions inspire others to dream more, learn more, do more, and become more—you are a leader.

—John Quincy Adams

The five core skills you have learned, combined with the understanding of how to make a first and lasting impression, now bring you to the next phase in the curriculum. The Old School Advantage training program is ultimately designed to support your leadership capabilities and aspirations. There are two kinds of leaders.

First, there are those who are *transactional*. They have followers who simply provide certain outputs in exchange for some kind of return. The other kind of leader is *transformational*—or, to put it in old-school terms, a *life-changing* leader. This kind of leader is one who senses and satisfies the higher needs of his followers in a way that *transforms* both the leader and the followers.[1]

With *life-changing leadership*, the concepts of vision, stewardship, uncommon wisdom, and service must be included. It is irrefutable that leaders who change lives at this level have certain characteristics in common. Among them are:

- They have a plan and a vision for the future.
- They manage their time and resources well.
- They value and nurture relationships.
- They make well-informed decisions.
- They continually seek wisdom.

Given these commonalities, let's look at the following areas to enhance your leadership abilities:

1. The Personal Purpose Statement
2. Discipline and Habits of Life-Changing Leaders
3. Finding Your Place to Lead
4. Decision Making
5. The Wisdom Vault

The first area deals with "who you are."

THE PERSONAL PURPOSE STATEMENT (PPS)

In *Drive*, Daniel Pink related this story concerning President Kennedy:

> In 1962, Clare Boothe Luce, one of the first women to serve in the US Congress, offered some advice to President John F. Kennedy. "A great man," she told him, "is one sentence." Abraham Lincoln's sentence was: "He preserved the union and freed the slaves." Franklin Roosevelt's was: "He lifted us out of a great depression and helped us win a world war." Luce feared that Kennedy's attention was so splintered among different priorities that his "sentence" risked becoming a muddled paragraph.[2]

Pink explains that one way to position your life toward a greater purpose is to think about "your sentence."[3] At the Old School, this concept was renamed the *Personal Purpose Statement,* or *PPS.* Some might call this a "personal mission statement."

As with my personal note card in the last chapter, I wanted to be consistent with my PPS. Again, I value books, writing, and lifelong learning because I am seeking truth and wisdom in order to pass it on. To convey the description of my life's philosophy more succinctly, I created this five-word Personal Purpose Statement: *"Seek truth. Pass it on."*

Your Personal Purpose Statement should reflect who you are. I am a truth seeker who is passionate about passing on that truth to those I care about. This principle guides me. No matter how busy I might get, I keep an eye on the clock of my life—not with a worry that it is running out but with a sense of determination to fulfill my purpose.

Another way to think about this concept is to create a PPS that could be easily used in your eulogy. If, for example, they said at my funeral, "He sought truth and wisdom and passed it on to the next generation at every opportunity," that would be a life well invested, in my estimation. What would you want mourners to say about you on the day your life is officially commemorated?

The Personal Purpose Statement is the mantra that guides how you conduct yourself even in the small things, because the small things always point to this bigger mission. You can ask yourself, "Is this activity or way of thinking consistent with my PPS—the larger mission of my life?" This undercurrent of virtuous actions in all aspects of your life will make you a person who can lead well.

Perhaps you are wondering where to start in creating your PPS. One good place is to revisit your answer to the interviewer's question from chapter 6: "How would you describe yourself?" Go back and find those words that describe you. There is no need to rush this process. By crystallizing your thinking concerning what you want to be and do with your life, you will create a compass for life-changing leadership.

> The secret of success is constancy to purpose.
>
> —Benjamin Disraeli

DISCIPLINES AND HABITS OF LIFE-CHANGING LEADERS

In 1912, the president of the Bethlehem Steel company in the USA was Charles M. Schwab. His company was struggling with inefficiency and Schwab didn't know how to improve it, so he called in Ivy Lee, a well-known efficiency expert at the time.

Lee agreed to help the company, with his fee being whatever Schwab felt the results were worth after three months.

Lee's advice to each member of the company's management team was to write a to-do list at the end of each day, which consisted of the six most important tasks to be done the following day. Then they were told to organize the list based on the highest priority tasks.

The next day, the employees worked through the list from top to bottom, focusing on a single task at a time. At the end of the day, anything left on the list would get added to the top of tomorrow's list when the employees once again planned for the following day.

As the story goes, the company was so much more efficient after three months that Schwab sent a check to Lee for $25,000[4] (Equivalent to more than $500,000 today at 3 percent inflation).

Mr. Schwab was obviously impressed with Lee's advice because he clearly understood the age-old concept that "time is money."

This story might seem trivial because of its simplicity. It is a concept we all understand: make a list and check off the tasks as you complete them. It's not rocket science. However, very few people actually *follow* this simple advice. Those who do know the secret of its power.

Learning some basic principles of time and money management at an early age can mitigate the danger of falling victim to their mishandling.

Time Management—The Scheduling Process

Time management and life management are really the same. Time management is having control over the next task. Your ability to distinguish the important from the unimportant is a key determinant of your success in life and work. A life-changing leader does what needs to be done *when* it needs to be done. Nineteenth-century philosopher William James said, "The art of being wise is the art of knowing what to overlook."

Another successful leader who understood the importance of time management predated even Mr. Lee and Mr. Schwab by more than a century.

Benjamin Franklin used lists to boost his own self-improvement. He created a thirteen-week plan to exercise virtues such as cleanliness and temperance. Each day, he tracked his progress on a chart. This strict daily routine included time for sleeping, meals, and working—all set for specific times of the day. Franklin combined the importance of having a list of tasks with the corresponding time they should be completed. The image below shows how he aimed to spend his time:[5]

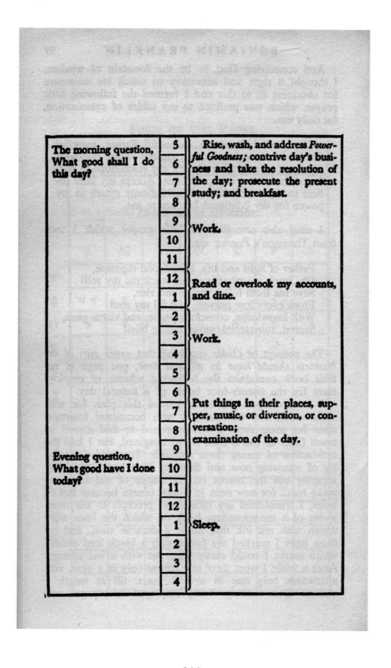

The morning question, What good shall I do this day?	5	Rise, wash, and address *Powerful Goodness;* contrive day's business and take the resolution of the day; prosecute the present study; and breakfast.
	6	
	7	
	8	
	9	Work.
	10	
	11	
	12	Read or overlook my accounts, and dine.
	1	
	2	
	3	Work.
	4	
	5	
	6	Put things in their places, supper, music, or diversion, or conversation; examination of the day.
	7	
	8	
	9	
Evening question, What good have I done today?	10	
	11	
	12	
	1	Sleep.
	2	
	3	
	4	

Conquering the Tyranny of the Rectangles:[6]

The rectangles of technology have trained us to "look down." We are hyperconnected yet distracted. We are always available yet rarely present. But life should be lived with our "heads up"—looking "out there," looking ahead, dreaming, anticipating—living out our purpose. Here are ten suggestions that might help you sift out the encumbrances technology brings but that still allow you to take advantage of the extraordinary tool that technology is.

1. Charge your cell phone *outside* of your bedroom at night.

2. Designate "No Tech Time" for *one hour* each day. (Schedule it *in writing* on your hardcopy schedule.) In office environments, the first hour after arriving is a good time for a "no tech hour" to make progress on your most difficult no-tech task of the day.

3. When working or studying, wait until the end of your time block to check messages. A typical office worker works on a task only eleven minutes continuously before interruption. Also, 60 percent of work interruptions are due to social media.

4. If your employer will allow it, check work e-mail *only* while at work. (You will be surprised at how much more efficient you will be during working hours if you apply this. You don't have to spread your work out over twenty-four hours.)

5. Reduce your digital footprint on Facebook by changing every setting to "private," "not shared," or "off."

6. No phones on the table at meals. Leave it in your car, or put it in silent mode in your pocket or purse. (Unless you're expecting a call; then, be polite and tell your companions before the meal.)

7. At mealtime, an alternative to omitting phones is to have some fun by playing "phone stack." The diners all stack their phones on the table, face down, one on top of the other. The first one to grab his or her phone pays the check!

8. Experience it first and post about it later (if you must). Checking comments about a post distracts from the enjoyment of the experience—not to mention that it can be rude.

9. Leave your phone behind when working out or taking a walk (to contemplate).

10. Vacation *without* the constant snapshots. Face it—you will likely never again look at most of the pictures you are impulsively taking. "Strike the right bargain between the present and posterity, between keeping a scrapbook of your life without scrapping the essence of life itself."

Bonus: Consider a social media *fast*. It is becoming more common to completely set aside phones and tablets for a full week to disconnect and decompress. Those who have tried this almost universally extol the benefits of the experience. Try it!

Here are five old-school principles to give you command of your valuable time:

1. Use the Traffic Light System.

A few years ago, my company implemented a simple system of time management with the goal of freeing up more time for profitable activities, which we generally defined as face-to-face client interaction. In the business arena, more time in front of customers and prospective customers means a healthier bottom line. Administrative activities—while important—can adversely affect revenue generation. (For students, concentrated study is the most profitable activity.)

The "Traffic Light System" involves carefully reviewing a *hard copy* of your daily schedule and coloring in time blocks as either wasted (red); necessary, but non-revenue generating, such as meetings, planning, or other administrative tasks (yellow); or face-to-face, including any type of customer communication—telephone, e-mail, handwritten cards, etc. (green).

The result of this simple exercise was quite revealing for our company. We discovered, on average, that we were losing about 30 percent of our time to red activities. By reallocating even a portion of this poorly spent time to green activities, we added enormously to the bottom line. (It works for your GPA too, students.)

This revelation did not result in an onerous new program, only a simple time reallocation. Simply by identifying the opportunities, we were able to dramatically improve our time management skills. Again, how did we do it? We just looked.

2. **Review your schedule the evening before—*on paper.***

Wordsworth said, "To steer is heaven, to drift is hell." Great leaders don't fly by the seat of their pants. They plan ahead—in writing. The mere act of having a definitive written schedule and action plan reduces your stress. Preparing tomorrow's activities *the night before* doubles that peace of mind.

You might prefer not to think about the activities of tomorrow because it might keep you from falling asleep at bedtime. This is a common belief, but the opposite is true.

By organizing your schedule and list of activities the evening before, you actually can put your mind at ease by knowing where your attention should be directed the next day. There are no lingering questions or things to remember. You know what they are because you have reviewed them. Additionally, by reviewing tomorrow's tasks sometime in the evening, your mind can actually be working on issues you face the next day—while you are sleeping.

Research by a leading expert on the positive benefits of napping suggests that rapid eye movement (REM) sleep enhances creative problem solving. The findings might have important implications for how sleep, specifically REM sleep, fosters the formation of associative networks in the brain.[7] Furthermore, research shows that your brain becomes very active when you sleep, and that during certain phases of sleep, your brain becomes even more active if you've just learned something new.[8] That "something new" can be the tasks you just reviewed that are on tap in the morning or the study material you just learned for the exam tomorrow.

Also, your list and schedule need to be *on paper*. Yes, that means a hard copy. It is acceptable—and even beneficial—to have it on your phone or tablet as well. But the ability to hold, write on, color (red, yellow, green), and otherwise "feel" your activities is important.

Here is more research on the matter:

> When we write something down, research suggests that as far as our brain is concerned, it's as if we were *doing* that thing. Writing seems to act as a kind of mini-rehearsal for doing. I've written before about how visualizing doing something can "trick" the brain into thinking it's actually doing it, and writing something down seems to use enough of the brain to trigger this effect. Again, this leads to greater memorization, the same way that visualizing the performance of a new skill can actually improve our skill level.[9]

There is a connection between the pen and the brain. Now you know.

Habits, like trees, are strengthened by age.

—J. C. Ryle

3. Schedule in time blocks.

I bought a plastic running watch in college and used it for at least two decades. Even after I stopped running every day, I kept wearing it because of the timer feature it had. I would constantly set a countdown for finishing a task. I took some ridicule for this from my "cooler" friends, but it worked well for me.

You are no doubt familiar with the mantra "A goal without a deadline is just a dream." It is generally applied to long-range planning goals. By scheduling time blocks throughout the day, you are applying this principle of "working to a deadline" on a short-term basis as well. This technique will provide much greater efficiency in the completion of your daily "things-to-do" list.

For example, if you arrive at your workplace at 8:00 a.m. and have a 12:30 lunch meeting, the four-and-a-half hours between can be broken into three time blocks of ninety minutes each. By then looking at your prioritized list of tasks, you can evaluate which tasks fit into each ninety-minute segment. It is fine to "re-block" the time segments if you get things done in less time than you planned for in the first block. (This will happen often after you implement this simple tip.) Instead of using my old plastic running watch, your smartphone, tablet, or laptop all have the countdown feature available, and the graphics are outstanding.

If you are a student, use the time block method to segment your study time. This assists you in prioritizing the more difficult or time-urgent subjects instead of leaving them for last—as is always the temptation. I estimate this simple tip will add a quarter- or half-point to your GPA.

Finally, wait until the *end* of each time block to check texts and e-mails. Not only will the attention to organized segments of time help you manage your tasks more efficiently, avoiding these every-other-minute distractions could do more for your production at work or school than anything else.

4. Have a to-do list tournament.

If you are an avid sports fan, you love tournaments. Most competitive leagues at all levels engage in end of season single-elimination tournaments in order to crown a champion. You should also have a tournament with your task list every day.

Rather than an elimination tournament, however, it needs to be a round-robin event. A round-robin tournament is one in which each task ("team") is pitted against every other task in order to determine its priority on your list. (A typical sports league season is actually a round-robin tournament. At the end of the season, each team has played every other team, and the records of wins and losses determine their standing.) Another term for this method is "paired comparisons."

If you have six tasks to complete, for example, begin by matching Task 1 on your list with Task 2. You determine which task "wins" between the two of them by placing the highest priority on it. Then do the same with Task 1 vs. Task 3, and so on, until each task has "played" the other five. Put a mark by each task when they "win," and the list will organize itself into the proper priority after you have completed the tournament. You might find that the highest-priority items are easy to discern without this exercise. But when you have eight, ten, or fifteen items to prioritize, this tool comes in handy.

"In study after study of men and women who get paid more and promoted faster, the quality of 'action orientation' stands out as the most observable and consistent behavior they demonstrate in everything they do. Successful, effective people are those who launch directly into their major tasks and then discipline themselves to work steadily and single-mindedly until those tasks are complete."[11] The to-do list tournament is a simple technique that helps you achieve optimal action orientation.

One other caveat: It is actually best to have your daily tournament in the *morning* instead of the night before when you review your schedule. This is because you might think of things to add to your list subconsciously while you are sleeping—or in that great think tank known as the shower. This might change your priorities for some tasks. Playing the tournament as late as possible, yet before you begin your workday, eliminates having to reorganize your day.

Use the tournament, have fun, and you will be a champ every day!

5. **GMAD (not ASAP).**

The generic answer to the question "When do you need it?" is most often "As soon as possible"—or ASAP for short. This is not a good answer if you want to get things done efficiently because no one really knows what ASAP means. (It seems that many people believe the S stands for "slow.") It is not definitive, and because it is so overused, it actually loses its meaning of urgency.

A better answer is "Give me a deadline"—for short, GMAD.[10] This serves to create a specific day and time that all parties can understand. When you are assigned a task, by asking for the "GMAD," you are saying, "Give me a specific day and time when this is needed." This will make planning easier and you will get a lot more done as well.

Too Many Tasks!

It will not be unusual for you to find yourself in a place where you have twenty-five, fifty, or one hundred tasks on your list and are asking yourself, "How did I get here?!" What do you do? You must become *ruthless*.

Typically, this issue is a result of either not fully understanding how to prioritize (not uncommon), or, more frequently, you have a hard time saying no. As you become more successful, the requests for help will increase. You must learn to refuse some requests and prioritize until it hurts. The alternative of taking on so many items that you drown every day in a sea of over-activity is a sure route to burnout.

But take it easy on yourself. Take baby steps. Try reducing your task list to a comfortable number by gradually eliminating a few unnecessary items every day or week until you get it to a more manageable number.

MONEY MANAGEMENT

We are surrounded by financial mismanagement in our culture. We see the way our government wastes money, and we find our own behavior influenced by the poor spending habits of family and friends. With an estimated three hundred sixty thousand television commercials inundating us by the time we are twenty years old, the average American is continuously tempted to make unnecessary purchases.[12]

Unfortunately, some parents have done a poor job of teaching their children about money. The optimum age to begin teaching children about money management is six to eight years old. Fortunately, it is never too late to learn. With just a few basic principles, you can get your house in order. And this is essential to becoming an effective leader.

Becoming adept at managing financial resources is less daunting than you might fear. By employing a few common sense practices, you can eliminate many of the problems associated with personal money management. Here are three that will take you a long way toward good financial stewardship:

1. **Set up a dual entry budget.**

    Just as tracking green, yellow, and red time in your daily schedule allows you to "find" more hours in the day, the act of *tracking* your expenditures is 90 percent of the money management game. And, yes, that means you will likely "find" more dollars as well. If you don't make a reasonable estimate of your monthly financial outlays, you will inevitably create issues of excessive debt or budget shortfalls. A simple Excel spreadsheet composed of four columns is all you need.

    Column one is for the date paid. Column two is for the monthly expense category. Column three is for the amount actually paid during the month, and column four is for the budgeted amount for the item for that month.

"Unbelievable!"

When asked the question, "How are you doing?" try this: answer with just one word—an enthusiastic "UNBELIEVABLE!" Here are three reasons to do so: **1)** It is an "interrupter." People expect you to say a standard and boring, "Fine, how are you?" Instead, you get their attention with one word. **2)** Even though the word "unbelievable" does not necessarily connote things are going well for you, when said with a positive, upbeat tone, you are seen automatically as an optimist—and everyone loves positive people—especially in *leadership*. **3)** Saying it usually elicits at least a chuckle from your companion. That makes YOU feel better too— no matter how things are going. Use it! It's UNBELIEVABLE!

March

Date Paid	Expense	Actual	Budget
03-01	Mortgage	1745	1745
----	Household	611	500
----	Utilities	555	650
03-05	Insurance	450	450
03-10	Auto	445	445
03-11	Credit Card	1109	1250
03-05	Life Ins.	330	330
----	Charity	800	800
----	Misc.	422	500
		6467	6670
	Surplus	203	

Mark the date paid and the actual amount paid for each expense item. There are some categories—such as *household* or *miscellaneous*—that might require several entries to maintain during the month. In those cases, use a light gray entry in the spreadsheet so you can easily refer to it (or write lightly in pencil if using a hard copy). It is best to update the spreadsheet on the day in which an expenditure on the spreadsheet occurs throughout the week. *At minimum*, update it once per week—perhaps on Saturday morning. You can easily compare columns three and four to get a quick feel for the over/under status of your spending for the month. For debit or credit card expenditures, you can have a notepad in a centralized location on which you can jot down charges or stack receipts to add up later when you do your weekly updates.

Once these small habits are implemented, they will come naturally. This "Ivy Lee-esque idea" (due to its obvious simplicity) will most assuredly help you stay on track each month.

2. Save early and often.

How much difference does ten years make?

Suppose you are settled in your first job and just celebrated your twenty-fifth birthday. If you are able to set aside $5,000 in a tax-deferred retirement account each year for the next forty years earning a 7 percent rate of return after management or administration fees, your account would be worth *$1,068,047* on your sixty-fifth birthday.

Alternatively, if you decide to have a little fun and enjoy yourself, deferring the same savings plan until your thirty-fifth birthday, how much will be in your account (earning the same 7 percent rate of return) when they give you that gold retirement watch (in thirty years)? *$505,365*. (And this does not take into consideration the taxes you would have saved each year due to the deductibility of the retirement plan deposit—assuming you qualified.)

One more scenario: What if you were the twenty-five-year-old prudent investor who saved $5,000 per year for ten years, but then had to stop at age thirty-five for some reason? You could never save another dime. How much would you then have at age sixty-five? *$562,682*. That's right. Even if you had to stop saving after ten years, you would still have more at age sixty-five than if you had waited till age thirty-five and saved for thirty years. Not only that: by starting at thirty-five, you would have put in *three times* as much money over the course of your career ($150,000), but you would still have more at retirement by taking advantage of the early savings plan even though your total investment was only $50,000.

NOTE: For those approaching retirement: If you are in a position to delay retirement from age sixty-two to age seventy, you can reduce [your] required savings rate by some two-thirds.[13] Life-changing leaders have financial maturity. This means they understand the benefits of delayed gratification. Regardless of your current age, save now.

[Compound interest] is the most powerful force in the universe.

—Albert Einstein

3. Avoid debt.

In spite of what some would tell you, not all debt is bad. For example, a home loan—if you put more than 20 percent as a down payment—can be a prudent choice instead of renting. However, this is not a blanket endorsement of mortgage debt. It depends on the facts of your particular situation. (It is best to get professional advice on any big-money move.)

Debt that places an undue burden on your financial standing *is bad*. In particular, credit card interest, which can approach an incredible 30 percent per year, can devastate a family's financial position. Just as compounding works for you when investing for the long run, it works *against* you when you borrow. It can ruin your credit rating if you get behind, not to mention the stress and emotional pressure it creates, which can adversely affect not just your pocket book but your job performance and relationships as well. (Surveys indicate that 50 percent of those who divorce include financial hardship as a reason.)

The key is to minimize borrowing. The best way to control borrowing is to simply spend less than you earn. But when you take on debt, the economic *benefit* of borrowing money must be greater than the economic *cost*. Borrowing money simply to create a certain lifestyle can eventually be devastating. Peace of mind is important for good leaders to have as they make important decisions on behalf of those in their charge. A clear mind leads to clear thinking and better decisions. Knowing for sure that you have a way to repay a loan—or avoiding unnecessary debt altogether—are sure ways to be at peace in the financial area of your life.

Bonus financial advice: Don't try to pick stocks or time the ups and downs of the market in your investment accounts. Passive, evidence-based investment strategies (such as index funds) have been shown to likely be the most efficient way to invest in the long run. Don't get duped into believing that a "guru" you hire can tell the future. They can't. And that is exactly what you are asking them to do when you expect them to pick rising stocks and avoid market downturns. The earlier you understand this, the better.

HEALTH & FITNESS

In the early 1900s, President Teddy Roosevelt was a physical fitness advocate and famously challenged Americans to exist "not for the life of ease but for the life of strenuous endeavor."

Life-changing leaders set an example concerning their health. Poor physical appearance and fitness belies a leader who is encouraging self-discipline. Healthy teammates are happier and more productive. A physically fit team is less likely to get sick, thus boosting attendance and reducing healthcare costs. Here is a summary of the benefits of getting and staying in shape:[14]

NOTE: Just like any other task, exercise time must be scheduled. Otherwise, it won't happen! Generally, two hundred minutes per week will keep you where you need to be physically. And this does not have to be strenuous exercise. Simply walking or taking the stairs when possible counts too.

- Paradoxically, more exercise provides *more energy* throughout the work or school day.
- Studies show that *confidence and creativity increase* even with moderate levels of exercise.
- Exercise *increases mental stamina.*
- Exercise is one of the best ways to *manage stress* because of an increase in "feel-good" neurotransmitters called endorphins.
- Exercise *improves sleep patterns.*

Far better it is to dare mighty things, to win glorious triumphs, even though check-ered by failure, than to take rank with those poor spirits who neither enjoy much nor suffer much, because they live in the gray twilight that knows not victory nor defeat.

—Theodore Roosevelt

Finding Your Place to Lead

As you have seen, keeping your own house in order through certain personal disciplines is important to development as a leader. Additionally, wisely *positioning* yourself in order to best use your leadership gifts is also key. Since the majority of your leadership opportunities will occur in the workplace, you must identify what aspects of your vocation are important to you in order for you to optimize your talents within an organization. Furthermore, since the success of a business never rises above the quality of its leadership, the decision you make concerning where you should offer your services should be made carefully based on that organization's leadership.

Find a job that you like so much that you'd do it without compensation; then do it so well that people will pay you to continue.

—Walt Disney

Making the wrong selection of associates in business is one of the most common reasons for failing professionally. Whether you are considering an initial, entry-level job or looking at opportunities to rise in your profession, you need to choose an employer who is not just successful and intelligent but also wise and inspirational. "We emulate those with whom we associate most closely. Pick an employer who is worth emulating."[15] And find an occupation that you love and into which you can throw yourself completely.

Here are seven things to consider:[16]

1. **You can't do it all.** You must understand that you can't be all things to all people. Know your strengths and limitations, and communicate them well. Find your niche, and be authentic.

2. **Embrace failure.** You are more valuable to an organization when you try many times and sometimes fail than when you rarely try in order to stay under the radar. Ironically, the key to success has always been frequent failure. That is how you learn best. Leaders know this and recognize it in others. The only real risk in your career is *not* taking a risk with your career.[17] Your attitude when it comes to risk-taking should simply be, "Sometimes you win, and sometimes you learn."

   Failure is not fatal, but failure to change might be.

   —Coach John Wooden

3. **Network.** Big breaks in your career are most likely to come from someone you know. Use your current network, and meet as many new people each day as you can. You are now equipped with Old School communication skills that make this an easier task. The more folks you know outside of your own organization, the higher your chances of finding a better opportunity. (By sending one to three handwritten cards per day, you will ensure that your personal network is ever expanding.)

4. **Think long term.** Having a long-term perspective is more important than your education, intelligence, or connections. You will make better decisions when you have a clear *future orientation* because it improves your short-term decisions by fully aligning them with the long-term future you desire. Simply put: future intent influences and often determines present actions.[18] So when you identify an employment

opportunity, learn the long-term prospects and plans for that company. This means investigating whether their industry growth trajectory is up or down over the next decade. For example, service industries in the United States are currently growing much faster than manufacturing companies. Make sure your industry is not going to replace you with an algorithm, sending you on an unwanted career detour.

Before you begin scrambling up the ladder of success, make sure that it is leaning against the right building.

—Stephen Covey

5. **No one gets there alone.** No matter how gifted you are, you need help. Choosing an opportunity where you will be mentored by the best is a sure way to increase your leadership opportunities. Assistant coaches become head coaches and then general managers. It follows in any profession—if your boss succeeds, you likely will, too. This goes for your coworkers as well. Make sure the team you join is one that is supportive. Positive peer pressure is another vital component of success.

Every man I meet is my superior in some way; and in that I can learn of him.

—Emerson

6. **Have an idea.** On the night before he died, Victor Hugo wrote, "Nothing, not all the armies of the world, can stop an idea whose time has come." Great leaders have great ideas. Become an "idea person" by drinking deeply from the waters of not only your field of expertise but others as well. This well-rounded, 360-degree perspective can take you to the top of your field and provide leadership opportunities you cannot now imagine. (More on this in chapter 8.)

7. **Get into your "flow," and "AMP" up.** When you are in the state of *optimal* challenge, then you are in a state otherwise known as *flow*.[19] Note that this is not the state of *maximum* challenge. That leads to burn out. Optimal challenge means that your skill set and the task at hand are in equilibrium, and you truly love what you do. The most satisfying experiences in peoples' lives happen when they are in flow. In order to reach and maintain flow in your work environment, Daniel Pink (*Drive*) explains that you need three primary factors to be present and available. You can use the acronym *AMP*.

- **Autonomy.** Having a feeling of independence when accomplishing your tasks has a powerful effect on performance and, most importantly, attitude. It "promotes greater conceptual understanding, better grades, enhanced productivity, less burnout, and greater levels of psychological well-being."[20]

- **Mastery.** Whereas flow is a daily occurrence, mastery takes place over the long term. Geoff Colvin's research indicates that mastery occurs with ten years or ten thousand hours of practice.[21] It is a *mindset* that requires perseverance. As professional basketball Hall of Famer Julius Erving once said, "Being a professional is doing things that you love to do, on the days you don't feel like doing them." Also realize that mastery can never really be achieved because you can always get better. But having an environment that allows you the *pursuit of perfection* is a key component of achieving flow.

- **Purpose.** "The most deeply motivated people—not to mention those who are most productive and satisfied—hitch their desires to a cause larger than themselves."[22] (Emerson said, "Hitch your wagon to a star.") While most companies look to maximize profit, you should look to maximize *purpose*. If you can find a team that also aspires to a greater purpose, then you have a potential match.

The selection of any career leadership opportunity—whether your first or your last—has other important and far-reaching implications. Consider this:

A 2011 study conducted by a team of social scientists at the University of Canberra in Australia concluded that having a job we hate is as bad for our health and sometimes worse than not having a job at all. Levels of depression and anxiety among people who are unhappy at work were the same or greater than those who were unemployed. Another study, conducted by researchers at University College London that same year, found that people who didn't feel recognized for their effort at work were more likely to suffer from heart disease. And according to a Gallup poll conducted in 2013 called "State of the American Workplace," when our bosses completely ignore us, 40 percent of us actively disengage from our work. If our bosses criticize us on a regular basis, 22 percent of us actively disengage.[23]

If you choose the wrong work environment, you likely will surround yourself with unhappy people who make those around them unhappy. And stress, anxiety, and happiness at work have less to do with *what* we do and more to do with *who* is doing it with us.[24] You can see why choosing the best leadership opportunity in your vocation is vitally important not only for you but for your family as well because your unhappiness can affect others.

Gratitude List

Gratitude affects happiness. When you are grateful about *specific* things from your past, dwelling on triumphs and not disappointments, you tend to be more satisfied with the present.

In his book *A Whole New Mind*, Daniel Pink offers some thoughts on three ways to increase your gratitude—and thus your happiness:[25]

1. **The gratitude visit letter.** Think of a person who has been particularly helpful and special to you, but you have not thanked this person the way

you wanted to. Write a detailed letter, and then visit in person to read it. Tears will flow in a good way.

2. **The birthday gratitude list.** Each year on your birthday, make a list of all you are grateful for up to the number of years you have been alive. Your list obviously grows by one each year. The older you get, the more grateful you become. Make new lists from scratch each year—knowing there will be overlap—but keep your lists over the years to pull out on your birthday.

3. **The gratitude one-a-day.** Once per day, think of something you are grateful for. To do this, pick a time when you will make it a daily habit of focusing on something good in your life. It could be during your morning reading time, first cup of coffee, when shaving, at bedtime, or some other time. It doesn't matter when. Just make it a routine, and see each day produce a positive thought to live by.

DECISION MAKING

> The risk of a wrong decision is preferable to the terror of indecision.
>
> —Maimonides

It is said that Columbus "didn't know where he was going when he left, didn't know where he was when he got there, and didn't know where he had been when he got back."[26] The same should never be said of you because you are going to now learn a method of decision making that will help to guide you in the right direction.

We make thousands of decisions each day. The vast majority are minor and mundane. Some are important; a few are profound and life changing. But all of our decisions shape who we are. Greatness comes through making right choices. Therefore, having a system to make good decisions—rather than relying on a heavy dose of guesswork and "gut" feelings—is a life-changing leader's responsibility. In this section, you will explore the principles of effective decision making by utilizing a straightforward, quantitative process. You will learn the barriers that keep you from making high-quality decisions and implement an objective, ten-step process to wise decisions.

Seven Barriers to Good Decisions

1. **Too rushed.** "Haste makes waste." This one is easy—you learned it from your grandmother. Another common form: "The hurrieder I go, the behinder I get."

2. **Too much information.** When we are overwhelmed with data or alternatives—as is often the case in our information-laden age—we can become frozen with indecision ("paralysis by analysis"). And indecision actually IS a decision . . . to do nothing.

3. **No process.** Having no organized way to decide means you are "going with your gut," and this is effectively the same as a coin flip.

4. **No skill.** You are uninformed in the area in which the decision needs to be made.

5. **You answer the wrong question.** Knowing the right question to ask is often difficult. But asking the correct question gets you halfway to the answer.

6. **Overconfidence.** Ignorance and arrogance can both lead to overconfidence, which can lead to bad decisions.

7. **Groupthink.** Taking the "everyone is doing it" approach gets you no further now than it did when you were a child saying this to your mom.

The good news is that by applying some solid decision-making principles, each of these barriers can be removed. Increasing the amount of time you have to make an important decision is usually a matter of planning ahead. Also, focusing on the question *first*—and then the answer—allows you to prioritize properly. And finally, if you can avoid the emotional traps in your decision making by seeking wise counsel, this will set you on a course to decision-making success.

TEN STEPS TO WISE DECISIONS[27]

The following is a robust, *criteria-based* process that organizes your thinking and maximizes *objectivity*. This type of process will give you the *confidence* to make an informed decision every time.

Furthermore, this decision-making process is useful for all major life decisions, such as choosing a college, selecting a career or employer, or deciding where to live. It can also be used for less monumental but still important decisions, like selecting a car or choosing a vacation spot.

"Choosing a college" is the decision example I will use to show how this process works. Either you have A) already been through a college selection process and can therefore relate to the methodology, or B) this is a decision awaiting you—and thus the timing is perfect.

The first step is to define each area of the decision-making process.

1. **Identify the question.** At this initial stage, ignore a "right" answer. Focus only on defining the decision that is to be considered. You can gain clarity by simply asking questions such as:
   - "What is the heart of the matter?"
   - "Am I thinking long term, or am I thinking short-term expedience?"
   - "How many alternatives are there?"

   Be aware of the binary trap of simply looking for a yes or no answer that could eliminate consideration of all the appropriate alternatives.

2. **Clarify your objectives.** What are you trying to optimize with this decision? What will it cost you in the way of money and time? List your qualitative and quantitative objectives, imagining what each will look like when it is accomplished.

The Big Fish / Little Pond Effect

The more elite an educational institution is, the worse students feel about their own academic abilities.

That is the conclusion Malcolm Gladwell came to while doing research for his book *David and Goliath*. He explains:

"The likelihood of someone completing a STEM degree—all things being equal—rises by 2 percentage points for every 10-point decrease in the university's average SAT score. The smarter your peers, the dumber you feel; the dumber you feel, the more likely you are to drop out of science. Since there is roughly a 150-point gap between the average SAT scores of students attending the University of Maryland and Brown, the "penalty" [a student] paid by choosing a great school over a good school is that she reduced her chances of graduating with a science degree by 30 percent. . . . That's a very large risk to take for the prestige of an Ivy League school.

"The very thing that makes elite schools such wonderful places for those at the top makes them very difficult places for everyone else. . . . The Big Pond takes really bright students and demoralizes them."

3. **Prioritize your objectives.** In this step, you are listing the "*must* haves" in order to distinguish them from the "*want* to haves."

- *Must haves* are nonnegotiable. "Intuitively, most people think that experts consider more alternatives and more possible diagnoses rather than fewer. Yet the mark of true expertise is not the ability to consider more options, but the ability to filter out irrelevant ones."[28] List only those items related to this decision that you truly cannot live without.

- *Want to haves* need to be scored on a scale of 1 to 10. This is not a ranking, but a *relative* score. In other words, if attending a college within three hours of home is the most important of your criteria, then score it a 10. All other categories would be scored in comparison to this priority. Here is an example:

Must Haves:
Desired major
Academic prestige
Within budget

Want to haves:	Priority Rating
Culture fit	8
Three hours or less from home	10
Scholarship opportunity	8
Co-ed	7
Good athletics atmosphere	8
Good living arrangements	6
Car-friendly campus	4
Strong career center	8
Library space	4
Student camaraderie/traditions	7
Campus beauty	3
Competitive pricing	7
Good corporate reputation	9

4. **Identify alternatives.** You must avoid the binary trap and be creative when listing the alternatives. There is no reason not to push the envelope in this step.

	Community College	Texas	Vanderbilt	Oklahoma	Texas A&M

5. **Evaluate the alternatives.** If any alternative does not stack up against the "must haves," it is no longer viable. Now, all the attention turns to the "want to haves." Focus on *facts,* not opinions, as much as possible. Don't forget that you are comparing alternatives against the objectives—not ranking them against each other.

Want to haves:	Priority Rating	Community College	Texas	Vanderbilt	Oklahoma	Texas A&M
Culture fit	8	1	2	9	7	10
Three hours or less from home	10	10	10	1	10	10
Scholarship opportunity	8	8	1	7	5	7
Co-ed	7	6	9	9	8	9
Good athletics atmosphere	8	1	8	5	8	10
Good living arrangements	6	1	6	6	6	6
Car-friendly campus	4	8	1	7	5	5
Strong career center	8	2	8	8	6	9
Library space	4	2	3	5	4	7
Student camaraderie/traditions	7	0	5	7	7	10
Campus beauty	3	4	4	9	6	4
Competitive pricing	7	10	8	2	7	9
Good corporate reputation	9	3	9	10	6	9

6. **Make a preliminary choice.** Multiply the evaluation rating times the priority rating from step 5. Total them at the bottom of each column. The highest score is the best preliminary choice. However, there are four steps remaining.

Must Haves: Desired major Academic prestige Within budget Want to haves:	Priority Rating	Community College		Texas		Vanderbilt		Oklahoma		Texas A&M	
Culture fit	8	1	8	2	16	9	72	7	56	10	80
Three hours or less from home	10	10	100	10	100	1	10	10	100	10	100
Scholarship opportunity	8	8	64	1	8	7	56	5	40	7	56
Co-ed	7	6	42	9	63	9	63	8	56	9	63
Good athletics atmosphere	8	1	8	8	64	5	40	8	64	10	80
Good living arrangements	6	1	6	6	36	6	36	6	36	6	36
Car-friendly campus	4	8	32	1	4	7	28	5	20	5	20
Strong career center	8	2	16	8	64	8	64	6	48	9	72
Library space	4	2	8	3	12	5	20	4	16	7	28
Student camaraderie/traditions	7	0	0	5	35	7	49	7	49	10	70
Campus beauty	3	4	12	4	12	9	27	6	18	4	12
Competitive pricing	7	10	70	8	56	2	14	7	49	9	63
Good corporate reputation	9	3	27	9	81	10	90	6	54	9	81
			393		551		569		606		761

7. **Assess the risk.** Ask these questions: What is the worst thing that could happen? How likely is it that this will happen? In the case of choosing Texas A&M as the college you wish to attend, let's say that the worst that can happen is you are not accepted to enroll. If you determine the chance of this is 30 percent, then it would be prudent to apply to two to three additional schools in order to guard against this risk.

8. **Make the decision.** (There are still two more steps.)

9. **Seek wise counsel for confirmation.** As we grow older, our perspective enlarges. Run your decision-making process by an older, trusted advisor in your life. If you have two, show both of them. Seeking wise counsel shows wisdom on *your* part. Be sure to take the time to explain the process you used in arriving at your decision in case the person is unfamiliar with this particular methodology. Seeking this wise counsel will either cement your choice or help you consider aspects of the decision you might have overlooked or misunderstood.

10. **Set a timetable to implement.** Once your mentor(s) have signed off, then you can ask about logistics. For example, "When should I apply for admission to each school?" (Perhaps your top three.)

In summary, good decisions are made using a *process* because it not only solidifies the right decision but also brings out issues that you did not consider when you thought about your choices initially. Now you also know that there are many traps in decisions that can be eliminated or dealt with accordingly and that a decision can never be any better than the data and the known alternatives allow.

Mentors

A good friend of mine, Dave, implemented a unique method of becoming a protégé when he turned twenty years old. On each of his "zero" birthdays, he finds a person ten years older than he is that he considers wise enough to be his mentor. He then interviews this person about his or her own life journey, starting with the simple question, "What did you learn in the last decade—the one I am entering—that would be a lesson you could pass on to me?"

Why is it so important to seek counsel from the "older and wiser"?

John Stonestreet, referring to David Brooks, explains: "The first life skill he notes [about older people] is *bifocalism,* the ability to see a situation from multiple perspectives. That only comes with experience. Next is *lightness*, the ability to be at ease with the downsides of life. Again, the accumulation of years can help us not take ourselves so seriously. And then there's the *acquired wisdom* of responding to competing demands. Finally, Brooks notes that older people often have an intuitive grasp of what other people are thinking, leading to greater *empathy*."[29]

So don't hesitate to follow my friend Dave's advice and seek out an "older and wiser" mentor at any age!

THE WISDOM VAULT

In chapter 5, you read about developing a corporate Story Vault in order to efficiently disseminate a company's stories amongst its employees and customers. In similar fashion, the *Wisdom Vault* provides words and phrases that convey wisdom in terms easily used in a variety of settings, whether in the corporate world or within your inner circle of family and friends. It can be fun to collect new terms and ideas. Here is a baker's dozen of examples that makes a good starter list. I invite you to use it as a catalyst to build your own.

"Crossing the Rubicon." *To take an irrevocable step that commits one to a specific course.* When Julius Caesar led his troops from Gaul to the Rubicon River, he paused on the northern end of a bridge, debating whether to cross. It would be a crime against Rome for proconsul Caesar to bring his troops in from the province. Caesar crossed the Rubicon in January 49 BC, thereby starting a civil war that inevitably gave him his power.

"Kairos."[30] *Rhetorical timing.* The ability to seize the perfect persuasive moment. Always look for the best *kairos*, and utilize it as part of your rhetorical strategy.

"Flow."[31] *The optimal state of challenge.* The highest, most satisfying experiences in life happen when you are in *flow.* Flow is sometimes called "the zone." The experience is challenging but not overwhelming, precisely suited to your abilities. Everything seems to be going right, and you love it!

"The wisdom of crowds."[32] *The aggregation of imperfect personal perspectives into collective intelligence.* In spite of our individual limitations, our collective intelligence is often excellent. (Note: A fun and easy experiment to demonstrate this concept is to fill a large jar with jelly beans and ask at least thirty people to guess the number it contains. With few exceptions, the average of the estimates will be within 5 percent of the actual number. Do it and see!)

"Procrustean bed."[33] *A plan or scheme to produce uniformity or conformity by arbitrary or violent methods.* Named after Procrustes, the bandit from Greek mythology who stretched or amputated the limbs of travelers to make them conform to the length of his bed.

"Acres of diamonds."[34] *The idea that in a free-market economy, a man can find all he needs to be successful in his "own backyard," where plenty of "diamonds" are waiting to be found.* It is the antithesis of "the grass is greener on the other side of the fence."

"The race to free." *The concept that as supply or access to a product or service becomes more widespread, the cost goes down—sometimes precipitously.* This occurs with the commoditization of products or services. A good example of this is the continued dropping of technology prices over the last two decades and the outsourcing of left-brain jobs. This can be good for the consumer but bad for the producer of goods and services. (Both manufacturing and service sectors of a free economy are susceptible.)

"Watergate strategy." *Asking for more than one needs as a negotiating ploy.* This term refers to the method used to get funding for the Watergate Hotel break-in of 1972. Instigators asked originally for $1 million but settled for $250,000. This was plenty to get the ill-fated and ill-advised (and illegal) job done.

"The Russian Winter." *Overextension in either time or resources or both.* This reference is to the fatal miscalculation Napoleon Bonaparte made in taking his soldiers to Russia only to get caught in the grip of an early October winter. His huge army was unprepared and decimated. It spelled the beginning of the end of his reign. (Interestingly, even though Hitler studied Napoleon extensively, his army also got caught up in similar circumstances, which led to his defeat in Russia as well.)

"Satisfice."[35] *This term means to settle for something that is good enough and not worry about the possibility that there might be something better.* It is the opposite of the paralyzing tendency to "maximize" every decision we make. By being a satisficer, you are able to avoid paralysis by analysis and make decisions more efficiently, thus providing time for other, more important endeavors.

"Thin slice."[36] *The ability to make an assessment with very limited information.* You are able to extrapolate the full meaning or identity based on this narrow amount of information.

"Invisible gorilla."[37] *An unexpected item or action which is not readily seen or noticed by virtue of its non sequitur nature.* Otherwise known as "inattentional blindness," the name is based on a famous experiment where a gorilla invades a circle of people passing around a basketball. Here again is the link to see this concept of selective attention: http://www.theinvisiblegorilla.com/videos.html.

"Dog whistle." *A coded message for a target group and no one else.* In his 2003 State of the Union message, George W. Bush spoke of "power, wonder-working power, in . . . the American people." Christians recognized the "wonder-working power" phrase from a well-known gospel hymn "There is Power in the Blood."

Keeping a Daily Journal—For Leaders[38]

Super Mentor Michael Hyatt offers the following advantages for keeping a daily written journal:

1. **Process previous events.** What happens to me is not as important as the meaning I assign to what happens to me. Journaling helps me sort through my experience and be intentional about my interpretation.

2. **Clarify my thinking.** Writing in general helps me disentangle my thoughts. Journaling takes it to a new level. Because I am not performing in front of a "live audience," so to speak, I can really wrestle through the issues.

3. **Understand the context.** Life is often happening so quickly I usually have little time to stop and reflect on where I am in the Bigger Story. Journaling helps me to discern the difference between the forest and the trees.

4. **Notice my feelings.** I understand feelings aren't everything, but they also aren't nothing. The older I get, the more I try to pay attention to them. They are often an early indicator of something brewing.

5. **Connect with my heart.** I'm not sure I can really explain this one, but journaling has helped me monitor the condition of my heart. Solomon said "above all else" we are to guard it (see Proverbs 4:23). It's hard to do that when you lose touch with it.

6. **Record significant lessons.** I'm a better student when I am taking notes. Writing things down leads to even deeper understanding and, I hope, wisdom. I want to write down what I learn, so I don't have to re-learn it later.

7. **Ask important questions.** A journal is not merely a repository for the lessons I am learning but also the questions I'm asking. If there's one thing I have discovered, it's the quality of my questions determines the quality of my answers.

> **BONUS IDEA:** Keep a "parallel journal." By using the same journal (with dates) for multiple years, you can see where you were on the same day each year.

Conclusion

When we look at the synonyms for *leadership* found in the first several entries of the dictionary, we see words such as *management, stewardship, influence, command, guidance,* and *direction.*[39] But the characteristic that rises above all others when it comes to being a *life-changing leader* is *empathy*—the ability to understand and share the feelings of others. And empathy always leads to humility.

Humble leadership might seem countercultural when we observe leaders on television so often exhibiting anything but an unassuming nature. But leaders who have empathy and humility facilitate a following like none other.

> Humility doesn't mean you think less of yourself but that you think of yourself less.
>
> —Max Lucado

I once came across the term *humbition* (humility plus ambition). It reminds me that to be humble does not mean to sacrifice success or have limited ambition. But those who would be humble also know that failure is the main ingredient in the recipe of success and therefore will take the necessary risks with careful calculation and consideration. They understand that challenges are the best teachers and that, ultimately, the most useful degree comes from the University of Adversity. They know that with every stumble, a diamond can be found. This fundamental attitude concerning the value of failure as the precursor to success makes them uniquely qualified to lead because they understand a prime element of the human condition. They understand that to err is human.

Even in such technical lines as engineering, about 15 percent of one's financial
success is due to one's technical knowledge
and about 85 percent is due to skill in
human engineering-to personality and the
ability to lead people.

—Dale Carnegie

Empathetic leaders resist becoming ideologues. When necessary, they can rest comfortably in a bed of ambiguity because they love truth. There is a great irony with truly great leaders. Because of their empathetic disposition, they are equipped to be the greatest *servants* of all. As such, they exhibit the characteristics you have just explored. They:

1. Know *who* they are and *where* they are going.
2. Are disciplined (have good habits).
3. Are involved with, and surround themselves with, good people.
4. Make sound decisions.
5. Seek and use wisdom.

In this chapter, you have learned ways to engage in all of these leadership qualities. But now it is time to complete your study—and it is going to be *life changing* for you.

CHAPTER 8
Learn

It's what you learn after you know it all that counts.

—John Wooden

Shakespeare said, "The readiness is all." Years of structured learning in the classroom have given you a foundation. You also now have the Old School Advantage tools to help you accelerate your progress. But now it is time to look to the most important factor pertaining to a successful and significant future—*lifelong learning.*

Hopefully, you have come to understand that a formal education is meant to teach you how to continuously learn on your own. Knowledge is not a destination—it is a journey. Life is richer when you are learning. When you stop learning, you stop living. Like many, I didn't become a serious student until after my formal academic career was complete. Perhaps this is your experience as well. But *regardless of your age*, you have only begun to learn.

It is one of the paradoxes of success that the things and ways which got you there are seldom those that keep you there.

—Charles Handy

We looked earlier at the idea of seeking truth diligently through honest and open discussion. Socrates "was always suspicious of the obvious, and he [felt that he] could nearly always show that the obvious was untrue, and [that] the truth is very rarely obvious."[1] He also believed that the role of education was to "show an individual that he possessed far less knowledge than he thought he did, and thus to encourage him to acquire more." He believed that wisdom consisted largely in knowing his own ignorance.[2] Ironically, the more we learn, the more we realize what we don't know. So why learn more?

"Successful men, in all callings, never stop acquiring specialized knowledge related to their major purpose, business, or profession. Those who are not successful usually make the mistake of believing that the knowledge acquiring period ends when one finishes school. The truth is that schooling does but little more than to put one in the way of learning how to acquire practical knowledge."[3]

But what is the best reason for lifelong learning? *Because that is what life-changing leaders do.* They leave their comfort zone to explore and make the way safe for those who follow. They strive to learn *how* to think—not only what to think. They understand these words from Cicero: "They who wish to do easy things without trouble and toil must previously have been trained in more difficult things."

To lead, you must "escape the gravity of the ordinary"[4] and live in a state of *constant curiosity.*

> Curiosity is more important than knowledge. I have no special talent. I am only passionately curious.
>
> —Albert Einstein

Curiosity depends both on being aware of your own ignorance and on not depending on the supposed omniscience of your electronic rectangles. Truly curious people ask "why" as well as "what." Our electronic devices can make us ignorant of our own ignorance. This is the worst state in which you can find yourself if you desire to be a lifelong learner.

In order to prepare you for lifelong learning and thus help you to quench your constant curiosities, we will focus on these three areas:

1. The Wisdom Factor
2. Overcoming the Challenge That Is Changing Our Brains
3. *Your* LifeLong Learning GamePlan

Let's get to work!

THE WISDOM FACTOR

Information is everywhere, yet wisdom is rare. And paradoxically, to seek wisdom *shows* wisdom. The Old School student must always endeavor to pursue wisdom.

When I was a boy, my mom used to say, "What a shame that youth is wasted on the young."[5] This was always a thought-provoking statement for me. The older I get, the clearer the meaning of this quote becomes. In our youth, we have optimal energy and physical capabilities, but we lack the knowledge and experience that leads to wisdom. An ancient proverb says, "Knowledge in youth is wisdom in age." I want to introduce a concept that I believe will bear this truth out, and that I hope will motivate you to seek wisdom at every age.

In chapter 5, I mentioned an equation whose product is wisdom. I will now expand on this concept.

$$(\text{Intelligence} + \text{Knowledge}) \times \text{Experience} = \text{Wisdom}$$

or

$$(I + K) \times E = W$$

The first element—*intelligence*—is generally fixed. Naturally, such things as proper nutrition, exercise, and certain methods of learning can enhance this to some degree—especially in the formative years of childhood. Conversely, things like trauma or substance abuse can harm your intellectual capacity. But for the purpose of quantification of the Wisdom Factor, we will assume that intelligence is static. Therefore, the level of your inherited cognitive abilities *generally* determines your capacity to obtain and apply what you learn. (For the purposes of Wisdom Factor calculations, a score of 6 represents average intelligence for an adult, or an IQ of 90 to 110. A 10 in our scale would be intellectual giftedness of an IQ of 130 or more.)

However, extensive research indicates that your IQ only accounts for a small portion of your career success. How small? Only 4 to 10 percent![6] That leaves a big opportunity in the rest of the equation. It says, vocationally at least, that the outcome (product) of your equation—*your* Wisdom Factor—is largely *within your control.*

> Men are anxious to improve their cir-
> cumstances, but are unwilling to improve
> themselves; they therefore remain bound.
>
> —James Allen

Ancient proverbs state that "the wise listen and add to their learning"; they remain teachable. They heed instruction and "store up knowledge." "By paying attention to the wise, [the simple] get knowledge."[7]

Notice the emphases: *listening, learning,* being *teachable* (I like the word *coachable*), *instruction, paying attention to the wise.* These terms imply openness to new ideas, willingness to put forth effort, and eagerness to learn from those who are wiser than you are. This requires the availability of and access to two things: people and information.

Remember, *the people you meet and the books you read change your life.*

Time is only one aspect of experience. The people with whom you associate will also dictate your experience and subsequently the *wisdom* you acquire. (We learn *something* from everyone we are with—*every time* we are with them.) Given this, investing your time with wise people and good books is a critical factor in acquiring wisdom. Furthermore, if you are young and your experience is calendar-limited, you can leverage wisdom from others who are older and wiser.

Why Does Wisdom Reside with Age?

"*Phronesis* is the ability to think about how and why we should act in order to change things, and especially to change our lives for the better. According to Aristotle, phronesis isn't simply a skill since it involves not only the ability to decide how to achieve a certain end, but also the ability to reflect upon and determine that end. Aristotle claimed that the acquisition of phronesis requires time, as one must gain both the habit and understanding of correct deliberation:

> While young men become geometricians and mathematicians and wise in matters like these, it is thought that a young man of practical wisdom cannot be found. The cause is that such wisdom is concerned not only with universals but with particulars, which become familiar from experience, but a young man has no experience, for it is length of time that gives experience.

Phronesis is concerned with *particulars*, because it is concerned with how to act in particular situations. One can learn the principles of action [book learning], but applying them in the real world, in situations one could not have foreseen, requires experience of the world."[8]

How Is the Wisdom Factor Used?

Few would argue with the notion that having more knowledge is a good thing. And gaining more knowledge is straightforward: it is dependent on the time and effort you devote to the task. Experience is largely the same. It takes time and effort to be involved with others, and better experiences have a direct effect on the wisdom that comes as a result. As the Wisdom Factor equation dictates, experience helps you synthesize your knowledge into wisdom. This is why the importance of positioning yourself to gain the best training and experience possible is so important as you select a college and make career choices. (Your wisdom factor is equally important in the area of choosing a mate, but that is for another book.)

Note that, in the formula, knowledge is *added* to intelligence, but experience *multiplies* the sum of intelligence and knowledge. Why is this?

To best illustrate why experience carries so much weight in the Wisdom Factor calculation, consider this. Have you ever known people that you would describe as "very smart" yet who were without a college degree? Perhaps for some reason they were not afforded the opportunity to gain additional formal education because of life circumstances. Yet we describe them as "very bright," having "street smarts," or maybe having a great deal of "common sense."

They are often very successful in their endeavors because they were gifted with a good mind. If these same people have a great deal of life experience and have read and studied on their own, we have ample reason to consider them to be very wise. Their experience and autodidactic undertakings mitigate their lack of formal education to a large degree. I have known many great men and women in this category who have had a significant impact on my life. Some of them were close mentors from whom I learned many valuable lessons.

On the other hand, I have known people who possessed extraordinarily high IQs and three college degrees but who had little or no experience in the "real world." This is a person we might describe as very well educated, but not necessarily wise. The contrast between these two types of people shows why the equation places a much higher value on experience than knowledge.

Let's look at some examples of various types of individuals and their Wisdom Factors.

On a scale of 1 to 10, a person with extraordinary intelligence (even genius level) with limited experience and no lifelong learning motivation results in lower wisdom. That equation, $(I + K) \times E = W$, would look like this:

$$(10 + 4) \times 1 = 14$$

His attitude will directly affect his wisdom, and thus, his options will be limited.

Another example: High intelligence (3.0 GPA), just graduated, but has a great drive to learn from books and mentors—and works hard. Here is her equation:

$$(7 + 7) \times 1 = 14$$

Her high lifelong learning score (for knowledge acquisition) puts her Wisdom Factor on par with the honors graduate in the first example.

There's an old saying: "School is a place where former A students teach B students to work for C students." While it is an extreme generalization meant to be somewhat humorous, the spirit of this quip represents the essence of lifelong learning and the importance of getting the right kind of experience and turning it into practical wisdom for life.

NOTE: The knowledge score of 4 might seem low because it is also measuring an *ongoing commitment* to learn—not only the base knowledge acquired from his formal education. The knowledge element has this weighting characteristic because, in our information age, most of his learning will be obsolete in a matter of years. "Increasingly, anything you learn is going to become obsolete within a decade," says Larry Summers, the former secretary of the Treasury and president of Harvard. "The most important kind of learning is about how to learn."[9]

Freshly minted graduates like we've seen in our first two examples are naturally going to have limited total scores because of the low experience (time) factor. Their commitment to lifelong learning will be a difference maker as the experience comes. Here are other examples of those with more working years under their belts.

This person has high intelligence, earned a college degree, and has been working in her field for ten-plus years. She has also been fully engaged in a formal lifelong learning curriculum (more on this later) for five-plus years:

$$(8 + 8) \times 4 = 64$$

You can see the enormous difference in her Wisdom Factor as a commitment to aggressively acquiring knowledge *times* experience brings leverage to bear in an exponential way. Remember, experience is not just time; it is also affected greatly by good positioning decisions. That means finding good opportunities, mentors, and companions who make you better.

It also means being able to *learn* from your experience—including mistakes. Sometimes we don't learn the right lesson from experience, which can actually drop our Wisdom Factor. Learning from others' experience is also important. I have a favorite maxim that says, "Learn from the mistakes of others. You don't have the time or money to make them all yourself."

One more example: A person who did not have the opportunity to get a formal education, but who has above-average intelligence, has been a voracious reader for ten-plus years (a dedicated lifelong learner), surrounds himself with wise people, and has twenty-plus years of experience in the working world:

$$(7 + 8) \times 7 = 105$$

In analyzing all three elements—intelligence, knowledge, and experience—we can conclude that the *most* controllable factor, which is dependent completely on you—and which will determine your life's successes more than any other—is *lifelong learning*, i.e., obtaining more knowledge that you can pour into your experiences. (Finding wise advisors in the experience category is also *mostly* dependent on you.)

By understanding and applying the Wisdom Factor Equation, you are combining your formal educational training with the Old School Advantage tools and will soon be

NOTE: In chapter 7, during step 9 of our decision-making section, we talked about "seeking wise counsel for confirmation." By assessing *their* Wisdom Factor, you can now evaluate a prospective mentor's advising qualifications using a more quantitative approach.

implementing a LifeLong Learning GamePlan as well. This is a prescription for an ever-rising Wisdom Factor. Imagine what this means! As you gain more knowledge and experience, there will be no limits to acquiring more wisdom, and you can thus pursue your personal purpose with confidence. And you can start *now*. The results are *inevitable*.

> Is not wisdom found among the aged? Does not long life bring understanding?[10]

Here is a simple yet important example from American manufacturing history in which an everyday working man drew on his knowledge and experience—then took an idea to the right person and changed industry forever.

"The art of analogy flows from creative re-categorization and the information that we extract from surprising sources. Take the invention of the moving assembly line. Credit for this break-through typically goes to Henry Ford, but it was actually the brainchild of a young Ford mechanic named Bill Klann. After watching butchers at a meat-packing plant disassemble carcasses moving past them along an overhead trolley, Klann thought that auto workers could assemble cars through a similar process by adding pieces to a chassis moving along rails.

> Overcoming significant management skepticism, Klann and his cohorts built a moving assembly line. Within *four* months, Ford's line had cut the time it took to build a Model T from 12 hours per vehicle to just 90 minutes. In short order, the moving assembly line revolutionized manufacturing and unlocked trillions of dollars in economic potential. And while in retrospect this innovation may seem like a simple, obvious step forward, it wasn't; the underlying analogy between moving disassembly and moving assembly had eluded everyone until Klann grasped its potential."[11]

The American economy has never been the same because a young man—without a college degree but wise beyond his years—looked in the window of a butcher shop and said, "Aha!"

Which of *your* ideas will change the world?

Accomplished to a Degree
—Even Without One

Conventional wisdom dictates that if you can get a college degree, by all means, do so. I still hold to this view, and so should you. However, the following list proves that if you apply yourself to obtaining knowledge and experience (for yourself and from others)—no matter the circumstances—you can succeed in your *vocation*.[12]

- **History's most eminent figures**—da Vinci, Galileo, Beethoven, and Rembrandt—received only a moderate amount of education, equal to about the middle of college or less.

- **Abraham Lincoln** dropped out of school at age twelve yet became a self-educated lawyer and the sixteenth president.

- **Harry Truman** was the only twentieth-century president without a college degree. As a voracious reader, he often dazzled visiting dignitaries with the breadth of his knowledge.

- **Walt Disney** dropped out of high school at sixteen, joined the Red Cross, left for Europe, and later founded the Walt Disney Corporation.

- **F. Scott Fitzgerald** left Princeton University due to poor grades. He became one of the most famous American authors of all time.

- **Ralph Lauren** left Baruch College after two semesters to serve in the US Army and then became CEO and founder of Polo Brand.

- **John Lennon** was expelled from Liverpool College. He decided to join a band.

- **Wolfgang Puck** quit school at fourteen, became a cooking apprentice at a hotel, and is now one of the most well-known chefs in the world.
- **Steve Jobs** dropped out of Reed College and became founder of Apple.
- **Bill Gates** dropped out of Harvard, founded Microsoft, and became the wealthiest man in the world.
- **Oprah Winfrey** dropped out of Tennessee State University. She became a television icon.
- **Brad Pitt** was on track to become a journalist but dropped out of the University of Missouri *two weeks* before graduation.
- **Mark Zuckerberg** left Harvard, invented Facebook, and became one of the richest men in the world.

Becoming *wise*, however, is a different matter . . .

Overcoming the Challenge That Is Changing Our Brains

Now that you understand that *you can take control* of the pace at which you acquire wisdom, I will show you *why* gaining wisdom is so difficult in our age. Even so, know this: you can not only overcome this challenge but thrive in the midst of it.

I stated earlier that wisdom is rare. Sadly, this has been the case in all ages. But today, it seems to be so scarce that we might actually be living in an *anti-wisdom* age. By this, I don't mean to imply that wisdom is not desired nor sought after. Rather, I fear that wisdom is presumed to exist in our *machines*. In chapter 1, you learned how the electronic information age is affecting our memories. Regretfully, it is affecting our acquisition of wisdom as well.

We are being led to believe that because artificial brains are more efficient in many ways, this efficiency can equate to wisdom. This is a misnomer of the highest order. We might be able to transfer data to our computers, but decisions that are meant for our deepest discernment must be seen and understood through the prism of our unique human personalities and *experiences*.

As author Michael Harris terms it, we are living in a world of "continuous partial attention." He cites Nielsen research showing that the average teenager now manages upward of four thousand text messages every month.[13] And this number will only increase. Glowing rectangles give us little time for *creating* content because we spend so much time simply *managing* it. We live in an "ecosystem of interruption technologies."[14]

A prime example of this "interruption" is the act of communicating *about* an experience in real time, which actually supplants the experience *itself* (pan to a family of four on vacation in a unique restaurant, all peering soullessly into their smartphones). We must reverse this and other recent lifestyle trends because our slavery to technology is literally *changing our brains*.

More Information, Less Wisdom.

Roman philosopher Seneca said, "To be everywhere is to be nowhere." In consuming data, we ourselves are being consumed. As Nicholas Carr, author of *The Shallows*, explains, "We no longer have the patience to await time's slow and scrupulous winnowing. Inundated at every moment by information of immediate interest, we have little choice but to resort to automated filters, which grant their privilege, instantaneously, to the new and the popular. On the Net, the winds of opinion have become a whirlwind."[15] We have a decision to make. We can be under the direction of cyberspace traffic cops, or we can seize the opportunity and do things differently.

As our time staring at rectangles increases, contemplation time—the place where wisdom takes hold—is reduced dramatically. We are paying a high price for this. We need to understand the value difference between information we get from the rapid-fire pace of the cyber world versus the deeper value gleaned from an old-school habit of *scheduled* deep reading, with its beneficial impact on our right brains.

When discussing how memory works in chapter 1, we briefly touched on the concept of neuroplasticity of the brain. Evidence indicates that our brain cells grow bigger with use and weaken when not used. We also learned that our brain cells and pathways change continuously; it is just a matter of how they are changing. We naturally skim newspapers and articles, but if skimming text (as we also do on digital devices) has become the primary mode of reading, this is a problem. In this mode, we become "mere decoders of information."[16] This means that the part of the brain that makes rich connections, which are formed when we read and contemplate deeply without distraction, is disengaged.[17]

In other words, *we lose the bed of knowledge that we must draw from in order to gain and then apply wisdom.* Nicholas Carr provides a fuller explanation in *The Shallows*:

> If working [short term] memory is the mind's scratch pad, then long-term memory is its filing system. The contents of our long-term memory lie mainly outside of our consciousness. In order for us to think about something we're previously learned or experienced, our brain has to transfer the memory from long-term memory back into working memory. It was once assumed that long-term memory served merely as a big warehouse of facts, impressions, and events, that it played little part in complex cognitive processes such as thinking and problem-solving. But brain scientists have come to realize that long-term memory is actually the seat of understanding. It stores not just facts but complex concepts.

Carr quotes Australian educational psychologist John Sweller, who says, "Our intellectual prowess is derived largely from the schemas [complex concepts] we have acquired over long periods of time. We are able to understand concepts in our areas of expertise because we have schemas associated with those concepts."

"The depth of our intelligence [wisdom]," Carr himself continues, "hinges on our ability to transfer information from working memory to long-term memory and weave it into conceptual schemes. But the passage from working memory to long-term memory also forms the major bottleneck in our brain. Unlike long-term memory, which has a vast capacity, working memory is able to hold only a very small amount of information."

In explaining the transference of information from our working memory into our long-term memory, Carr provides the illustration of using a thimble to fill a bathtub with water. He points out how media play a strong role in the process by controlling the speed and intensity of information flow. For example, during the time we are reading a book, the "information faucet," as Carr describes it, provides a steady drip that we can regulate by determining how fast we read. In essence, through our single-minded focus on the book's text, we can transfer the information thimbleful by thimbleful from the text into our long-term memory "and forge the rich associations essential to the creation of schemas."

Carr goes on to explain that the Internet provides numerous information faucets. Our "thimble" quickly overflows, and thus we cannot possibly transfer all the information to long-term memory. Therefore, "we're unable to retain the information or to draw connections with the information already stored in our long-term memory. . . . Our ability to learn suffers, and our understanding remains shallow (thus his book title). . . . We become mindless consumers of data."

The serious implication here is that if we are unable to extract what we have learned from our brains, it is as if we have *never* learned it. Practically speaking, an experience not remembered is an experience that *never* occurred—and thus wisdom *never* acquired or shared. A continual diet of information acquired only through electronic mediums, with no contemplative supplementation, is like eating only "comfort food" at every meal. The satisfaction we get is short term, and the long-term effects are dire.

Given this, what is the solution?

DEEP READING

Deep reading is a meditative act that allows the "disengag[ing] of attention from the outward flow of passing stimuli in order to engage more deeply with an inward flow of words, ideas, and emotions."[18] The words in books strengthen our ability to think abstractly and enrich our experience of the physical world outside the book.[19] This is the antithesis of rectangle surfing.

Deep reading is intellectually rewarding because it "understimulates the senses," allowing you to minimize distractions and engage in deep *thinking*. The mind is calm.[20] Today, the challenge is to find time for both gathering data and contemplating the data we have gathered. The first is done in the manic world of the information age matrix; the latter is done in the quietness of a back porch swing.

Guaranteed Mediocrity

"I never read books." If this sentence is coming out of your mouth, you are chaining yourself to a post of mediocrity for life.

Napoleon Hill, legendary author of *Think and Grow Rich*, said:

"The person who stops studying merely because he has finished school is forever hopelessly doomed to mediocrity, no matter what may be his calling. The way of success is the way of continuous pursuit of knowledge."

Tom Corley, author of *Rich Habits*, found that rich people read (and listen to) books at a much higher rate than poor people: "63 percent of wealthy parents make their children read two or more non-fiction books a month vs. 3 percent of poor." Also, "63 percent of wealthy listen to audio books during commute to work vs. 5 percent of poor people."

Reading nonfiction (as well as fiction) can help reduce stress, enhance creativity, and boost your memory.

The wisest men would tell you they are always learners, and they are humbled to find how little they know after all. The great Sir Isaac Newton used to say that "he felt himself no better than a little child, who had picked up a few precious stones on the shore of the sea of knowledge."[21]

If you read—you succeed. It is that simple.

As I mentioned in the introduction, we don't often "go on a walk" anymore. But studies have revealed that after spending time in a quiet setting, close to nature, we have greater attentiveness, better memory, and improved cognition. Our brains become calmer and sharper. Why? Because we aren't being barraged by external stimuli. We can relax. Our working memories (short-term) are off duty because of the absence of distractions. The result is that we find a state of contemplation. This is the same thing that happens during deep reading. The net, on the other hand, diminishes our capacity to contemplate. It not only alters our thoughts but hinders our deep emotions as well.[22]

This introspective ability is exemplified in the lives of the notable men and women of history. As William Powers explains, "Great artists, thinkers, and leaders all have an unusual capacity to be 'grasped' by some idea or mission, an inner engagement that drives them to pursue a vision, undaunted by obstacles. Ludwig van Beethoven, Michelangelo, Emily Dickinson, Albert Einstein, Martin Luther King, Jr.—we call them 'brilliant,' as if it were pure intelligence that made them who they were. But what unites them is what they did with their intelligence, the depth they reached in their thinking and brought to bear in their work."[23] It is not a coincidence that these greats knew the importance of meditating on their life and their work—and that they did not have to deal with the technological distractions we experience today.

One book, printed in the heart's own wax /
Is worth a thousand in the stacks.

—Jan Luyken, Dutch Poet

"Augustine was said to be so steeped in the Psalms that they, as much as Latin itself, comprised the principle language in which he wrote."[24] The ancient way of reading was totally different from how we read today. People didn't read books; they *meditated* on them.

The practice of deep reading, which became widespread even among the masses after Gutenberg's historic invention, could well continue to fade in our lifetimes, "becoming the province of a small and dwindling elite."[25] In fact, deep reading might ultimately be considered nothing more than a brief "anomaly" in our intellectual history.[26]

John Adams said Thomas Jefferson was chosen as the writer of the Declaration of Independence because he had a "happy talent for composition and singular felicity of expression." Translation: He was wise beyond his years (only thirty-two at the time), largely because he was so well read—thus, he was the right man for the job. (By the time the British burned the US Capitol and the Library of Congress in 1814, Jefferson had acquired the largest personal collection of books in the United States. Jefferson sold his library of more than sixty-four hundred volumes to Congress as a replacement.)

A modern day example of a successful business leader who was a voracious reader at a young age is investor extraordinaire Warren Buffett. "[He] says by age eleven he had read every book on the subject of investing in the Omaha Public Library. Today he's a billionaire forty-five times over."[27]

So, could those who employ a disciplined and purposeful strategy of deep reading become a powerful "reading class," thus owning an increasingly rare form of cultural capital?[28] I am convinced this is indeed what *will* happen.

And if I am right, you will have the *opportunity of a lifetime.*

Grad School, Anyone?

If you are a freshly minted college graduate and want to continue your formal education, or if you are considering going back for more, consider this.

If you have a left-brain degree already—business, engineering, math, science, etc.—then your vocation and area of expertise is ever more susceptible to being turned into an algorithm and commoditized. Consider diversifying your knowledge base.

It is critical to develop your right-brain capabilities as the world of commerce increasingly demands creativity. In fact, according to Geoff Colvin in his book *Talent is Overrated*, the right-brain shift is now widespread enough that the MFA—master of fine arts—is gaining ground on the MBA as the preferred graduate degree for young adults heading into business fields.

NOTE: Two subjects that are not specifically listed amongst the four quadrants are Math and Science. There is some overlap with these areas in the quadrants. Because these two areas tend to be covered more thoroughly in formalized education programs, they will be picked up under the "Miscellaneous" category on occasion.

Your LifeLong Learning GamePlan

It is time to create your LifeLong Learning GamePlan. This plan is predicated on the concept of *360-degree instruction* through various books that provide a balanced approach to new knowledge. Each of the 90-degree quadrants deals with a different aspect of life. They are: History/Government, Economics/Finance, Psychology/Sociology, and Family/Faith/Miscellaneous.

A person who won't read has no real advantage over one who can't read.

—Mark Twain

Step 1 is to create a curriculum of the books you read within the "360-degree view."

Let's say that you happen to be in the financial services business. You would naturally have an interest or *leaning* in that direction. Therefore, the Economics/Finance quadrant would weigh heavier in your curriculum. Economics/Finance could be considered your "Old School major." If you also loved history (like me), that, too, would be a leaning. It could be considered your minor. You then could weigh the other categories accordingly. Assuming you decided that you wanted to read *two books per month* this year, you might set these parameters based on your leanings:

History/Government	6
Economics/Finance	9
Psychology/Sociology	4
Family/Faith/Fiction/Misc	5

With this plan in place, you get the bulk of your learning in the areas where your primary interests lie, yet you also get ample exposure to other areas, broadening your knowledge base and perspective. This helps you in three ways:

1. You can take advantage of the *crossover effect* of all subject areas. For example, economics is affected by government, history, and psychology—at a minimum. Not only does this give you a clearer understanding of other subject areas; you will also be amazed at how much better you will become in the areas where you already feel proficient. Don't worry about acquiring knowledge that is not immediately useful. It will reside in your long-term memory for use at some opportune time in the future.

2. You can *connect on a personal level* with *anyone*, from *anywhere*, with any *vocation* or *interests*. (You are about to become the most interesting person in *any* room. Remember LAVA?)

3. You can *optimize* your *Wisdom Factor*.

NOTE: Don't panic if you are thinking that two books per month are more than you want to commit to. This is just an example. One book per month is still twelve per year. The average American reads *fewer than one book per year*. What a tremendous opportunity this is for you to soar above the average! That said, I know there are some of you—once you grasp the value of this process—who will exceed one hundred books per year. You think that is crazy? We'll see.

Step 2 is to drill down to more specific topics for your books that fall within your broad parameters from Step 1. To arrive at the right mix for your LifeLong Learning curriculum, you simply filter various aspects of your life through the four categories contained in the LAVA technique introduced in chapter 3. Using me as an example, here is how this information can guide you:

Locations: Where you are *from*, live *now*, or *wish* to live? Where do you like to go on *vacation*?

Answer: I grew up in West Texas. I now live in Dallas. I most enjoy vacations where I need a sweater or light jacket and am open to traveling anywhere in the world.

How can these answers guide me in my LifeLong GamePlan book selections? Well, for example, I might be interested in a history book on the Dustbowl since my hometown was located at ground zero. Maybe the JFK assassination is especially interesting since I now live in the city where that fateful day in 1963 changed our nation. Or I might want to study Napoleon in preparation for an upcoming visit to France.

The idea is to match books to your life events, interests, talents, and so forth in order to make you a more well-rounded person and thus provide ample opportunity for knowledge synthesis to raise your Wisdom Factor.

Let's continue.

Associations: Where did you go to school? To which organizations do you belong? Whom do you most want to emulate?

Answer: My alma mater is Texas A&M. I belong to Toastmasters. My boyhood hero was Coach John Wooden.

If I am looking for a recreational book in the miscellaneous category, I might want to read anything about SEC football because I am an Aggie. A biography of John Wooden is also an obvious choice (I have read them all). *The Psychology of Public Speaking* would be a book title that interests me.

Can you see how this works? I would then go through the same exercise in the areas of *Vocations* and *Avocations*, and I would choose books in each of the 90-degree quadrants that fit my profile. The available books are unlimited. (In 2012, more than 290,000 books were published in the United States alone. An estimated 2.2 million are published *each year* worldwide. And Google estimates there to be more than 130 million books available in the world.[29])

For the first year of your reading plan, you should start with a short list of "must reads" to get you up to speed in some critical areas. These might or might not be in your area of expertise or your leaning. These can be interspersed throughout your first year. After that, you don't have to choose all the books for your plan each January. I recommend choosing books one to three months ahead of time because there are so many that will get your attention throughout the year. The key is to stay disciplined as a life-changing leader and to end the year having covered all the quadrants as they were allocated. I will warn you—in nearly every case where the LifeLong Learning GamePlan is implemented, the number of books the readers actually read exceeded their January projection.

> All great books point out the emerging truth in a way that allows us to stop overlooking it.
>
> —Annette Simmons

You might ask, "Why do I need a 'GamePlan' just to read books?"

The LifeLong Learning GamePlan is a plan put *in writing*. Again, life-changing leaders know that their chances of success are dramatically increased when they write things down and track them. When you do this, you are using the Commitment and Consistency influence technique on yourself! (This is the same concept used for keeping a household budget, as discussed earlier.)

And here is a LifeLong Learning bonus for you if you happen to be a technophile: by entering the contemplative world of good books, you can enhance your knowledge and wisdom to make your *social media* encounters more meaningful as well. The idea is simple: to lead happy, productive lives in a connected world, we must [strategically] disconnect.[30] The LifeLong Learning GamePlan helps this happen.

How to Read Twenty-Five Books in One Year

Leaders are readers. It is undeniable. "But twenty-five books is a lot!" you say. Truly, it is. Especially when you consider that, according to a HuffPost/YouGov poll of one thousand Americans in 2013, almost a third of Americans read *zero* books each year, and fewer than three out of ten read more than ten books per year.[31] If you are a full-time student, you get a pass for now. Your lifelong learning can start ninety days after graduation. You deserve a break. But for the rest of you, here is some practical advice to help you become a voracious reader and great leader:

- **Start each day reading.** Having your reading time first thing in the morning is refreshing, stimulating, and allows you to always say you accomplished something today—even if nothing else great happens. If you tell yourself, "I will do it later," you most assuredly will not do it consistently. Forming this daily habit is a discipline that will pay off for you again and again in both your personal and professional life.

- **Defining "reading time."** This can include time for meditation, prayer, and contemplation. But it should definitely include reading books (not just periodicals). Contrary to popular belief, you *can* read several books at once just like you can multitask at work or watch different television programs at different times of the day. I prefer the Faith/Family and Psychology/Sociology genres in the morning, Economics/Finance at lunch, and History/Fiction and all others in the evening. Fit your reading "channels" to your moods.

- **E-reader or hard copy?** The obvious old-school answer here is hard copy. But I must admit that my personal reading reached a voracious pitch in early 2009 after I purchased my first e-reader. The ability to download a book within ten seconds (at a generally cheaper price) and carry all of my books with me, allowing me to "change channels" (books) depending on my reading mood, trumps the nice feel of a paper book for me. A study in 2012 confirmed my own preferences and revealed that e-readers read nearly twice as many books each year as readers of hardcopies.[32] (To redeem some of my old-school cred with you, I always buy the hardback version for my shelf.)

- **Only twenty-five minutes, twice per day.** That is all it takes to read twenty-five books per year. This assumes an average book size of 250 pages at a reading pace of only about twenty pages per hour. (This is plenty of time to highlight frequently and contemplate fully.) You can also accomplish this by reading fifty minutes at one sitting each day. *Here's an easy formula:* The number of books you wish to read per year is equal to half the minutes you read per day. (E.g., if you want to read fifty books per year, then spend fifty minutes *twice* per day reading.)

Get started today!

Heraclitus said, "No man ever steps in the same river twice." This is an understood truth for the dedicated lifelong learner. Once you implement your LifeLong Learning GamePlan, your life will change—for the better, forever. There is no avoiding it. The rest of Heraclitus's quote is ". . . for other waters are ever flowing on to you." Each volume you read brings "new waters" that affect *who you are*—and thus enhance your ability to live out your personal purpose.

The inspired text says, "A wise man is surrounded by a multitude of advisors" (Prov. 15:22). Those "advisors" can come in the form of humans that you surround yourself with or the books wise men and women from every age have written. Both sources will enrich your level of success and significance.

> When you sell a man a book, you don't sell him just twelve ounces of paper and ink and glue—you sell him a whole new life.
>
> —J. Gottschall

Combining LAVA and LifeLong Learning

"Everyone who was ever a guest of Theodore Roosevelt was astonished at the range and diversity of his knowledge. Whether his visitor was a cowboy or a Rough Rider, a New York politician or a diplomat, Roosevelt knew what to say. And how was it done? The answer was simple. Whenever Roosevelt expected a visitor, he sat up late the night before, reading up on the subject in which he knew his guest was particularly interested. For Roosevelt knew, as all leaders know, that the royal road to a person's heart is to talk about the things he or she treasures most."[33]

THE PERIODIC TABLE OF BOOKS

As you add books you have read to your Old School résumé, there will come a time when you can't keep up with them all. My solution was to create a "Periodic Table of Books" (PTB) that not only visually documents my progress but is also an invaluable tool for easily referencing material I might need for writing, speaking, or making book recommendations to a friend, coworker, or Old School student. (It also looks very cool on your wall.)

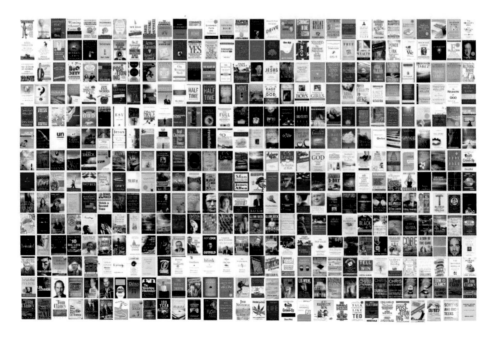

NOTE: Revisit the classics. Consider rereading books that you read years ago in high school or college. You might be surprised by the different perspective you will discover. This is because your Wisdom Factor has increased!

I use mine every day.

What does your PTB look like today? What will it look like five years from now?

Now imagine the enjoyment and advantage you would have if you were engaged with other like-minded lifelong learners as they grow their own PTBs. For several years, I have hosted monthly luncheons where approximately twelve to eighteen friends of all ages come together to share our individual perspectives on the books we read together. (At times, more than half of the participants were over sixty-five years of age. Talk about a gathering of wisdom! One gentleman—age eighty-two—reads more than sixty books per year!) The richness of those discussions adds a significant dimension to our lives as we interact with those from different backgrounds and disciplines.

Surrounding yourself with wise thinkers on all sides of your life creates a "living think tank." It is an effective way to take John Stuart Mill's advice to heart: "Very few facts are able to tell their own story, without comments to bring out their meaning. The only way in which a human being can make some approach to knowing the whole of a subject, is by hearing what can be said about it by persons of every variety of opinion."

LifeLong Learning in Real Life

Here is a true story about a young professional and his results from becoming a LifeLong Learner.

Mike was valedictorian of his high school class. (I've changed his name here, as he is a humble man.) As a freshman, he earned a scholarship to one of the largest and most prestigious state universities in the country. Even then, to make ends meet, Mike worked fast food jobs on the side while taking a full load of classes. After a successful academic career, combined with marriage to the love of his life, Mike became successful in his vocational endeavors as well. Three beautiful daughters were added along the way, and he continued on a rising professional trajectory—now fifteen years in.

Yet, while his foundational education was excellent and he was dedicated to staying on pace with the expertise he needed to excel at his profession, Mike was not a reader, per se. One day, his employer "suggested" a unique opportunity. Mike was given a chance to enroll in a lifelong learning program at work.

He began reading, and some of the books had nothing to do with his vocation. But he trusted his mentor and kept reading. He was reluctant at first, but then . . . something happened. Mike liked it. He came to understand the 360-degree concept and the power of the crossover effect. He felt more comfortable in business and social situations and, quite frankly, he just felt wise beyond his years. Humble, mind you, but wise.

The proof of the lifelong learning pudding became clearly evident one evening for Mike when he was on the road visiting a client. Thirty-something Mike found himself at a dinner party arranged especially for him in order to meet a dozen of his client's closest friends. It was a great opportunity to meet some high-quality people and perhaps even start relationships that could lead to new friends and maybe even some new business relationships. The trouble was, the average age of the guests was over seventy—with the youngest still being north of sixty. A generation and a half is a big gap. Most people Mike's age would see this as an intimidating atmosphere—watching the clock and hoping to escape the evening without a major faux pas. Not Mike.

He relished it. He seized it. And upon arriving back at his office, he related the experience to his boss and mentor, exclaiming, "I have *never* felt more comfortable in a business or social situation. I had complete command of the room. There was no topic of conversation I did not feel comfortable engaging in. The eighty-plus books I have read in my LifeLong Learning 360-degree program prepared me unimaginably well. I am so blessed to have crossed paths with you. Thank you."

In fewer than five years, Mike's Wisdom Factor (WF) went from this:

$$(9 + 4) \times 3 = 39$$

To this:

$$(9 + 8) \times 6 = 102$$

NOTE: If you lead a team in any organization, the lifelong learning/360-degree concept will allow you to create "living libraries"[34] full of experts who can provide a constant stream of knowledge to customers and colleagues alike. You can develop a culture of institutional brainpower that will be powerfully beneficial.

He took his solid formal education and excelled as a young professional with a moderate amount of working experience. But then, because he positioned himself for great opportunities and surrounded himself with good people who challenged him and sharpened his skills, he accepted the challenge of LifeLong Learning. And the payoffs have only just begun, because his knowledge and experience scores are both headed to 10.

It is time for you to join Mike.

Children are the living messages we send to a time we will not see.

—John W. Whitehead

A Legacy Gift

Life is so busy it seems we rarely take the time to ask questions of our family, whether questions about the big "important" things or the small, lovely things. Then, when our family members are gone, it is too late to get the answers. I learned this the hard way when my wife passed at the young age of forty-four. She left me with two boys aged ten and fourteen. We have been blessed to be able to move on to happiness and fulfillment in new relationships and new circumstances. However, it motivated me to document things for my boys as a father that they did not get from their mom.

This is so important because individual character is passed down from parents to children through stories and experiences. Parents pass on the life narratives that describe what they have lived through, where they came from, and how they acted during the different seasons of their lives. These accounts provide the next generation with a foundation and understanding of their family values and create an underlying belief system to help guide them in their own lives. Given this, I chose to do as much as I could for my children.

To accomplish this, I used a wonderful little book titled *Questions for My Father* as a guide to answer dozens of questions. I then gave the handwritten document to each of my boys as a high school graduation gift. The questions it contains can be used for moms too. Take the opportunity to pass on your wisdom, and give a gift to your loved ones they will never forget.

CONCLUSION

I suspect you now realize that *The Old School Advantage* has been about lifelong learning all along. The five tools you learned in the first half of this book are designed to put you in the best possible position to achieve the purpose for your life. But learning the Old School Advantage skills and then not developing and implementing a LifeLong Learning GamePlan is tantamount to having the tools for digging out the gold but not going to the mine to draw it out. This goldmine consists of the wise counselors you come to know and the mountain of great books you will read over the decades you have remaining. To forgo this great opportunity is a recipe for perpetual entry-level career status and personal mediocrity. You can instead carry out a plan that effectively provides you with *"CE credits for life,"* and every day is another chance to start.

Regardless of your age, your knowledge and skills become obsolete at a rapid rate. As legendary basketball coach Pat Riley said, "Anytime you stop striving to get better, you're bound to get worse." You must continually upgrade your skills. The advantages are substantial: greater capabilities, motivation, and confidence. The equation is simple: the more you learn, the more you *can* learn. As Brian Tracy says, "School is never out for the professional."

Each time I teach an Old School Advantage workshop, I ask the same question at the end of it. "What would happen to our country if every citizen had learned what you have learned today?" The answer is always essentially the same. "It would change the world, forever, for the better." The exciting thing is that this same question can be asked and answered the same way after *every* book you read along your journey. Every worthy book is life changing—and thus world changing.

Cervantes said, "The journey is better than the inn." Though you might not know exactly where you are going, it won't matter because you are equipped. And even when searching for something that you might not find, you will almost certainly find things you don't expect. Some of them will be great discoveries along the way.

And so changing the world starts with you—*today*. The biographies of great people are full of accounts of long hours they spent sitting by a river, roaming through the woods, and simply daydreaming. Developing your inner life is one of the most constructive and important things you can do. It starts with you finding your "sacred space" and, even if only for a few minutes each day, being quiet and still—first in meditation or prayer and then by diving deep into good books. In those times of reflection, you will replace the noise and distractions the world offers with the tried and true practices of the Old School.

> Live as if you will die tomorrow. Learn as though you will live forever.
>
> —Mahatma Gandhi

AFTERWORD

The only thing worse than being blind is
having sight but no vision.

—Helen Keller

There are reminders throughout this book that *it is not just what you do, but who you are* that is most important. You are now due a more complete explanation of what I mean by this.

The counterfeit success of simply "getting more" or "getting mine" has led to what has been called a "Monday to Friday sort of dying."[1] It is a "failure by success" condition that ironically creates stress and anxiety because as you get more, you worry more about losing what you have.[2] This is an all-too-common American lifestyle mentality that focuses on *what you do*. But your life must instead have a *calling*. And when you are called, you must go.

You learned about the importance of definitions. Defining success as "pertaining to those things that are significant, good, and lasting" will satisfy your soul. And who you become in your pursuit of excellence is worth exponentially more than any personal achievement. This is because the success you achieve for yourself is most valuable when it is conveyed to others—thus transforming success into *significance* and a transcendent *purpose*.

You must pursue your *purpose* not only by employing personal strengths and talents but also by being intentional about finding leaders, mentors, and opportunities that bring out your gifts. You must position yourself to have a "multiplier effect" in your community—which includes family, work, and other associations. Nelson Mandela said, "Your playing small does not serve the world." You are at your noblest, most virtuous, and largest when you are given over to a cause that is greater than you are.

Augustine said that asking yourself, "What do I want to be remembered for?" is the beginning of adulthood. It speaks to your legacy. And how *do* you want to be remembered? As just a "nice" or "good" person? What if you instead considered what type of "capital" you will leave behind? And *capital* could certainly refer to *financial* assets, such as an inheritance might comprise. That would be great. But what about leaving *social* capital—the family traditions and values you hold dear? Or *spiritual* capital, which gets to the heart of *who you are* and the *wisdom* you want to pass on?

Consider this. If you have your first child at age thirty, then in forty years, you might be talking to your ten-year-old grandchild. Whatever you teach that grandchild when you are seventy, assume that, at age seventy, he will teach *his* ten-year-old grandchild in the same way. If that great-great-grandchild of yours then lives only to age seventy—and he chooses *not* to pass on the wisdom that started with your child and carried on to your grandchild—then your instruction will *still* have affected the lives of your family for the next 150 years. Imagine what our world will look like a century and a half from now. The need for discernment and wisdom will be greater than ever.

And if you are retired and banking on a life of leisure that you feel you have earned, may I humbly extend to you a new and greater challenge? UNretire. At least to the extent that you can. We need you. And the question of the hour is this: What wisdom will you pass on to the coming generations—including and especially your own family?

I encourage you to live with your *eulogy* in mind, not your *résumé*. Résumés are about power, wealth, and achievement. Simply put, they are about *what you do*. Eulogies are about developing the qualities of character that friends and relatives will speak of while standing over your casket. Honesty, humility, self-control, courage—these things take time and intentionality to develop and are ultimately worthwhile.[3] They are about *who you are*.

Character is destiny.

—Heraclitus

I am reminded of a man named Daniel who lived in Israel circa the sixth century BC. He is perhaps best known for his survival in the "lion's den"—a story heard by many children in Sunday school. Many don't know that Daniel was around eighty years old in that story, but long before, he had made a name for himself as a young man. He and his people were captured and carried into exile in a foreign land when he was in his late teens. Because of his extraordinary natural talents—and the fact that he was also a fast learner, hard working, tactful, and well educated—Daniel was consistent in character and integrity. He was uncompromising in his values—even in the face of danger, which threatened his very life on *multiple* occasions. These are the character traits by which he was noticed so that he could influence the leaders of his day. In fact, Daniel rose to prominent leadership positions under all three kings he served.

My hope and prayer for you as a reader of this book is that you too will be prepared to "sit before kings." As you continue to seek truth unto wisdom—with goals that are purpose filled and not only success oriented—you will surely influence those around you for good, whether they be rulers, employers, co-workers, friends, or family. Don't just look at your accomplishments to date. Be a life-changing leader who is continually reading more, learning more, and helping to build solid families, businesses, and communities. Focus on the impact you can have by leading a people-centered, cause-oriented life. Realize that your life here is only a vapor. Continually ask yourself, as Ben Franklin did each morning, "What good shall I do this day?"—and then, each evening, "What good have I done today?"

Finally, I want to say thank you. I appreciate your attention to the end. My original purpose for writing this book was my four kids—all Millennials. If you're a parent, you know there is no greater motivator than your children. If only one copy of this book existed, I would give it to them. If it helps them get on in life, then it was worth every one of the thousand hours it took to write it. But my hope is that it will help many others as well.

If you learned something within these pages, then I am humbled. To quote the undisputed genius Sir Isaac Newton, "If I have seen farther, it is by standing on the shoulders of giants." I have simply tried to be an earnest messenger of men and women of every age who are much wiser than I. I wish you the very best in all of your future endeavors.

James N. Whiddon

The purpose of life is a life of purpose.

—Unknown

ACKNOWLEDGMENTS

Augustine said that asking yourself, "What do I want to be remembered for?" is the beginning of adulthood. It speaks to one's legacy.

This book helps answer that question for me. I originally wrote it for my four children, who have many steps yet to take—and many questions left to ask. I pray this effort answers at least some of those questions as they endeavor to become life-changing leaders. I decided to publish this book so that their friends, my grandchildren, and others I could never meet might in some way also benefit—or perhaps even be inspired. All whom I acknowledge here continue to inspire me.

First things first: I am not an author as much as a compiler. The brilliant men and women whose excellent work I have referred to the reader deserve the credit for any worthy content. I admire and thank them for their dedication.

To those working on the ground day to day: Thank you to Calli Galati for her tireless devotion to the Old School mission. The countless hours she spent supporting me in this effort were vital to its completion. Gratitude is owed to my lifelong friend and coworker, Sid Walker, PhD. Your wise counsel and passion for this movement are forever appreciated. Thank you to Melanie Reeves as well for your energetic and "spot-on" coaching.

My early manuscript readers, who humored me when the idea was first presented, were critical in helping me find my direction. Thank you Dave Berry; David Anderson; Dr. Tom Pledger; Mike Warren; Carol Stall; Dr. Lee Jagers; Alex Booras; Mike Jorgensen; Dr. Frank Turek; Oran Cogdill; Joel Holyoak, PhD; David Vierling; Madelaine Pfau; Charles Jones; Sanjive Agarwala; Dawna Guzak; Ed Wales; Mark Hendricks; Chuck Lee; and my venerable and longtime mentor, Don Wass, PhD, whose counsel has been life-changing.

Thanks to my editors—Tim Boswell, PhD, and Mike Towle—for your professional guidance and also to Milli Brown and her extraordinary team at Brown Books. I am glad to be back home!

Thank you to my dear and adored wife, Nizie. You are my faithful companion and inspiration. Your bright intellect, vibrant personality, unwavering support, and sweet heart always keep me grounded and leaping for joy all at once. And to my children, who are my motivation: Johnathan, Analiese, Daniel, and Alexandra. Thank you for embracing the Old School ways. I love you.

Lastly, I thank my parents, Lawrence and Mary Jim. While gone now, they taught me to diligently seek truth and that the only life that can be called "successful" is one that also longs to be *significant*—by passing on Truth.

APPENDIX

MORE OLD SCHOOL RESOURCES FOR STUDENTS

Test-Taking Tips[1]

You might yet be in the formal education stage of your learning journey, in which structured testing is still required. If so, these test-taking pointers will help ensure your success.

General:

- Before the test, eat light. Avoiding heavy foods will keep blood in your brain, not your stomach.
- Have your memory palaces loaded and ready.
- Round One: Answer easy questions first—skip the more complex.
- Round Two: Count remaining (harder) questions and divide your remaining time. Leave ten minutes to review.
- Circle crucial words in questions.

Multiple-Choice Rules:

- Questions usually have two obviously wrong answers. Eliminate them first. Then, one of the remaining two or three is correct.
- Take each remaining option as an independent true or false question.
- Don't be intimidated by *multiple-multiple* choice tests. They, too, are simply a group of true or false questions.
- C is *not* always the best answer to guess. Be more methodical.

Essay Rules:

- The grading is *relative* to other students, so the more *facts* you include, the better.

- Draw your mind map using a memory palace *before* writing.

- Use stock phrases from lectures (professors like seeing their own terms).

- Ask the professor: "I am not sure what is meant by number three when it says . . ." She might indirectly give you the answer!

- If you *don't know* the answer to the essay question(s) asked on the exam, *answer one you do know*. You will likely get credit for it—even if not full credit. (It's better than nothing, and showing that you know the subject well in some way cannot hurt you.)

NOTE: Scientists at the University of Washington found that the accuracy of ninety copy editors increased 21.3 percent when they listened to light classical music. What's more, thirty-six undergraduates at the University of California listened to ten minutes of Mozart's Sonata for Two Pianos in D Major (K. 448) and scored eight to nine points higher on their spatial IQ tests.[2]

Term Paper Rules:

- Understand clearly what is expected.

- Outline or mind map first, or do both.

- Check in with the professor early to see if you are on track.

- Write the first draft *early* in the process so you can edit *several* times. (The secret to good writing is *re*writing.)

Don't forget: It never hurts to get to class early and stay late or to sit on the front row and smile. Stay off your phone during lectures! Remember to study in time blocks—alternating subjects.

Writing Tips:

1. **Accumulate more material** for your writing project than you could ever use. Avoid using only obvious sources.

2. **First drafts** are meant to be cut. As much as 40–50 percent can be removed without compromising your message.

3. **First person** is more natural. "I," "me," "us," and "we." "One" and "it is" are impersonal.

4. Use **short sentences and paragraphs.**

5. **The last sentence of a paragraph** is the bridge to the next. Using humor or surprise here is good.

6. Most **adverbs and adjectives** are not needed. "He squinted narrowly." (There is no other way to squint.) "Ugly wild hog." (They are all ugly.) Instead, make sure your adjectives "do something" while describing a situation. "He saw an angry sky with low clouds."

7. **Use these contractions:** Use "I'll," "won't," and "can't" when comfortable. **Avoid** "I'd," "we'd," and "she'd."

8. **Avoid** "surprisingly," "predictably," and "of course." Let the reader decide.

9. **Use exclamation marks sparingly.**

10. **Colons** are for itemized lists. Semicolons can substitute for periods and dashes. But use them rarely.

11. **Strange facts** can be very effective. Look for opportunities to include them.

12. **Clichés** can ruin any work. Be careful.

13. Look for opportunities to **turn sentences into questions.** It creates a more introspective environment for the reader.

14. **Rewriting** is the key to good writing.

15. **Read out loud** when editing or rewriting.

Mind Mapping[3]

A Mind Map is a visual diagram utilized as a powerful learning technique that can be used for:

1. Brainstorming
2. Summarizing
3. Memorizing information
4. Interpreting complex problems
5. Decision making
6. Illustrating the overall structure of the subject

Popularized by British psychologist Tony Buzan in the 1970s, the thinking technique behind the Mind Map has been used by brilliant minds such as Leonardo da Vinci, Darwin, and Beethoven. Mind Mapping uses images and associations that create stronger connections between information, which in turn enhances memory; this then leads to a more effective way of learning.

Associations ➜ Connections ➜ Memory ➜ Thinking

A Mind Map can be used in a variety of ways. In school, it can be utilized as a powerful tool for summarizing and reviewing information. It is similar to creating an outline except that the information is being drawn out. Mind Mapping is a two-dimensional form of transferring information from your mind to paper as opposed to the linear, one-dimensional form of taking notes in an outline or list format.

Mind Mapping engages the brain to think "radiantly." Radiant thinking is when our brain associates several ideas to a central concept. Thoughts from the central concept branch out and expand into multiple networks that can be connected. Mind Mapping engages our mind to learn in the natural way it was designed to, and it allows us to interpret new concepts more holistically.

It is a good form of note taking when reading textbooks, reviewing PowerPoints, or taking lecture notes. Learn how you study best, and utilize the tools that best suit you; each individual learns best differently (auditory learners, hands-on learners, visual learners, etc.). It is worthwhile to try out Mind Mapping because it is a powerful learning method that integrates your left and right cortical skills. Left cortical skills include logic, words, lists, lines, numbers, and analysis. Right cortical skills involve imagination, daydreaming, color, spatial, and gestalt.

Mind Mapping is a bit time consuming when you first start learning how to use it, but you can learn to do it faster with more practice. It is a good way to connect what you learn into one cohesive picture. Essentially, you should create your Mind Maps according to what makes sense to your brain. Try it out to see if it helps you learn information better.

How to Make a Mind Map

Create a Mind Map when reading a textbook or reviewing a PowerPoint. Steps:

1. Write the main subject in the center.
2. Pick out the main ideas as you read the paragraphs or the PowerPoint, and create branches for those ideas.
3. Seek out the subtopics of those main ideas, and create branches off of the main ideas.
4. Simply branch out from the subtopics as you discover new pieces of information that relate to the subtopics.
5. Branch out from those subtopics as you discover details.

MIND MAPPING PROCESS

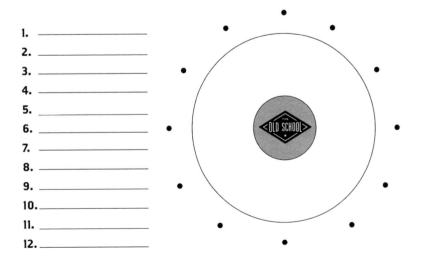

1. _____
2. _____
3. _____
4. _____
5. _____
6. _____
7. _____
8. _____
9. _____
10. _____
11. _____
12. _____

How to Create Effective Mind Maps

1. Use key words and phrases.
   A. Be able to distinguish the most important idea that the author is trying to get across in the paragraph or Personal Purpose Statement section.
2. Color-code your Mind Maps.
   A. Differentiate the information you write according to what makes sense to you.
      i. For example: you can highlight the different main ideas or create your own color-coding system (e.g., a green line means these two ideas are connected; a pink line means this is an exception to a rule, etc.)
3. Draw pictures or get pictures from online to help you remember concepts.
4. Use curved lines as opposed to straight lines.
5. Make the curved lines the same length as the words or pictures they hold.

Benefits of Mind Mapping

Mind Maps illustrate the structure of a subject, which makes it easier to recall pieces of information and see how all of the concepts are connected. Because of this, Mind Maps are the ideal memory palaces to create for studying.

Mind Maps are good memory palaces to create.

The different concepts are mapped out in their own branches, and you can simply "visit" each branch as you try to remember a certain concept. Another advantage of Mind Mapping is that information can be more easily added onto Mind Maps without disrupting the flow of ideas of the overall picture. Through Mind Maps, it is easier to connect the big picture.

In order to create an effective Mind Map, be sure to illustrate the *shape* of the subject, emphasize the most important points, and demonstrate how all of the concepts are connected.

Please note: each of the following three Mind Map examples contain text that is too small to be easily read. Rather, these examples are provided to depict a proposed format or layout as a guide for your own personal Mind Maps. You can be as creative as you wish!

Example 1: Organic Chemistry: Nomenclature of Alkanes

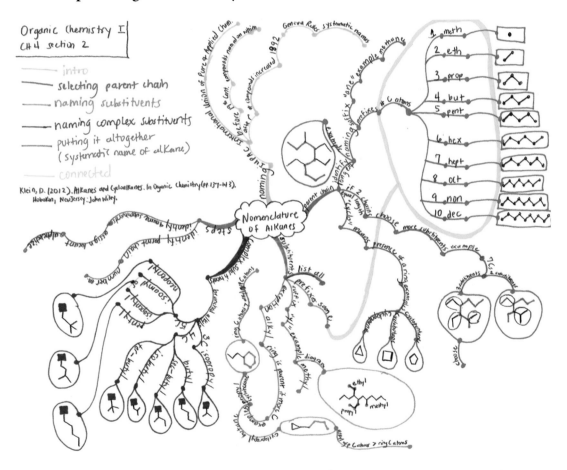

Example 2: A Topic for Presentation—Use Software

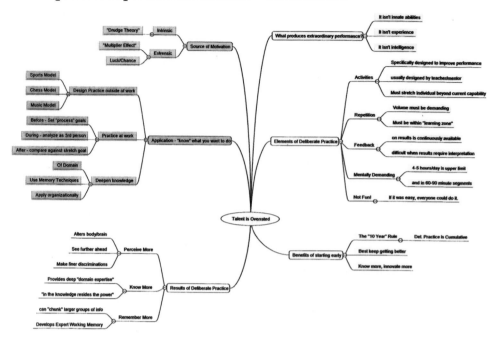

Example 3: Goals/Decision Making/Planning

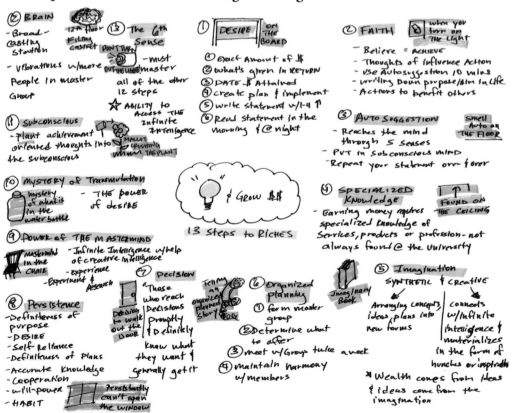

Make Your Own

1. Draw it yourself
2. Mind Map–creating software
   - Easily transfer your Mind Maps onto Word document or PowerPoint presentations
   - Where to find it:
     - Free: Coggle.it
     - Free trials: Bubbl.us, Mindmeister, MindGenius, iMindMap

"Commonplaces"

Classical Dutch Renaissance scholar Erasmus recommended that every reader keep a notebook for the purpose of collecting memorable quotations. This suggestion became enthusiastically followed, and the notebooks became known as "commonplace books" or "commonplaces." Every student kept one, and by the seventeenth century, they were used outside schools as well. Commonplaces became known as a "given" for the educated mind.[4]

Erasmus would have been blown away by the tools we have today. Here are three suggestions on how to use technology for your commonplaces:

1. **Tablet excerpts.** If you read your books in iBooks or Kindle, for example, both of these apps have phenomenal highlighting and cut-and-paste features.
   A. **Highlighting.** Use different colors to indicate importance or denote types of passages. For example, in iBooks, I use the following color-coded system:
      i. Yellow: historical facts or anecdotes.
      ii. Green: important passages.
      iii. Purple: *really* important concepts.
      iv. Blue: memorable quotes or words I did not know.
      v. Pink: passages I want to share with my wife in particular.
      vi. Red underline: topics that are followed by lists or questions in the text.

This highlighting technique allows you to locate passages more quickly. For example, if you know you are looking for a quotation, go the index in the front of the books and scan only blue highlights. Kindle and other reading apps have similar tools. Create your own system that is comfortable for you.

You can also cut and paste passages directly into your Notes app or into an e-mail for quick dissemination. The ability to share your excerpts (and your wisdom along with it) is extraordinary!

2. **Categorize as you go.** You can start an excerpt log on your Notes app on your tablet and categorize by topic with one or two words describing the excerpt. Then number them as well. This makes for easier lookup.

3. **Business cards.** This is more old school, but get in the habit of taking any business cards you acquire and attaching them to a five-by-seven card. Then write down everything you remember about the encounter with that person. Use the LAVA system to remember details about the person, the date, the reason for the introduction, etc., then simply file in a manual "recipe box" that is always at your fingertips. You can do the same thing electronically if you prefer. *Always send a personalized note card* to make a lasting impression with your new acquaintance.

Can you imagine what Erasmus would have thought of *these* commonplace books?

BIBLIOGRAPHY

Budziszewski, J. *Ask Me Anything*. TH1NK Books, 2004. iBooks.

Buford, Bob P. *Beyond Halftime*. Zondervan, 2008. iBooks.

Carnegie, Dale. *How to Win Friends and Influence People*. Simon & Schuster, 2009. iBooks.

Carr, Nicholas. *The Shallows: What the Internet Is Doing to Our Brains*. W. W. Norton & Company, 2010. iBooks.

Carter, Joe, and John Coleman. *How to Argue like Jesus*. Crossway Books, 2009. iBooks.

Chabris, Christopher, and Daniel Simons. *The Invisible Gorilla*. Crown Publishers, 2010. iBooks.

Cialdini, Robert B. *Influence: The Psychology of Persuasion*. HarperCollins, 2007. Kindle eBooks.

Colvin, Geoff. *Talent Is Overrated*. Penguin Group, 2008. Kindle eBooks.

Conwell, Russell H. "Acres of Diamonds." Waxkeep Publishing, 2014. iBooks.

DeMoss, Mark. *The Little Red Book of Wisdom*. Thomas Nelson, 2011. iBooks.

Denning, Stephen. *The Leader's Guide to Storytelling*. John Wiley & Sons, Inc., 2011. iBooks.

Deresiewicz, William. *Excellent Sheep*. Free Press, 2015. iBooks.

Detweiler, Craig. *iGods*. Baker Publishing Group, 2013. iBooks.

DeYoung, Kevin. *Crazy Busy*. Crossway, 2013. iBooks.

Elko, Kevin. *The Pep Talk*. Thomas Nelson, 2013. iBooks.

Farrell, Chris. *Unretirement*. Bloomsbury Publishing Plc, 2014. iBooks.

Fisher, Roger, William L. Ury, and Bruce Patton. *Getting to Yes*. Penguin Group, 2011. iBooks.

Foer, Joshua. *Moonwalking with Einstein*. Penguin Group, 2010. iBooks.

Geisler, Norman L., and Frank Turek. *I Don't Have Enough Faith to Be an Atheist.* Crossway Books, 2004. iBooks.

Gladwell, Malcolm. *Blink: The Power of Thinking Without Thinking.* Back Bay Books, 2007. iBooks.

Gray, Dave, Sunni Brown, and James Macanufo. *Gamestorming.* O'Reilly Media, 2010. iBooks.

Guber, Peter. *Tell to Win.* Crown Business, 2011. iBooks.

Harris, Michael. *The End of Absence.* Penguin Group, 2014. iBooks.

Heinrichs, Jay. *Thank You For Arguing, Revised and Updated Edition.* Three Rivers Press, 2013. iBooks.

———. *Word Hero.* Three Rivers Press, 2011-10-04. iBooks.

Hill, Napoleon. *Think and Grow Rich.* North Points Classics, 2010. IBooks

Hogan, Kevin, and James Speakman. *Covert Persuasion.* John Wiley & Sons, Inc., 2010. iBooks.

Johnson, Paul. *Socrates: A Man for Our Times.* Penguin Group, 2011-09-05. iBooks.

Kahneman, Daniel. *Thinking, Fast and Slow.* Macmillan, 2011. iBooks.

Koukl, Gregory. *Tactics.* Zondervan, 2009. iBooks.

Lucado, Max. *Facing Your Giants.* Thomas Nelson, 2009. iBooks.

Luntz, Frank. *Win.* Hachette Books, 2011. iBooks.

———. *Words That Work.* Hachette Books, 2007.

Mansfield, Stephen. *Mansfield's Book of Manly Men.* Thomas Nelson, 2013. iBooks.

Mayer-Schönberger, Viktor, and Kenneth Cukier. *Big Data.* Houghton Mifflin Harcourt, 2014. iBooks.

Paulos, John Allen. *Innumeracy.* Hill and Wang, 2011. iBooks.

Pink, Daniel H. *A Whole New Mind.* Penguin Group, 2006. Kindle eBooks.

———. *Drive.* Penguin Group, 2010. iBooks.

Powers, William. *Hamlet's BlackBerry.* HarperCollins, 2010. iBooks.

Reiman, Joey. *Thinking for a Living.* Taylor Trade Publishing, 2012. iBooks.

Richards, Jay W. *Money, Greed, and God.* HarperCollins, 2009. iBooks.

Ries, Al, and Jack Trout. *Positioning: The Battle for Your Mind*. McGraw-Hill, 2001. iBooks.

Roberts, Russ. *How Adam Smith Can Change Your Life*. Penguin Group, 2014. iBooks.

Ryle, J.C. *Thoughts for Young Men*. Amazon Digital, 2011. Kindle eBooks.

Schwartz, Barry. *The Paradox of Choice*. HarperCollins, 2004. iBooks.

Shepherd, Margaret. *The Art of the Handwritten Note*. Broadway Books, 2010. iBooks.

Simmons, Annette. *The Story Factor*. Basic Books, 2011. iBooks.

Sims, Ronald R., and Scott A. Quatro. *Leadership: Succeeding in the Private, Public, and Not-For-Profit Sectors*. Taylor & Francis, 2015. iBooks.

Sinek, Simon. *Leaders Eat Last*. Penguin Group, 2014. iBooks.

Surowiecki, James. *The Wisdom of Crowds*. Knopf, 2005. iBooks.

Tracy, Brian. *Eat That Frog!* Berrett-Koehler Publishers, Inc., 2007. iBooks.

Twain, Mark. *The Quotable Mark Twain*. Golgotha Press, 2010. iBooks.

Warren, Rick. *The Purpose Driven Life*. Zondervan, 2012. iBooks.

Wass, Donald. *Six Secrets to Success in High School and College*. Book Publishers Network, 2011. Kindle eBooks.

Woodward, Orrin, and Oliver DeMille. *LeaderShift*. Grand Central Publishing, 2013. iBooks.

NOTES

Introduction

1. Craig Detweiler, *iGods.*
2. Ibid.
3. Ibid.
4. William Deresiewicz, *Excellent Sheep.*
5. Stephen Mansfield, *Mansfield's Book of Manly Men.*
6. Gregory Koukl, *Tactics.*
7. Frank Luntz, *Words That Work.*

Chapter 1

1. Jay Heinrichs, *Word Hero.*
2. Joshua Foer, *Moonwalking With Einstein.*
3. Ibid.
4. Ibid.
5. Ibid.
6. Ibid.
7. Ibid.
8. Ibid.
9. "Curve of Forgetting," University of Waterloo, accessed July 23, 2015, https://uwaterloo.ca/counselling-services/curve-forgetting.
10. Kevin DeYoung, *Crazy Busy.*
11. Nicholas Carr, *The Shallows.*
12. Ibid.
13. Ibid.
14. Foer.

15. Paul Johnson, *Socrates: A Man for Our Times.*

16. Foer.

17. Ibid.

18. Ibid.

19. Denison Forum on Truth and Culture, June 4, 2014.

20. Orrin Woodward and Oliver DeMille, *LeaderShift.*

21. Ruben Berenguel, "Learn to Remember Everything: The Memory Palace Technique," *Mostly Maths* (blog), March 27, 2011, http://www.mostly-maths.net/2011/03/learn-to-remember-everything-memory.html.

22. Foer.

Chapter 2

1. Proverbs 18:21. Bible, English Standard Version (ESV).

2. Proverbs 11:25.

3. Mark Twain, *The Wit and Wisdom of Mark Twain.*

4. Frank Luntz, *Win.*

5. Ibid.

6. Ibid.

7. Ibid.

8. Mark DeMoss, *The Little Red Book of Wisdom.*

9. Luntz. *Win.*

10. Ibid.

11. Luntz. *Words That Work.*

12. Luntz. *Win.*

13. Ibid.

14. Ibid.

15. Ibid.

16. Robert B. Cialdini, *Influence: The Psychology of Persuasion.*

17. Luntz. *Win.*

Chapter 3

1. Roger Fisher and William Ury. *Getting to Yes.*

2. Ibid.

3. Ibid.

4. Christopher Chabris and Daniel Simons, *The Invisible Gorilla.*

5. Ibid.

6. Daniel Kahneman, *Thinking, Fast and Slow.*

7. Ibid.

8. Ibid.

9. Robert B. Cialdini, *Influence: The Psychology of Persuasion.*

10. Ibid.

11. Ibid.

12. Ibid.

13. Russ Roberts, *How Adam Smith Can Change Your Life.*

14. Paul Johnson, *Socrates: A Man for Our Times.*

15. Fisher and Ury.

16. Cialdini.

17. Fisher and Ury.

18. Cialdini.

19. Gregory Koukl, *Tactics.*

20. Chabris and Simons.

21. Daniel Kahneman, *Thinking, Fast and Slow.*

22. Ibid.

23. Cialdini.

24. Ibid.

25. Fisher and Ury.

26. Ibid.

27. Ibid.

28. Cialdini.

29. Fisher and Ury.

30. Ibid.

31. Kevin Hogan and Jim Speakman, *Covert Persuasion.*

32. Cialdini.

33. Ibid.

34. Hogan and Speakman.

35. Ibid.

36. Dale Carnegie, *How to Win Friends and Influence People*.

37. Kahneman.

38. Hogan and Speakman.

39. Ibid.

Chapter 4

1. *Dictionary.com*, accessed July 23, 2015.

2. Frank Turek, *I Don't Have Enough Faith to be an Atheist*.

3. Ibid.

4. Ibid.

5. J. Budziszewski, *Ask Me Anything*.

6. Paul Johnson, *Socrates: A Man for Our Times*.

7. Gregory Koukl, *Tactics*.

8. Al Ries, *Positioning*.

9. Johnson.

10. Christopher Chabris and Daniel Simons, *The Invisible Gorilla*.

11. Koukl.

12. Ibid.

13. Ibid.

14. Ibid.

15. Ibid.

16. Ibid.

17. Dale Carnegie, *How to Win Friends and Influence People*.

18. Koukl.

19. Ibid.

20. Ibid.

21. Jay Heinrichs, *Thank You for Arguing*.

22. Frank Luntz, *Words That Work*.

23. Heinrichs.

24. John Allen Paulos, *Innumeracy.*

25. Ibid.

26. Adapted from: Jay Heinrichs, *Thank You for Arguing.*

27. Heinrichs.

28. Ibid.

29. Ibid.

30. Ibid.

31. Ibid.

32. Harvey Mackay, accessed July 23, 2015, www.harveymackay.com/P= Speaking+Tips.

Chapter 5

1. Brian Tracy, *Eat That Frog!*

2. Daniel H. Pink, *A Whole New Mind.*

3. Ibid.

4. Ibid.

5. Viktor Mayer-Schönberger and Kenneth Cukier, *Big Data.*

6. Ibid.

7. Peter Guber, *Tell to Win.*

8. Annette Simmons, *The Story Factor.*

9. Stephen Denning, *The Leader's Guide to Storytelling.*

10. Simmons.

11. Ibid.

12. Ibid.

13. Ibid.

14. Ibid.

15. Dave Gray, Sunni Brown, and James Macanufo, *Gamestorming.*

16. Simmons.

17. Guber.

18. Rick Warren, *The Purpose Driven Life.*

19. Guber.

20. Joe Carter and John Coleman, *How to Argue Like Jesus*.

21. Denning.

22. Simmons.

23. Ibid.

24. Ibid.

25. Ibid.

26. Ibid.

27. Ibid.

28. Denning.

29. Ibid.

30. Simmons.

31. Kevin Hogan and James Speakman, *Covert Persuasion*.

32. Simmons.

33. Ibid.

34. Ibid.

35. Ibid.

36. Denning.

37. Ibid.

38. Simmons.

39. Ibid.

40. Ibid.

41. Ibid.

42. Ibid.

43. Ibid.

44. Ibid.

45. Denning.

46. Pink.

47. Simmons.

48. Kevin Elko and Robert L. Shook, *The Pep Talk*.

49. Denning.

50. Simmons.

51. Ibid.

52. Ibid.

53. Ibid.

54. Russ Roberts, *How Adam Smith Can Change Your Life.*

55. Denning.

56. Roberts.

57. Simmons.

58. Chris Seidman, Senior minister at the Branch Church, Farmers Branch, Tex.

59. Annette Simmons, *The Story Factor.*

Chapter 6

1. Agencies, "Judgments about Trustworthiness Are Made in the First Second of Meeting," *Telegraph*, August 5, 2014, http://www.telegraph.co.uk/news/science/science-news/11013780/Judgements-about-trustworthiness-are-made-in-the-first-second-of-meeting.html.

2. Frank Luntz, *Win.*

3. Ronald R. Sims and Scott A. Quatro, *Leadership: Succeeding in the Private, Public, and Not-For-Profit Sectors.*

4. "How to Remember a Person's Name," wikiHow, accessed July 23, 2015, http://www.wikihow.com/Remember-a-Person%27s-Name.

5. Napoleon Hill, *Think and Grow Rich.*

6. Adapted from work by psychologist Martin Seligman.

7. HRNasty, "Job Interview Questions," HRNasty.com, accessed July 23, 2015, http://www.hrnasty.com/job-interview-questions.

8. Lia, "Interview Tips," Everyday Job Interview Tips, accessed July 23, 2015, http://www.everydayinterviewtips.com/interview-tips.

9. Vivian Giang, "The Best and Worst Colors to Wear to a Job Interview," *Business Insider*, November 22, 2013, http://www.businessinsider.com/best-and-worst-colors-to-wear-to-job-interview-2013-11.

10. Catherine Conlan, Monster.com contributing writer. Website not live as of July 23, 2015.

11. Mark DeMoss, *The Little Red Book of Wisdom.*

12. Margaret Shepherd, *The Art of the Handwritten Note.*

13. Ibid.

14. Ibid.

15. Ibid.

16. Ibid.

17. Ibid.

18. Ibid.

Chapter 7

1. KingdomAdvisors.com, accessed July 23, 2015.

2. Daniel H. Pink, *Drive*.

3. Ibid.

4. Belle Beth Cooper, "The Surprising History of the To-Do List and How to Design One That Actually Works," *Social* (blog), Buffer, October 3, 2013, http://blog.bufferapp.com/the-origin-of-the-to-do-list-and-how-to-design-one-that-works.

5. Ibid.

6. "How to Cut Back on Technology," *Karatomlin* (blog), April 27, 2012, http://karatomlin.wordpress.com/2012/04/27/how-to-cut-back-on-technology.

7. ScienceDaily.com, June 9, 2009, accessed July 23, 2015.

8. Joanne Cantor, PhD, "Sleep for Success: Creativity and the Neuroscience of Slumber," *Psychology Today*, May 15, 2010, http://www.psychologytoday.com/blog/conquering-cyber-overload/201005/sleep-success-creativity-and-the-neuroscience-slumber.

9. Dustin Wax, "Writing and Remembering: Why We Remember What We Write," Lifehack, accessed July 23, 2015, http://lifehack.org/articles/productivity/writing-and-remembering-why-we-remember-what-we-write.html.

10. First heard "GMAD" from Scott Bornstein via WordPower.com. Website not live as of July 23, 2015.

11. Brian Tracy, *Eat That Frog!*

12. KingdomAdvisors.com.

13. Chris Farrell, *Unretired*.

14. Brent Gleeson, "5 Reasons Why Good Fitness Makes for Better Entrepreneurial Leadership," *Forbes*, October 22, 2012, http://www.forbes.com/sites/brentgleeson/2012/10/22/5-reasons-why-good-fitness-makes-for-better-entrepreneurial-leadership.

15. Napoleon Hill, *Think and Grow Rich*.

16. Adapted from: Al Ries, *Positioning*.

17. Joey Reiman, *Thinking for a Living*.

18. Tracy.

19. Pink.

20. Ibid.

21. Geoff Colvin, *Talent Is Overrated*.

22. Pink.

23. Simon Sinek, *Leaders Eat Last*.

24. Ibid.

25. Pink, *A Whole New Mind*.

26. Max Lucado, *Facing Your Giants*.

27. Adapted from KingdomAdvisors.com training program, 2009, Session 18.

28. Christopher Chabris and Daniel Simons, *The Invisible Gorilla*.

29. John Stonestreet, "Old Age, Happiness, and Virtue," BreakPoint, December 19, 2014, http://www.breakpoint.org/bpcommentaries/entry/13/26580.

30. Jay Heinrichs, *Thank You for Arguing*.

31. Pink, *Drive*.

32. James Surowiecki, *The Wisdom of Crowds*.

33. Dictionary.com.

34. Russell H. Conwell, "Acres of Diamonds."

35. Barry Schwart, *The Paradox of Choice*.

36. Malcolm Gladwell, *Blink*.

37. Chabris and Simons.

38. Michael Hyatt, "The 7 Benefits of Keeping a Daily Journal," July 17, 2012, http://michaelhyatt.com/daily-journal.html.

39. *Dictionary.com*.

Chapter 8

1. Paul Johnson, *Socrates: A Man for Our Times*.

2. Ibid.

3. Napoleon Hill, *Think and Grow Rich*.

4. Bob P. Buford, *Beyond Halftime*.

5. My mom was quoting George Bernard Shaw.

6. Daniel H. Pink, *A Whole New Mind*.

7. All phrases from the book of Proverbs; (1:5, 13:1, 10:14, 21:11).

8. Joe Carter and John Coleman, *How to Argue Like Jesus*.

9. William Deresiewicz, *Excellent Sheep*.

10. Job 12:12.

11. *Wall Street Journal*. November 8, 2014.

12. Ashly Perez, "23 Famous Dropouts Who Turned Out Just Fine," BuzzFeed, June 18, 2013, www.buzzfeed.com/ashleyperez/23-famous-dropouts-who-turned-out-just-fine.

13. Michael Harris, *The End of Absence*.

14. Nicholas Carr, *The Shallows*—Note 23.

15. Carr.

16. Ibid.

17. Ibid.

18. Ibid.

19. Ibid.

20. Ibid.

21. J. C. Ryle, *Thoughts for Young Men*.

22. Adapted from Carr.

23. William Powers, *Hamlet's BlackBerry*.

24. Joshua Foer, *Moonwalking with Einstein*.

25. Carr.

26. Ibid.

27. Mark DeMoss, *The Little Red Book of Wisdom*.

28. Carr.

29. Russ Roberts, *How Adam Smith Can Change Your Life*.

30. Powers.

31. "POLL: 28 Percent of Americans Have Not Read a Book in the Past Year," *Huffington Post*, October 7, 2013, http://www.huffingtonpost.com/2013/10/07/american-read-book-poll_n_4045937.html.

32. "How Many Books Does the Average American Read a Year?," Division of Libraries' Blog, August 5, 2012, http://library.blogs.delaware.gov-/2012/08/05/q-how-many-books-does-the-average-american-read-a-year.

33. Dale Carnegie, *How to Win Friends and Influence People*.

34. Joey Reiman, *Thinking for a Living*.

Afterword

1. Daniel H. Pink, *A Whole New Mind*.

2. Frank Luntz, *Win*.

3. David Brooks, *New York Times* columnist and author

Appendix

1. Donald Wass, *The Six Secrets to Success in High School and College*.

2. Joey Reiman, *Thinking for a Living*.

3. "Mind Mapping," Tony Buzan, accessed July 23, 2015, http://www.buzan.com.au/learning/study_skills.html.

"Maximise the Power of Your Brain - Tony Buzan MIND MAPPING," YouTube video, 5:38, posted by "iMindMap," January 8, 2007, https://www.youtube.com/watch?v=MlabrWv25qQ.

"Mind Mapping: Learn How to use Mind Maps to Take Notes, Brainstorm, and Think Creatively," YouTube video, 2:55, posted by "MindToolsVideos," April 1, 2011, https://www.youtube.com/watch?v=k2paRXMKefQ

"Mind Mapping," Tony Buzan, http://www.tonybuzan.com/about/mind-mapping.

Elizabeth Eyre, "Mind Maps: A Powerful Approach to Note-Taking," Mind Tools Ltd., accessed July 23, 2015, http://www.mindtools.com/pages/article/newISS_01.htm.

MindMapping.com, accessed July 23, 2015.

"Mind Maps Club," accessed July 23, 2015, http://mindmapsclub.com/
details2.php?id=40.

4. Nicholas Carr, *The Shallows*.

ABOUT THE AUTHOR

J.N. "Jim" Whiddon, who has spent much of his career in the financial services industry, has owned and operated his own companies for more than thirty years. He hosted his own radio show for five years, including a stint with *CNN Headline News* in Dallas. He also has been often interviewed and quoted by national media outlets such as *Fortune* magazine, *The Wall Street Journal*, and CNBC.

Whiddon founded The Old School in 2014 with a mission of conveying timeless tools of interpersonal communication and wisdom to make life-long leaders among students, professionals, and mentors alike. With this goal in mind, he wrote *The Old School Advantage*, which is his fourth book. He prepared for it by reading more than four hundred other books for the purpose of research. His other published works are *There for the Taking, Wealth Without Worry,* and *The Investing Revolutionaries*. He earned his bachelor's degree from Texas A&M University and a master of science from The American College in Philadelphia.

Whiddon is involved in his local church, enjoys playing guitar, and loves all sports. He lives in Dallas with his wife, Nizie. They have four children, ages sixteen to twenty-three.